Jeremy Black is one of the UK's most respected and prolific historians. He is Emeritus Professor of History at the University of Exeter and a renowned expert on the history of war. He is a Senior Fellow at both Policy Exchange and the Foreign Policy Research Institute. His recent books include *Military Strategy: A Global History*, *A History of the Second World War in 100 Maps*, *Tank Warfare* and *The World of James Bond*. He appears regularly on TV and radio.

Other titles in this series

A BRIEF HISTORY OF

The Atlantic

....

JEREMY BLACK

ROBINSON

ROBINSON

First published in Great Britain in 2022 by Robinson

1 3 5 7 9 10 8 6 4 2

Copyright © Jeremy Black, 2022
Map © iStock

The moral right of the author has been asserted.

A CIP catalogue record for this book
is available from the British Library.

ISBN: 978-1-47214-591-8

Typeset in Scala by Hewer Text UK Ltd, Edinburgh
Printed and bound in Great Britain by Clays Ltd, Elcograf S.p.A.

Papers used by Robinson are from well-managed
forests and other responsible sources.

Robinson
An imprint of
Little, Brown Book Group
Carmelite House
50 Victoria Embankment
London EC4Y 0DZ

An Hachette UK Company
www.hachette.co.uk

www.littlebrown.co.uk

For Andy Horide

Contents

....

Preface

....

The scale of the Atlantic long daunted the humans on its shores for the coastal waters stretching into the horizon seemed to be the edge of the world. Even more recently, the Atlantic, once crossed, was still a mighty ocean instilling fear among voyagers and, at best, uncertainty. This fear and uncertainty were only tempered with the age of mighty steamships that began in the mid-nineteenth century and then, more conclusively, in the twentieth with aircraft that could cross with ease in five hours.

Indeed, the history of the Atlantic has gone into a reverse, suggesting a degree of human control that would have been inconceivable or, at best, fantasy to other generations. Thus, in 2020, scientists at the National Oceanography Centre in Southampton collected samples at ten locations in a line from Britain to the Falkland Islands. The average cubic metre of seawater was found to contain about 1,000 particles of polyethylene, polypropylene and polystyrene litter. The ocean now is still a mighty body of water and a major source of food, but also the sump of the surrounding societies.

Variety is the theme today, and necessarily so for an ocean that links four continents, but also variety in the past, from Norse voyages in exposed longboats to the misery and harshness of slave ships, from pirates to steamships 'rolling down to Rio'.

I have seen the Atlantic seemingly every shade of blue, green and black, in storm and stillness, and with trepidation and pleasure. I would like to thank those who have given me the opportunities and those who have shared the silence of a seemingly shoreless ocean. It is a great pleasure to note the continued friendship and support of Duncan Proudfoot, my commissioning editor, and not only for this but also for other books, including *A Brief History of the Caribbean*, which should be read by those interested in that sea and which I have not duplicated here. I am also most grateful to David Abulafia, Alejandro Amendolara, Sam Cavell, Helen Doe, Cheryl Fury, Bill Gibson, Armando Marques Guedes, Malyn Newitt, José Miguel Sardica and Neil York for their helpful comments on an earlier draft, to Howard Watson for helping as copy-editor, and Amanda Keats for overseeing the editing process. None is responsible for any errors that remain. Dedicating this book to Andy Horide is a very pleasant way to record a good friendship.

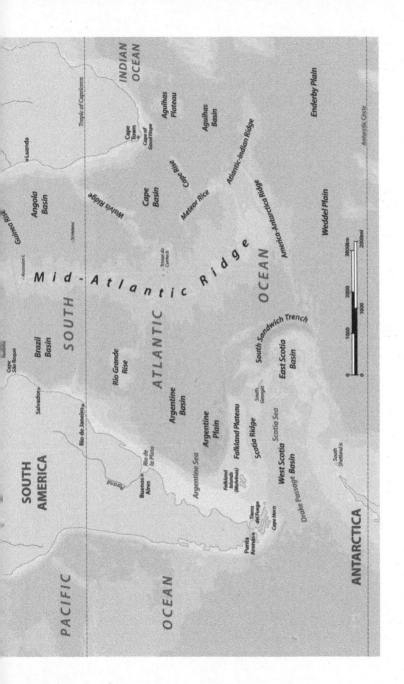

Physical History

....

Charles Dickens crossed the Atlantic twice, in 1842 and 1867. The first, a January crossing on the Cunard paddle-steamer *Britannia*, from Liverpool via Halifax to Boston, and the second on the Cunard *Cuba*, again arriving in Boston. *Martin Chuzzlewit*, a novel written in the aftermath of the first, and published in full in 1844, offers a vivid account of an Atlantic storm, one that presents the vulnerability of a transatlantic crossing:

> ... over the countless miles of angry space roll the long heaving billows ... all is but a boiling heap of rushing water ... a spouting-up of foam that whitens the black night ... the wild cry goes forth upon the storm 'A ship!'
>
> Onward she comes, in gallant combat with the elements, her tall masts trembling, and her timbers starting on the strain; onward she comes, now high upon the curling billows, now low down in the hollows of the sea, as hiding for the moment from its fury; and every storm-voice in the air and water cries more loudly yet, 'A ship!'
>
> Still she comes striving on: and at her boldness and the spreading cry, the angry waves rise up above each other's hoary heads to look; and round about the vessel, far as the mariners on the decks can pierce into the gloom, they press upon her, forcing each other down, and starting up, and rushing forward from afar, in dreadful curiosity. High over her they break; and round her surge and roar; and giving place to others, moaningly depart, and dash themselves to

fragments in their baffled anger. Still she comes onward bravely. And though the eager multitude crowd thick and fast upon her all the night, and dawn of day discovers the untiring train yet bearing down upon the ship in an eternity of troubled water, onward she comes, with dim lights burning in her hull, and people there, asleep: as if no deadly element were peering in at every seam and chink, and no drowned seaman's grave, with but a plank to cover it, were yawning in the unfavourable depths below.

The Atlantic is the world ocean. It is not the largest, that is the Pacific, but the Pacific was singularly little crossed in its entirety until the late eighteenth century and only really became a unit with the 'opening up' of China and Japan in the late nineteenth. The Atlantic, the world's second largest body of water, making up about a quarter of the Earth's water surface, is more compact, especially east–west, than the Pacific. Moreover, the Atlantic, unlike the Pacific or the Indian oceans, has had a close linkage from east–west since the end of the fifteenth century. This provides a way to look at one of the major means and regions of global history, and to do so in a period that coexists with that history, for the opening of the Atlantic world was one of the aspects, almost conditions, of modernity. The Atlantic was the centre of the so-called Age of Discovery, marking the emergence of Western European states to global significance and leading eventually to Western domination.

But this stage was long set and it is to that which we must turn first. In a process understood from the early twentieth century, and mapped from mid-century, the initial opening up of the Atlantic was a consequence of the lengthy breaking up of a supercontinent, Pangaea, about 200 million years ago, and the consequent moving apart of its new sections through continental drift. Europe and Africa (the Old World) shifted away from the Americas (the New World), although these constituent halves did not move apart at the same pace. As the European and American plates moved apart to create what is a relatively recent ocean, new seafloor was produced and, in turn, this helped drive the plates further apart. In a reminder of the continuing role of the geological narrative, this continues to be the case by about 3 centimetres a year, so that the ocean is getting larger at the expense of the human-occupied landmass even as, in a totally separate process, it is becoming more polluted by man. Due to the respective locations of the plates, there is no 'ring of fire' around the Atlantic as there is around the Pacific.

Ocean-floor mapping has clarified the situation. For example, the twenty-four-sheet *Carte générale bathymétrique des Océans* (1904) had many deficiencies, but wartime delays and the provision of new information from sonic and ultrasonic devices led to subsequent incomplete editions, before the data was digitised and a digital atlas published in 1994. Comparison of earlier editions, such as the first and the fifth (1980), indicated the increase in data availability.

The major use of acoustic echo soundings, by the *Meteor* in 1925–7, provided an understanding of the Mid-Atlantic Ridge, the border between the plates and the longest mountain range in the world. It sees much volcanic activity and earthquakes, activity below the ocean surface, but the magma that wells up at the Ridge can lead to volcanic islands, the largest of which is Iceland. Saint Helena, Tristan da Cunha and Ascension are all volcanic islands, as are the Azores and Canaries. At the Azores Triple Junction, the North American, Eurasian and African plates meet. Eruptions in the past were not restricted to the Ridge, including in the Canaries, the San Antonio (1677) and Teneguía (1971) volcanoes on La Palma, the Montañas del Fuega (1730) and Tinguatón (1824) on Lanzarote, and that at Garachico (1706) on Tenerife. Distinctive landscapes such as the calderas, for example, on the Canaries, the *Caldera de Taburiente* on La Palma, and the lava fields of Lanzarote where Malvasía wine is produced, are explained by the igneous rocks and volcanic history.

This history in turn has led to mythology. Indeed, it was only in 1750 that two Icelandic students climbed to the top of Mount Hekla, the most famous volcano there, and returned safely, which helped lessen the popular view of it as the main entrance to hell. Following up a coded note from a sixteenth-century Icelandic alchemist in a copy of a runic saga manuscript written by the (real) poet Snorri Sturluson (1179–1241), the protagonists in Jules Verne's novel *Journey to the Centre of the Earth* (1864) set off via the crater of the Snaefellsjökull volcano.

Surtsey: A New Atlantic Island

Thrown up in an eruption in 1963, Surtsey, named after a fire giant, is off southern Iceland. It has since been greatly affected by erosion, but plant species and bird colonies have been established and seals bask there. This new island is a different liveliness to that of the ocean's waters. A decade later, a volcano on the nearby island of Heimaey, the lava and ash from which buried houses, created a new mountain, Eldfell (Mount Fire). There were fresh eruptions in Iceland in 2021.

The igneous intrusion of magma at the Ridge ensures that the rock in the ocean deep is volcanic and muddy. There is a more complex geological history on the relatively shallow continental shelf – the area off the continental mainland, near the shoreline. That complexity includes the presence of oil and natural gas deposits, both already well worked, as off Nigeria and Brazil, and in development or prospect, as off the Guianas (Guyana, Cayenne and Surinam), Ghana, Senegal and Mauritania.

In turn, the Atlantic is topped and tailed by landmasses covered in ice: Greenland and Antarctica. Indeed, turning to more recent times, the Ice Ages saw a considerable restriction of the Atlantic. In the last Ice Age, ice sheets spread across the northern reaches of the ocean, joining Greenland via Iceland to Norway, and spread southwards to include most of the British Isles. There was a further southward expansion in the north-west Atlantic, with the Laurentide ice sheet covering the Labrador Sea and the Labrador Bay and encompassing Newfoundland. Much water was frozen into the ice sheets, ensuring that the ocean's water level was lower than at present and coasts therefore more extensive. Much of what is currently the continental shelf became dry land, and notably so off Argentina. So also with island groups, especially the Bahamas, which were linked to the landmass.

The end of the Ice Age was followed by the raising of water levels and the drowning of the continental shelf, so that the ocean expanded in size much more rapidly than it had been doing by the geological expansion from the mid-ocean Ridge. Some land, however, remained as islands. Thus, about 6000 BCE, the Breton island of Belle Île was separated from the coast.

Within the ocean, there are wind and current flows, the latter associated with the movement of cold and hot water. The wind pattern is one of trade winds blowing from the tropics of Cancer and Capricorn to the Equator, and westerly winds dominant between 35 and 60 degrees latitude, thus contributing in the northern hemisphere to the impact of the Gulf Stream. The most significant features are the gyres, large systems of rotating ocean currents with relatively still waters within them. In the North Atlantic, the Gulf Stream, part of the clockwise ocean currents system called the North Atlantic Gyre, takes warm water from the Caribbean north-east to the Atlantic shores of Europe, helping to make them warmer than they otherwise would be. In contrast, the Labrador Current moves cold water from the Arctic south-wards along the eastern seaboard of North America. In the South Atlantic Gyre, the Benguela Current moves cold water from the Antarctic north along the coast of South-west Africa. The equivalent of the Gulf Stream, but a weaker one, is the south-ward-flowing warm-water Brazil Current. Close to the Equator, there are westward-blowing tropical trade winds, and the North and South Equatorial Currents. The pattern and interplay of winds and currents helped make transoceanic maritime travel feasible.

The climate has very varied effects on the islands and coast-lines. Some, notably the Cape Verde Islands and the coasts of Mauritania and Namibia, are arid. Severe drought led to famine in the Cape Verde Islands, including in 1773–5, 1830–3, 1854–6 and 1863–6, and most recently in 1941–3 and 1947–8, with perhaps 45,000 people dying and many others emigrating in the last two. Other coasts and islands have high rainfall, particularly West Africa and Brazil, while the Azores have a higher rainfall than the Canaries let alone the Cape Verde Islands.

The Bermuda Triangle

This is part of the western Atlantic, with one apex of the triangle on Bermuda, another on Puerto Rico and a third on Miami, that, from the early 1950s, was allegedly an area of aircraft and ship disappearances. The supernatural and implausible magnetic claims are to the fore in much of the discussion; but many of the accounts are dubious and, given the size of the area, the number of ships crossing it and the extent of tropical cyclones, the numbers definitely lost are not disproportionate. Insurance rates reflect this situation. Bermuda was dangerous for its reefs and storms, and, combined with the sounds of birds and wild hogs, this helped give rise in the sixteenth century to reports of spirits and to the name 'Isle of Devils'.

Atlantic Monsters

Belief in Atlantic monsters includes that of the huge Devil Whale able to swallow whole vessels, and large enough to be mistaken for an island, as by Saint Brendan. In Norse mythology, the Kraken lives in the North Atlantic, notably the Greenland Sea, and is like a malevolent giant squid, able to swallow ships. There were certainly massive creatures in the Atlantic: about 100 million years ago, mosasaurs, huge marine reptiles up to 17.1 metres (56.1 feet) long, existed in the South Atlantic, and their bones have been found in Angola. Mosasaurs were the enemies of sharks.

The coastlines vary between areas, such as Namibia where there are no offshore islands and others where there are many, and where indeed the coast is an expression for a complex mélange of land and sea, including of coastal salt marsh and new alluvial barrier islands. Tidal movements change the situation daily, as, more occasionally, do storm surges. That is the case, for example, for much of the tropical coastlines of West Africa and South America, but also in other areas, notably South and North Carolina and Georgia. These inshore islands frequently support distinctive societies as with the Gullah of the Sea Islands of South Carolina and Georgia, formerly enslaved African Americans who speak a creole language. Large deltas contribute to the land–sea mélange, not only famous ones, notably the Amazon and the Niger, but also many others.

The varied pattern of the winds accentuates the difficulties of navigation in the Atlantic. Although skill and experience could ease the strain, ships were dependent on the weather. Too much or insufficient wind was a serious problem, and ships could only sail up to a certain angle to the wind. Insufficient wind obliged ships to turn to rowing, the ships' boats being used for towing. James Field Stanfield, a crewman, recalled of a slave ship crossing the Atlantic from east to west in the mid-1770s: 'In the torrid zone. In the calms . . . we were in the boat, rowing, from morning till night.'

The Skeleton Coast

The clash between the Benguela Current moving northward along the coast of South-west Africa, and warm air from the Hadley Cell, leads to very frequent fog which has helped cause frequent shipwrecks. The coast of northern Namibia and southern Angola has been called the Skeleton Coast since 1944, but that term, derived from shipwrecks, notably of the *Dunedin Star* in 1942, in fact originally arose from the whale and seal bones left by the whaling industry. Shipwrecks continue, the *Fukuseki Maru*, a Japanese fishing vessel, running aground near Durissa Bay in 2018.

Conversely, winds could make landings difficult, as for the British expedition that captured the Breton island of Belle-Île in 1761, the commander, General Studholme Hodgson, reporting, 'we could get nothing landed yesterday, it blew so excessively hard'. Such Atlantic storms, westerlies in the northern hemisphere, bring wet weather to coastal regions such as Ireland, the Scottish Highlands, Brittany and Galicia. I live 13 kilometres (8 miles) from the ocean and can see the storm-dark skies over it, and, at other times, clouds banked up to move forward. Weather conditioned how people viewed the Atlantic and must have heightened the awareness and sense of danger, even heroism, when fishermen, explorers and others took it on. Atlantic storms affected almost every era, as with the Great Storm of December 1703 which hit England very hard and wrecked warships, as well as destroying the Eddystone Lighthouse 20 kilometres (12 miles) south-west of Plymouth, which had only been completed in 1698. Replaced in 1709, the lighthouse was burned down in 1755.

It was far harder to counteract the impact of current and tide before the advent of steam power. For example, French ships could readily leave Brest, their major Atlantic port, only when the wind blew from the east, which it did at best only intermittently. The Atlantic's stormy character has been a problem ever since recorded history began, and presumably deterred earlier would-be navigators. The sailing of the ocean and encounters with its storms searched out the flaws in the construction, maintenance and sailing of individual ships, with inadequate caulking being a particular problem, as with the *Sea Venture* that was run aground on the reefs to the east of Bermuda in 1609 to prevent its sinking.

There also came storms that hit squadrons as a whole. For example, sailing with five ships from the River Plate in January 1741 to intercept George Anson's attempt to circumnavigate the world, Admiral José Pizarro lost two ships in a storm, had to return to harbour and, on the second attempt with two vessels, was demasted anew and returned to Montevideo. Storms hit the returning Spanish Armada off Scotland and Ireland in 1588, dispersed the Spanish invasion attempt on England in 1719 off Cape Finisterre, hit the French fleet going to Nova Scotia in 1746 and its British equivalent en route to North America in 1776, and affected the victorious British in the aftermath of the battles of the Saintes in 1782 and Trafalgar in 1805. Many people mentioned in this book were affected by Atlantic storms, John Byron, 'Foulweather Jack', being badly injured crossing to the Caribbean in 1779.

Storms remain a serious problem today, although large ships no longer disappear into uncertainty. I recall being on a ship trying to land passengers on the Caribbean island of Cayman Brac and, due to large waves, notably breaking hard on the shore, only succeeding after several hours.

The Bay of Fundy

The tidal range in this Canadian bay, between Nova Scotia and New Brunswick, is one of the largest in the world, usually about 13 metres (43 feet), compared to an average global range of 1 metre (3¼ feet). There are two high and two low tides daily. The very high tides are dramatic and powerful. The tidal bore on the rivers coming into the bay is fun to ride, while at the 'Reversing Falls' on the Saint John River, the bay's tides can be seen forcing the river flow to go into reverse.

Ice was also a hazard, most spectacularly claiming the *Titanic* in 1912, although human error in design, construction and operation were all serious in that case. In 1862, Henry, 3rd Viscount Palmerston, the British prime minister, underlined the role of ice in any possible conflict with the Union (North) during the American Civil War: 'We should have less to care about their resentment in the spring when communication with Canada opens, and when our naval force could more easily operate upon the American coast than in winter, when we are cut off from Canada and the American coast is not so safe.'

Atlantic Whales

There are a number of whale species in the Atlantic, and therefore there are migrations across the ocean. Humpback whales migrate from the Caribbean to feeding grounds further north, including off Iceland. Other whale species in the North Atlantic include right, fin, sei, sperm, minke and blue. Numbers are under pressure, with only about 410 North Atlantic right whales surviving in the western Atlantic, in part due to entanglement in fishing gear and to ship strikes. In the eastern North Atlantic, the right whale has been dying out. In 2020, Spain suspended yachting off its north-west Atlantic coast after killer whales (orcas) hit vessels while following tuna on their migration routes.

South Atlantic whales include humpbacks, which breed off Brazil and feed in sub-Antarctic waters, the southern right whale, blue, fin, sei, Antarctic minke, sperm and Bryde's whales. The South Atlantic has seen an increase in humpback and right whales. In 2020, Tristan da Cunha decided to set up a marine wildlife sanctuary around its waters, thus protecting humpback, southern right, fin and other whales; fishing was banned between 50 and 200 nautical miles from the island and from Gough Island. In 2019, a very large protected area was created around Ascension and in 2012 around South Georgia and the South Sandwich Islands.

Global warming brought more whales (including humpback, minke and killer), dolphins and porpoises to British waters in 2019, the animals following fish that in turn were attracted by the good conditions for the plankton. However, the impact of the dumping of chemicals is believed to have made Britain's pod of killer whales infertile.

Good sites to see whales include the Bay of Fundy off Nova Scotia in Canada and Skjálfandi, a bay in Iceland.

Atlantic Fish

Cod, halibut and shark are the most common fish in the Atlantic. The first two are extensively fished, as are pollock, hake, herring, mackerel, plaice, haddock, shrimp and squid.

As a source of food, including key protein and vitamins, Atlantic fish has been very important to the various shoreline communities. Aside from humans, seals are a major predator, which helps explain the importance to fish stocks of the number of predators on seals, principally sharks. Indeed, the attacks of orcas on yachts in Iberia in 2020 were attributed to the pressure of overfishing on their food, bluefin tuna. Cod is important to Atlantic fish diets, as in *bacalhau à brás*, a traditional Portuguese dish that includes potatoes, onions, eggs and olives. Alongside haddock and wolf fish, cod is one of the sources of Icelandic *harðfiskur*, dried fish. I recall a month's camping tour in 1975 in which villages had wooden racks with fish drying in the open air. The fish is then pounded with a mallet to make it edible, but the dish did not suit me.

Currently, it is climate-warming that is to the fore. The year 2020 was the eighteenth 'above-normal' Atlantic storm season since 1995, showing that the warming of the oceans and the atmosphere were wreaking havoc. Indeed, nineteen of the twenty warmest years had occurred since 2001. The warmer the air, the more moisture it holds. The warmer the ocean, the higher it rises as it expands and the more energy there is for storm systems. In particular, warming the tropical Atlantic leads to major storms, which then have an impact elsewhere in the ocean.

The post-Ice Age raising of water levels has very recently rapidly accelerated with climate warming and its impact on the ice caps. Each year, there is a melting of the ice caps during the summer and a freezing during the winter. In the Arctic there has been, in addition, due to warmer summers and winters, a net loss of ice every year since 1997, with the 'equilibrium line', where winter snow freeze and summer melt balance each other, moving toward the

North Pole. The amount of ice lost varies each year due to temperature changes: thus, in 2018, when the Arctic was very cold, only 19 billion tonnes were lost from Greenland, but, in 2017, 109 billion were lost and, in 2019, Greenland suffered a record loss of ice: 532 billion tonnes, with 12.5 billion on 1 August alone. In 2020, there was less ice in the Arctic (3.6 million square kilometres/1.4 million square miles) than at any point besides the summer for 2012 (3.4 million square kilometres/1.3 million square miles).

Greenland is highly significant to the Atlantic as its ice sheet is more than a mile thick and holds 8 per cent of the world's fresh water, enough to raise sea levels by 6 metres (20 feet). Crevasses and icequakes on Greenland indicate that the ice sheet is not only melting but also moving toward the sea, with the water melt helping to lubricate the ice sheet-bedrock join. This melting has led to projections of a rise in the Atlantic's water level, and to the realisation that cities directly on the ocean, such as Dakar, New York and Rio de Janeiro, or indirectly, such as London, will need to confront a much more difficult future. It is the relationship between the ocean and these cities that has been so significant to world history.

2

Confronting the Crossing:
The Ocean Before Columbus

....

ULYSSES IN THE ATLANTIC

Dante, in Canto 26 of the *Inferno* (*c.* 1308–20), came across Ulysses, one of the greatest heroes of the ancient world, in hell, suffering for his restless presumption to know:

> the experience that lies beyond the sun,
> the world that is devoid of human kind.

Rowing south for five days in this 'mad flight', Ulysses encountered his doom.

> gloomy in remoteness, there appeared
> a peak that seemed to soar to such a height
> there's nothing I had seen which could compare.
> We leaped for joy, but soon this turned to grief;
> for from the strange new land a whirlwind sprang
> and struck our vessel hard across its bows.
> Three times it churned the waters and the ship.
> and on the fourth it hoisted up the stern
> and, as Another willed, plunged down the prow
> until the ocean closed above our heads.

The Latin name for Lisbon, *Olisipo*, was said in Late Antique tradition to derive from Ulysses (*Ulixes*) going there in his wanderings. In Shakespeare's *Troilus and Cressida*, Ulysses referred to being 'parch in Afric sun'.

THE EDGE OF THE OCEAN

The edge of the world is the obvious response to an ocean that simply goes on and on, beyond the swimmers, the canoeists, the sailors and the fishermen, with nothing in sight, no sound or smell to suggest a limit to the water other than some edge somewhere, an edge from which no one returns. The edge of the world is how the Atlantic appears in the Hereford *Mappa Mundi* (map of the world) of the late thirteenth century, albeit as an inconsequential edge, not a terrible watery cliff into nothing. The idea of an edge encouraged speculation as to its identity and location. One long-standing view was that it was maybe off Cape Bojador in modern Moroccan-ruled Western Sahara. Its Arabic name Abu Khatar means 'the father of danger'. Ideas of the edge of the world continue to play a role in modern culture, whether novels or songs, as in 'Edge of the Ocean' (2001), a successful song that presents the edge as a place to go, by the American rock band Ivy.

That was not, however, the sole response, and the belief that the world was a sphere was present from classical Greece. Such a belief presumed that travelling westwards from Europe would eventually lead to returning to it from the east, although it was far from clear what would be encountered en route and whether as a result such a journey was possible.

Indeed, whether or not the world had edges, or was a sphere, or was an unknown shape, there was mystery; and the great source of mystery for Europeans, though not eventually for the Norse, the first to cross it, was the Atlantic. There is evidence of Neolithic movement along the 'Western Seaways', as from the Channel Isles to the Orkneys from *c.* 3900 to *c.* 3700 BCE, from France and the British Isles from *c.* 4500 to *c.* 4250 BCE, to Galicia, and between Iberia and Morocco, while, in opposition to the more established view, there is a theory that Celtic culture originated along the later Bronze Age Atlantic littoral before diffusing into Europe away from the ocean. The basis for this is the extent of evidence in 1300 to 700 BCE of exchange between Atlantic centres from the British Isles to Spain, with the ocean providing the links, notably the coastal waters between the Irish Sea and the Mediterranean.

The importance of very recent archaeology and analysis to this work suggests that similar research on non-European areas may offer important revisions to existing theses. At any rate, the importance of maritime routes for development is increasingly apparent.

Travelling eastwards from Europe there was land, and Alexander the Great had reached India, while trade routes stretched down the Red Sea and eastward in the Indian Ocean. Southwards, the Mediterranean was a finite body of water, but there was no Atlantic comparison. As a result, both real knowledge and imaginative creation looked east, from where there was the basis of travellers' tales, rather than westward. So also for North Africa, which from the seventh century looked eastward, within the world of Islam, to the holy cities of Mecca and Medina, as well as to political and intellectual centres, notably Baghdad and Cairo.

Atlantis

This is a fictional island from the period of antiquity, with Plato presenting it in an allegory on hubris as an opponent of Athens. Many took up the idea of an island in the Atlantic, but belief in Atlantis as fact has vied with discussion of it as a useful myth. The extent to which tsunamis and geological events indeed caused land to be suddenly or slowly flooded, led to the idea of lost places, and Atlantis, a variable location, became generally situated outside the Pillars of Hercules in the Atlantic. It was accordingly located in maps, for example by Ortelius, although also seen by some

---

Europeans from the sixteenth century as a precursor of knowledge of the New World, for example of Mayan or Aztec civilisation.

Utopianism was one characteristic in some accounts, notably Sir Thomas More's *Utopia* (1516), with the imaginary island located in the Atlantic of South America, and Francis Bacon's *The New Atlantis* (1627), but the latter, a mythical island called Bensalem, is located in the Pacific. In his *New Set of Maps Both of Ancient and Present Geography* (1700), Edward Wells revealed contemporary knowledge as being far more extensive: an entire hemisphere was 'unknown to the Antients' unless North America was their Atlantis, and, even if so, the ancients could not map it whereas the moderns could.

Belief was strengthened by Ignatius Donnelly's *Atlantis: the Antediluvian World* (1882), which presented this small continent as destroyed by the biblical Flood. In turn, the Theosophists, notably Helena Blavatsky in *The Secret Doctrine* (1888), offered a positive account of a pre-Aryan civilisation in Atlantis. Arthur Conan Doyle wrote *The Maracot Deep* (1929) about the discovery of Atlantis.

The mystery of the ocean remained the case even though the traders and warships of the Mediterranean were able to sail into the Atlantic. They did so by overcoming the difficulty posed in the Strait of Gibraltar as a result of the dominance of the Atlantic inflow in the surface waters, through finding a westward under-tow along the northern shore.

The Phoenicians

As a result, the Phoenicians' city states, mostly in Lebanon but with Carthage (near Tunis) ultimately the most significant, established an important base beyond the strait at Gades (Cádiz) in about 800 BCE. They also sailed south along the Moroccan coast certainly to Mogador and possibly further, and northwards along that of Europe. They obtained copper, tin (necessary for the production of bronze, the need for which increased greatly in the Mediterranean) and silver from Iberia (Spain and Portugal). In return, they brought Mediterranean goods, such as wine and textiles. There were bases north of Gades, including at Abul and Alcácer in modern Portugal, as well, in the eighth century, as Lisbon, which they called *Alis Ubbo* or calm harbour. How far the Phoenicians travelled is a matter of research, notably archaeological, nautical and oceano-graphical, as well as speculation. Himilco, a Carthaginian of the sixth or fifth centuries BCE, allegedly, according to a much later Roman source, sailed from the Mediterranean as far as the British Isles and may, less plausibly based on the description of him finding part of the ocean seaweed-covered, also have encountered the Sargasso Sea. Hanno the Navigator, a Carthaginian explorer of the same period, may have reached as far as Gabon, Senegal, Gambia or only southern Morocco. He may also have visited the Canaries. Possibly the Azores were reached by the Carthaginians/Phoenicians, and probably at least Madeira and the Canaries.

Herodotus reported that the Phoenicians circumnavigated Africa in about 600 BCE, sailing from the Red Sea. This idea might appear implausible, not least due to the problems of navigation without a stern rudder, and of securing sufficient fresh water on some of the coasts, especially that of Namibia. In an Atlantic version of the 1947 voyage of the *Kon-Tiki* from America to Polynesia, Philip Beale, using *Phoenicia*, a 20-metres (65-foot) long replica of a Phoenician ship, was able both to circumnavigate Africa in 2008–10 and to sail the Atlantic in 2019, but modern claims of Phoenician remains in Brazil, notably tools, inscriptions and linguistic influences, are problematic. In the far shorter distance of European waters, and with fresh water available on the coast, the Phoenicians definitely traded as far as Britain for tin for the production of bronze. The Greeks also reached as far as Andalusia.

THE ROMANS

In turn, the Romans reached the ocean, conquering Iberia and deploying warships into the Atlantic, with Julius Caesar using them in his expeditions against Britain in 55 and 54 BCE and in campaigning against the Veneti of southern Brittany. The Veneti were defeated in 56 BCE by Decimus Brutus who, at the battle of Morbihan, employed hooks mounted on poles to secure the opposing ships so that they could be boarded. As part of the Celtic trading pattern, the Veneti had impressive oak-built boats with leather sails, handled them well and transported tin from Cornwall and Devon. In his *Gallic War*, Caesar recorded: 'These Veneti exercise by far the most extensive authority over all the sea-coast in those districts, for they have numerous ships, in which it is their custom to sail to Britain, and they excel the rest in the theory and practice of navigation. As the sea is very boisterous, and open, with but a few harbours here and there which they hold themselves, they have as tributaries almost all those whose custom is to sail that sea.'

In 43 CE, the Roman invaders crossed the English Channel in force, and, thereafter, maritime links were crucial to the Roman presence in Britain. Moreover, these now focused on the short crossing from the Pas-de-Calais to Kent, and not on the Atlantic route from Brittany, although the Veneti appear to have continued their maritime links with the British Isles.

It is unclear whether, as reported for 83 or 84 CE, the first circumnavigation of Britain was undertaken by a Roman fleet. Furthermore, although Roman naval activity was important to the acquisition of geographical information about the British Isles, there was no extension of Roman power to further islands, whether Ireland or those of Scotland, let alone to Norway or into the North Atlantic; although there is evidence of the Romans trading with the Canary Islands, which both Plutarch and Pliny described. At this point, there is no sign of comparable naval activity on this scale by powers in the South Atlantic nor in the New World.

The Romans did not focus relevant colonies in modern Britain, France, Spain and Portugal on their Atlantic coastlines. Thus, Lusitania, the province covering much of what would become Portugal and western Castile, had its capital at *Emerita Augusta*, inland Mérida in modern Spain. Nevertheless, the Romans developed trade from Atlantic Iberia, with the Torre de Hércules in Corunna, built in the second century, the oldest still-functioning lighthouse. The vista into the ocean from the impressive site is windswept. Moreover, the prosperity of Gades, the key port for Andalusia, increased greatly under the Romans. Julius Caesar gave the inhabitants Roman citizenship in 49 BCE, and Augustus's census revealed considerable wealth. The young women of Gades were taken as slaves to Rome where they were prized for their expertise in dancing and singing.

Atlantic ports also included Oporto, Lisbon, Alcácer and Alvor, which ensured that minerals, wine, grain, olives, wool and salt could be exported to Italy. In Lisbon, where the population under the Romans may have been around 30,000, it is possible to see the remains of a temple and a fish-preserving plant, while at Cetóbriga, a town near Troía, the stone tanks in which fish were salted can be visited.

The Canary Islanders

The aboriginal inhabitants of the Canaries, genetically similar to the North African Berbers, probably arrived in the first millennium BCE, possibly in response to desertification in North Africa. Little is known about them. Polytheistic, they practised embalming the dead and had different governmental systems on the various islands, with kingdoms on Tenerife. The islanders were cave-dwelling and wore clothes made from goatskin or plant fibres. They did not have iron. Conquered by Castile in 1403–16, the islanders were killed, enslaved or intermarried with the conquerors.

Romans in America: Clive Cussler

Claims of Romans crossing the Atlantic are long-standing, and have been kept alive by the alleged discovery of Roman artefacts in the New World, but these have not commanded much support among scholars. In the prologue to Clive Cussler's fantastical adventure novel *Treasure* (1988), the Romans bury the treasures from the Library of Alexandria in Roma, Texas, before being killed by the local population. Prior to Cussler, Barry Fell, an expert on sea urchins, claimed that his study of inscriptions, beginning with *America BC: Ancient settlers in the New World* (1976), demonstrated that Phoenicians and others visited the New World, arguments that have been widely castigated as pseudo-archaeology.

THE DARK AGES

The post-Roman era is generally labelled the Dark Ages and seen as a period of a drawing in of European civilisation. In other perspectives, it was one of new relationships, notably the expansion of Islam, including to the Atlantic coasts of Morocco and Iberia. In Europe, there was destruction, for example of Gades and Lisbon by the Visigoths in the fifth century. Yet, the Dark Ages also saw greater engagement with oceanic possibilities, with, in particular, a move from the Mediterranean-based consciousness of the Roman world to one that for part of Europe was more concerned with the Atlantic, albeit primarily with Atlantic coasts rather than the deep ocean. Maritime links along the Atlantic coasts of what had been the Roman empire were strengthened and also supplemented by the development of the Irish Sea, eventually, in the tenth century, as a 'Celto-Norse lake', as well as by that of the North Sea: the southern North Sea linked to the English Channel and focused on the relationship between England and the Low Countries, while the more open northern North Sea linked Britain and Scandinavia, and thus looked toward the North Atlantic.

Saint Brendan's Island

St Brendan of Clonfert (c. 484–c. 577 CE), one of the Twelve Apostles of Ireland, was from the ninth century presented as a seafarer who not only sailed to Scotland, Wales and Brittany, but also to the Isle of the Blessed in an attempt to find the Garden of Eden. Brendan, in a coracle, an oval-shaped boat made of wattle covered in hides and powered by a sail, finds a number of islands, including that of the ageless monks of Ailbe, sea monsters, Judas seated on a rock, and an awareness of Christian justice, in what is a

---

religious allegorical presentation of the Irish *immram* or account of heroic voyaging, as seen for example in the eighth-century oceanic voyage of Bran in search of the Otherworld.

Saint Brendan's Island, which was frequently sighted into the eighteenth century, was marked on many maps and contributed to the idea of an Atlantic with numerous islands, as did Saint Ursula's Island and Antillia, the Island of Seven Cities. The myths around the islands largely focused on those who had left Europe, often as refugees, but there was also interest in non-European creatures, although largely in the form of sea monsters. Antillia drew on the legend of seven bishops and their flocks having fled the Muslim conquest of Iberia in the 710s CE and settled on an island where seven cities were established.

THE VIKING ODYSSEY

The most dramatic aspect of the Atlantic 'Dark Ages' was the Viking odyssey into the North Atlantic, an achievement that drew on a Northern European engagement with the Atlantic over a number of centuries. In European waters, Viking longboats, with their sails, stepped masts, true keels and steering rudders, were shallow, open and therefore exposed to the elements. Nevertheless, the longboats were capable, thanks to their shallow draught, of being rowed in coastal waters and up rivers, even if there was only 1 metre (3 feet) of water. The latter capability provided more opportunities in terms of the targets available and was more profitable, as it was easier thereby to benefit from the accumulation made by others. However, *knarrs*, larger vessels, were used by the Vikings both for trade and for sailing the North Atlantic.

Knarrs

The Viking ships used for raiding in Western Europe were slender, long, and sat low in the water. These were not the ships that sailed the North Atlantic. Those, the *knarrs*, were broader and deeper, with high gunwales, able to carry a larger cargo, and therefore supplies, and thus suited for longer voyages. The *knarrs* were also more seaworthy in terms of surviving storms. The ships were lapstrake clinker-built, with overlapping oak planks from a central keel. Rowing oars and a sail were supported by a steering oar. Navigation was made harder by cloud and white nights, both of which made it more difficult to see the stars.

The Viking diaspora was also looking for land for settlement, and North Atlantic islands provided that. The process was a gradual one, and understandably so given both alternative opportunities in Europe and the difficulties of the waters. The Danes found much better opportunities in Britain, and the Norwegians could look to the lands round the Irish Sea, but for the Norwegians there were also opportunities in the North Atlantic. However, the seas between the Faroes and Iceland were particularly stormy, while the journey was about 1,600 kilometres (1,000 miles). Although their effectiveness is controversial, the Vikings may have used crystal sunstones to navigate their ships through foggy and cloudy conditions. These sunstones, gemstones found in Norway, establish the sun's position as they enable the detection of polarisation, the properties displayed by rays of light depending on their direction, which is not visible to the human eye.

The Atlantic in the Icelandic Sagas

The Icelandic sagas are old tales, from 850 CE onwards, that were memorised and retold across the centuries, and were committed to writing in the forms now preserved from the twelfth century. The sagas record the life and strife of Iceland, as well as the Norse Atlantic explorers. Written in the vernacular, they focus often on feuds and honour. The *Greenland* and *Erik the Red* sagas were probably not written down until about 1300, and were therefore probably embellished. The sagas differ in their accounts of which explorers came first. *The Saga of Erik the Red* includes a tale of westward journeys in response to problems, Erik being outlawed from Iceland as a result of killings. Magic vies with Christianity. In the *Greenland Saga*, a series of voyages reflects the difficulties of mastering the Atlantic, with Erik losing ships between Iceland and Greenland, and Bjarni Herjólfsson lost due to fog and storms.

According to the traditional account, approximately 825 CE saw both the first settlement of the Faroe Islands by Vikings and the first discovery of Iceland by Irish monks. In this account, in about 860, the Viking Garðar Svavarsson made the first circumnavigation of Iceland, while, in the late 860s, the brothers Ingólfr and Hjörleifr reconnoitred the East Fjords. In about 870, Naddod was blown off course and landed on the east coast, but, finding no human settlement, soon left. In 873, Ingólfr, sailing from Norway, made the first permanent settlement. Separately, encouraged by Naddod's earlier sighting, Floki landed in the far north-east. The sea ice obliged him to winter there and he named the island Iceland.

In contrast, more recently, excavations at Stod in eastern Iceland have uncovered the richest longhouse yet found in the country. It dates from about 874 and the dig yielded 148 glass beads and 31 silver objects including coins from the Middle East. Within the walls are the remains of an earlier longhouse that have been carbon-dated to about 800. It is possible therefore that Viking hunters spent summers there over many decades, and, in turn, over time, some overwintered in addition, as a prologue to the main settlement traditionally dated to 873. This became the developing practice for Europeans in Greenland. DNA studies reveal Irish as well as Norse roots for the Icelandic population, the Irish probably coming in as enslaved people as the Irish ports were under Norse control and thus part of the North Atlantic world.

The Norse View of the World

Not affected, at least strongly, until late by Christian and Greek ideas of the world, and notably their focus on the Mediterranean, the medieval Norse also had an idea of the world as in four quarters. In this the Norse world was the northern and the Atlantic the western quarters.

Soon after the settlement of Iceland, there was the first sighting of Greenland by Viking sailors who had sailed across the Denmark Strait. Reducing any dependence on Norway, Iceland was to be an important basis for exploration there. Erik the Red began the colonisation of Greenland in about 986, when the settlements Godthåb and Julianehåb were founded in a climate mild enough for stock rearing. From there, Viking Greenlanders sailed north along the long coasts of Greenland in a quest for polar-bear skins, walrus ivory and other goods that could be used and traded. Meanwhile, across the Davis Strait, Bjarni Herjólfsson had spotted land west and south of Greenland in 985–6.

He was followed by voyages from Greenland, notably Leif Eriksson in 1003 and Thorvold Eriksson from 1005. North America was visited, a small settlement was established in L'Anse aux Meadows in northern Newfoundland, and the Norsemen sailed south to what they called Vinland as a result of the vines growing there. There were later to be claims of voyages further south, including to Newport, Rhode Island, but, although entrenched in local lore, they are implausible. So even more are suggestions of Viking voyages to South America and Yucatán, with the latter allegedly leading to contact with Mayas.

Although reliant on island stepping stones, and helped by the shorter distances to cover in higher latitudes due to the curvature of the Earth, the voyages across the North Atlantic were an impressive feat of seamanship and endurance. Moreover, the settlements established represented the furthest reaches of European power until the fifteenth century.

However, the lasting impact of these voyages and settlements was limited. Beyond Iceland, Viking expansion was very small-scale. Furthermore, affected by disease, the hostility of the local Inuit population, difficulties and deterioration in an already harsh climate, remoteness, and an inability to sustain them, the settlements in North America and Greenland were abandoned. The first went after the early eleventh century.

The commitment to Greenland was greater, but it ended in around 1500. Details are scanty. The failure to seek cooperation with the Inuit may have been a major flaw, but there is also a theory that the Norse eventually intermarried and were subsumed by the Inuit. The greater cold of the 'Little Ice Age' may have been a factor both in cultivation on land and in navigation at sea; and also the persistent stagnation in the European population following the mid-fourteenth-century Black Death.

The Kingdom of the Isles

A major part of the Viking diaspora became the basis of the Kingdom of the Isles, which includes the Isle of Man and the Hebrides. There were variable links with Norway, Ireland, England, Scotland and the Orkneys. Following Scottish victory at Largs in 1263, the Treaty of Perth of 1266 saw Alexander III of Scotland prevail over Norway, although he accepted that the Orkneys and Shetlands were Norwegian.

Within the ambit of European expansion, the Viking world dwindled to a sideshow. There were still distant fishing and whaling voyages, for example to Spitsbergen, but the basis for sustained long-range trade and territorial expansion was lacking. There were too few people, the climate and sailing conditions were hostile in the high latitudes, and the Danish state (which ruled Norway and dominated Iceland) lacked both the resources and the will to pursue options. Instead, there were much more promising opportunities for Denmark in Scandinavia, the Baltic and Germany, and this became more the case in the sixteenth century as the Reformation threw open the lands of the Crusading orders in the eastern Baltic for conquest.

The Vinland Map

Purchased in Switzerland in 1957 and subsequently deposited in Yale University, the map, allegedly dating from the mid-fifteenth century, was supposed to demonstrate eleventh-century Norse contact with North America, and thus compensate for the fact that the Norse of that period did not make maps. Chemical analysis and historical consideration have led most scholars to decide that the map is a fake produced after 1920.

THE EUROPEAN ATLANTIC

Meanwhile, the impact on Europe and, indeed, on the Atlantic of Norse expansion was limited. Knowledge of the fisheries there helped attract boats across to Icelandic waters in the late Middle Ages. Nevertheless, to sail west from the British Isles was to be exposed to prevailing westerlies and the Gulf Stream in those latitudes, whereas, further south, the Iberians (Portuguese and Spaniards) benefited greatly from supporting winds and the east to west North Equatorial current when they sailed to the Caribbean via the waters off North-west Africa and the supportive Canary Current.

As a result, the peoples of the British Isles had only limited experience of oceanic navigation. In addition, they lacked the stepping stones into the Atlantic offered the Vikings by the Faroes, Iceland and Greenland, and the Portuguese and Spaniards by the Canaries, Madeira and the Azores. There was also nothing comparable to the tradition of expansion at the expense of the heathen that the Portuguese and Spaniards had acquired from their long wars against the Muslims.

For all European peoples, however, there was the tradition of fishing. Inshore maritime experience was far more readily translated to deep-sea activities than is the case today; and by the late fifteenth century, over a hundred English boats per year were leaving the northern Atlantic, and staging round trips lasting six months, to sail to Iceland in order to fish or to buy cod. These voyages encouraged developments in shipbuilding and also led to greater knowledge of currents and winds in the North Atlantic, in particular of the brief season of easterlies from March to May, which permitted ships to sail to Iceland. As was typical of much European Atlantic activity, violence – not only the killing of fish but also armed struggles both with Hanseatic competition and with the Danish overlords of Iceland – played a key role.

In the last quarter of the fifteenth century, there were increasing signs of English participation in long-range naval activity.

Edward IV (r. 1461–83) was interested in trade and shipping, encouraged the development of both, and responded to merchant requests by unsuccessfully pressing Pope Sixtus IV in 1481 to reject the Portuguese claim of a monopoly over the trade to West Africa. Thomas Croft of Bristol and others who Edward licensed as traders in 1480 sent an expedition in 1481 to find Atlantic lands and it may have discovered Newfoundland, but the evidence is slim. The expedition took with it a lot of salt, which suggests that fishing was the prime purpose. John Jay of Bristol was reported to have sought the 'island of Brasylle' only to be driven back to Ireland by storms after nine weeks. Even if this or other expeditions from Bristol may have reached Newfoundland's offshore Grand Banks, if not North America, in the 1480s and 1490s, they proved no more than an adjunct to the quest for fish.

A Venetian Explorer?

In 1588, Nicolò Zen published a work *Dello Scoprimento (On the Discovery)* that suggested that his Venetian ancestor Antonio (died *c.* 1403) had reached the New World, finding gold, idol worship, cannibalism, nudity and Latin literature, although in part that account reflected a use of existing conventions on travel writings.

Rumoured voyages into the Atlantic from European coasts, not least from Ireland, are of interest, but it is the expansion of Portugal and Spain into the eastern Atlantic that was of key consequence. This expansion drew heavily on initiatives taken from Italians, who had the necessary maritime expertise, shipping, mercantile links and capital from investment. The most famous are Columbus and Cabot, but the first were Vandino and Ugolino Vivaldi who commanded two galleys that left Genoa in 1291 intending to travel to India 'by the Ocean Sea' in order to spread

Christianity but also to trade. They probably reached Cape Chaunar in southern Morocco, but thereafter speculation is to the fore. They may have gone to the Canaries, but there were later suggestions that they reached sub-Saharan West Africa, possibly Senegal. Reports of them circumnavigating Africa and reaching the Horn of Africa (Somalia) are implausible.

Subsequently, the Genoese navigator Lancelotto Malocello, in 1312, reached Lanzarote, which was named after him, in the Canaries. Allegedly he had wielded some control there before being thrown out by a revolt of the Canary Islanders, which would indicate the ability of the Atlantic to act as a setting for ambitions of power and position, one to be seen in the nineteenth century with American filibusters such as William Walker. Cape Chaunar was considered impassable, which led to the Portuguese calling it *Cabo de Naõ* (Cape No), but, from 1421, ships sent by Henry the Navigator were able to pass on and reach Cape Bojador, which was regarded by some as the southern limit of the human world. Italians who explored West Africa in the service of Portugal included the Venetian Alvise Cadamosto and the Genoese Antoniotto Usodimare, who discovered the Cape Verde Islands, and the Guinea coast between the Guinea and Geba rivers. In 1341, on behalf of Afonso IV of Portugal, the Florentine Angiolino del Tegghia de' Corbizzi and the Genoese Nicoloso da Recco, in command of three ships, cruised the Canaries and mapped them. Majorca, annexed by Aragon, also provided a source of explorers.

Reports of the native Canary Islanders led to European interest both in slave raiding and in conversion to Christianity, each of which was pursued in the Canaries in the late fourteenth century. Pope Clement VI had awarded the islands in 1344 to Luis de la Cerda, Admiral of France, and his heirs, so that he could lead a conversion crusade, but competing claims were advanced by Afonso and by Alfonso XI of Castile, and Cerda's death in 1360 brought the enterprise to an end although descendants continued to press the claim.

Iberian expansion was very varied because the Canaries were inhabited and their conquest involved lengthy fighting with the native population. In contrast, the Azores were uninhabited and the Portuguese were able to establish a colony with minimal difficulties, a process that was greatly eased by the fertility of its volcanic soils.

The Sargasso Sea

The sea, replete with Sargassum seaweed, was named by the Portuguese in the fifteenth century and is part of the western North Atlantic. It is where eel eggs hatch before the eels travel to European and American rivers, and after five to twenty years in fresh or brackish water they migrate back to the Sargasso Sea to spawn. This process has only been known since the early twentieth century.

The sea is surrounded by currents that leave the sea within largely undisturbed, and it has become part of the North Atlantic's garbage patch. The distinctive brown seaweed is important for the life cycle of a number of animals, notably eels, and is not the deadly carnivorous seaweed depicted in the Hammer Horror film *The Lost Continent* (1968). Nor are there the giant crabs, plants with human shapes, blood-drinking tentacle creatures, murderous humanoid 'weed-men' and other monsters of William Hope Hodgson's novel *The Boats of the 'Glen Carrig'* (1907). The Sargasso Sea is an area of mystery in much fiction, a form of living grave of trapped ships as in the novel *The Sargasso Ogre* (1933), which presents the descendants of Elizabethan pirates, and John Duffield's *Don Sturdy in the Port of Lost Ships* (1926). Another Atlantic myth is presented in *Don Sturdy in the Land of Giants, or, Captives of the Savage Patagonians* (1930) by the prolific Howard Garis, which is somewhat different in tone and content to his *Nannie and*

> *Billie Wagtail.* In *Twenty Thousand Leagues Under the Sea* (1870), Jules Verne describes the sea, providing a scientific explanation.

THE AFRICAN ATLANTIC

There was no known comparable activity by African peoples despite the presence of powerful states and sophisticated societies, notably in Morocco and West Africa, and Africa having a longer Atlantic coastline than Europe. Early inhabited sites in coastal Atlantic Africa included El Khil in Morocco, Casamance in Gambia, Cape Three Points in Ghana, and Bioko in Equatorial Guinea. The last, an island populated in the mid-first millennium BCE by Bantus from the mainland, indicated an ability to cross the water. However, the southward migration of Bantu people from 2000 BCE was essentially an inland process and there were no significant coastal sites in the equatorial rainforest areas.

In Morocco, the situation was very different due to Phoenician, later Carthaginian, trade. In turn, after Carthage declined, Mauretania, a Mauri Berber kingdom and not a major maritime force, traded in the Mediterranean, notably from Tingis (Tangier), re-establishing the manufacture of royal blue dye on the Iles Purpuraires off Morocco, the largest of which is Mogador Isle. From there, Juba II of Mauretania (r. 30 BCE–23 CE) sent an expedition to the Canary Islands, according to Pliny, who reported that huge dogs were brought back from the Canaries for Juba, which led to him naming the islands Islands of the Dogs, while there was also plentiful fruit, birdlife, honey and 'that these islands are plagued with the rotting carcasses of monstrous creatures that are constantly being cast ashore by the sea'.

However, Mauretania by then was under the Roman thumb. Conquered by the Romans in 46 BCE and turned into a province in 40 BCE, it became a Roman client kingdom in 30 BCE and was annexed in 44 CE, although it was never a particularly Romanised part of the empire. Subsequently, the Berber states that were able to compete with Rome for control of North-west Africa were based on inland peoples who lacked naval force, although Berber tribesmen were able to raid Roman Spain from the 170s.

Islamised and somewhat Arabised by Muslim conquest, medieval Morocco to a degree looked northwards into Iberia, which had been successfully invaded across the Strait of Gibraltar by Muslims in 711. There were close links throughout, not least due to Berber settlements and mercenaries in Spain, while Muslim Spain was for part of its history ruled by Moroccan-based dynasties: the Almoravids (1040–1147) and Almohads (1147–1244). The Marinids overthrew the Almohads in 1244, but, launched in 1333, their attempt, in alliance with the Sultanate of Granada, to establish themselves in southern Spain which was totally defeated by 1344.

The Almoravid sultan Ali ibn Yusuf (1084–1143) allegedly sent explorers, under his admiral Raqsh al-Auzz, into the Atlantic from Lisbon, reaching the Sargasso Sea. The contemporary Moroccan geographer Muhammad al-Idrisi (1100–65) described 'this ocean of fogs ... its waves are very strong ... its winds are full of tempests'. The account can be read to imply a voyage into the sea followed by a return via the Azores, Madeira or the Canaries. There have also been suggestions that al-Idrisi described Corvo in the Cape Verde Islands, but it is improbable not least as it is unclear how the boats would have returned northward against the Canary Current.

West African societies, especially Mali which had an Atlantic coastline, like their Indian and Persian counterparts, also focused on landed power. In South-west Africa, there were people on the coasts, notably the Strandlopers, who relied on beachcombing and a marine diet, which yielded whales, seals, fish and shellfish. However, there was not the basis for naval power there or elsewhere. The caves in Elands Bay, South Africa, contain rock art, but there is no suggestion of maritime activity of any range.

Looking for something that does not happen is always

problematic, because it assumes the desirability of outcomes and therefore the need for particular goals, and is, as a method of analysis, teleological and misleading. The Malinké empire of Mali dominated West Africa from the 1230s to the 1460s and, at its height, its coastal imprint included the rivers Senegal and Gambia. Inland trade routes, notably the trans-Saharan trade routes, were crucial, and the capital was at Niani, far from the Atlantic. The Wolof or Jolof empire was on a smaller scale but for a time, as a vassal of Mali, ruled part of the Atlantic coastal region, notably most of Senegal. The empire itself consisted of five coastal kingdoms that were tributaries of the landlocked kingdom of Wolof. Again, there was no long-distance maritime activity from settlements such as Guet N'dar, and, instead, the Portuguese, when they arrived, were the active players in trade to the region, which, indeed, helped cause rivalry between Wolof and the coastal kingdoms, leading to the overthrow of the former at the battle of Danki in 1549. This central event in the decline of the Wolof empire was an aspect of the creation of a vacuum of power that helped external influence, both European and Moroccan. Earlier coastal polities in West Africa, such as Kwa, in the region of Dahomey in the late first millennium CE, also give no sign of long-distance naval activity.

Nevertheless, Portuguese explorers found numerous native canoes in the fifteenth century, for example the long ones that Alvise Cadamosto encountered in 1456 in the estuary of the Geba River. Significant coastal traders, the Bissagos Islanders had a force of canoes. In coastal West Africa, there was also fishing, for example off modern Ghana.

The key developments in West Africa, notably the spread of Islam, bananas, cotton and sorghum, all occurred by inland routes. The major westerly routes in Africa from Sijilmasa in Morocco, founded in 757 CE from the north, ran to Timbuktu, far from the coast, or, from Marrakech via Ouadane (Wādān) in central Mauritania to Aoudaghost. There was no coastal route and therefore no need to cross estuaries. Moreover, the inland routes were shorter.

THE AMERICAN ATLANTIC

The Atlantic coasts of North and South America have archaeological sites reflecting coastal activity, notably frequent shell middens, the remains of shellfish. In addition, there are examples of shell rings, ceremonial sites constructed from shellfish remains. However, the forest-farming tribes that prevailed on the coasts of modern Brazil, the nomadic hunter-gatherers further south and their equivalent in North America, did not support ocean-going shipping, and their focus was on the interior. Marajó, an island in the Amazon estuary, contains earthen mounds that were used by the local people from at least the beginning of the first century and the culture included decorative pottery, but the aquatic resources employed, fish and shellfish, did not lead to significant long-range activity.

On the South American coast of the Caribbean, there are few sites prior to 10,000 BCE, notably Taima-Taima in Venezuela with occupation back to 12,200 to 10,980 BCE, and then, with the spread of agriculture, especially manioc and then maize, the development of sites round Lake Maracaibo and in the Lower Orinoco basin. Banwari Trace and Barrancas are early sites. Subsequently, the coastline saw some autonomous chiefdoms, notably the Tairona ones in modern Colombia, and the Orinqueponi and Llanos in Venezuela. Such chiefdoms shaded off into tropical forest farming villages, and the latter into hunter-gatherers, whether sedentary or nomadic.

Humans spread on to the Caribbean islands (by means of rowing boats). Trinidad was settled in the mid-sixth millennium BCE, and humans reached Hispaniola and Cuba by the mid-fifth; and with major consequences for other animals as humans proved the most successful predator. Subsequently, other peoples took the same route, the Saladoid from 400 BCE, the Barrancoid from 250 CE, the Arauquinoid (later called Taíno and Arawaks) from 650 CE and the Mayoid (later called Caribs) from 1200 CE.

However, this account underplays the complexity of the range of migrant groups, and the conventional categorisation can be actively misleading, a point supported by research on other areas of human settlement. This earlier sequence was not necessarily peaceful. In particular, the Caribs killed or enslaved the Arawaks where they encountered them. Separately, settlement on particular islands may have been affected by volcanism.

Other peoples appear to have come to the islands from the American mainland further north, either from Florida or Yucatán, both of which are close and with easy sea crossings. This was notably so to Cuba across the Yucatán Channel, which could well have been a settlement 'lifeline' whether or not it subsequently became the basis for an exchange network. The net effect was to produce considerable ethnic diversity and, as in the Pacific, very varied settlement histories, with Jamaica and the Bahamas not apparently settled until about 600 CE.

On the New World side of the Atlantic, the only powerful coastal states that appear to have been the basis of significant maritime trade were the Maya of Yucatán. There is no sign that they were capable of, or sought, naval power projection.

The bulk of Maya cities were inland, with additional sites revealed recently beneath the forest cover through the use of pulses of light from lasers mounted on an aircraft to create a three-dimensional map of the surface hidden beneath vegetation, as with the astronomical site at Aguada Fénix in the Mexican province of Tabasco, the discovery of which was revealed in 2020; and there will be more finds. There were also coastal settlements such as El Bellote, Jaina Island, Cozumel and Tancah, and ports such as Chactemal, Tulum, Moho Cay and Wild Cane Cay; and, necessarily so because of the impassable nature of much of the interior, coastal trade routes both westwards and eastwards. These routes appear to have hugged the coastline where water and food could be taken on by the crew and goods traded. Ports were located where coastal and inland routes converged, notably the latter in the shape of navigable rivers, and the absence of wheeled vehicles and draught animals encouraged reliance on water transport. Breaks in the sea cliffs, when accompanied by coves and landing beaches, were important for access to canoes. A major product of the Caribbean coast was salt, with brine boiled in ceramic pots, as in Punta Ycacos Lagoon in Belize, and the salt then traded. So also with maize, honey, fish, textiles, ceramics, cacao, gold, feathers and obsidian, the last of which has been found in particular at Tulum.

The extent to which the Maya navigated the Caribbean is unclear. Dugout canoes were probably made from hollowed-out cedar trunks made watertight with pitch, although archaeological evidence on the islands of the results of trade is limited. Ferdinand Columbus described one canoe encountered in 1502 near the Bay Islands during his father's fourth voyage. It was 'as long as a galley and eight feet wide' and 'in the middle' had a 'shelter of palm matting'. It contained up to twenty-five men as well as women and children and was full of trade merchandise from Yucatán. This was an impressive boat, but the Bay Islands were not far offshore. Moreover, watercraft designs and navigational techniques seen in many of the world's seas were not present, while seafaring traditions on the islands further from the shore may have waned after initial colonisation.

Conclusion

By 1490, the Atlantic world had outliers from Europe, outliers that encouraged both reports of other lands and exploration, but without comparable activity from the people of the other continents. There were, however, no signs yet of the transformation that was to occur within half a century. Nor was it the goal. Indeed, Columbus, like Henry the Navigator, wished to secure money and allies to further the reconquest of Jerusalem, which they regarded as a crucial preliminary to the Second Coming of Christ and thus to the end of human history. In this light, exploration was a form of militant theology, another version of crusading. Indeed, in his *Book of Prophecies*, compiled before his fourth voyage to the Caribbean in 1502, Columbus argued that the end of the world would occur in 155 years, and that his own discoveries had been foretold in the Bible.

Mermaids

In 1493, Columbus saw three mermaids near Hispaniola, complaining that they were less beautiful than hitherto reported. In fact, they were manatees, swimming mammals, but a belief in mermaids was a feature of sailors' tales. North Atlantic mermaids are part of modern folklore as well, and are presented as living in the North Atlantic Ocean Castle.

3

The Creation of an Iberian Atlantic, 1400–1600

....

Slaves and sugar, the plantation economy of Madeira, was a stark instance of what the Iberian Atlantic was to become. Portuguese settlement began there in about 1420, and Madeira became the leading producer of sugar in the Portuguese world. This fed the demand for enslaved people from Africa, whereas in the Canary Islands, which they began to colonise in 1341, albeit facing considerable resistance, the Spaniards were to rely initially on the conquered islanders as slaves on the sugar plantations, rather than on importing enslaved people from Africa.

The Conquest of the Canaries, 1402–96

Whereas most of the Atlantic islands taken over by Europeans were unsettled, this was not the case with the Canaries. Voyages there developed from the thirteenth century. Lanzarote, the northernmost and easternmost of the Canaries, was easily captured in 1402 by Jean de Béthencourt, a Norman noble sailing from La Rochelle having become a vassal of Enrique (Henry) III of Castile. However, in part due to divisions among the invaders, Fuerteventura only fell in 1405. El Hierro also fell that year.

The next stage, that of control by Castilian aristocrats, saw both agreement with some of the native Canary Islanders (the term Guanches only applies to Tenerife), but also rebellions, notably on La Gomera in 1488, caused by

---

mistreatment. Meanwhile, from 1478, the Spanish monarchs, Ferdinand of Aragon and Isabel of Castile, took greater charge, focusing on conquering Gran Canaria, La Palma and Tenerife, which had larger populations. The invasion of Gran Canaria began in 1478 when it was met with sustained resistance in the mountains of the interior. In 1483, key figures surrendered while others committed suicide. The island of La Palma was conquered in 1492–3, in part thanks to agreement with the chieftains, but also due to treacherously seizing Tanausú, the chieftain who held out, en route to talks.

Tenerife held out from 1464 to 1496, with the main effort made in 1494–6. The Guanches won the first battle, ambushing the Spaniards, but lost the second, which was fought on open ground, and the third. The Castilians benefited from the support of some Guanches, the use of firearms and cavalry, and the impact on the inhabitants of epidemics. The war ended with the submission of the remaining Guanches.

Meanwhile, Portugal was advancing southward on the coast of West Africa, as well as to offshore islands, bringing more of the Atlantic into the span of European interest. The Portuguese, who, in the largest expedition they were to mount for the century, had conquered Ceuta in Morocco, their first African base, in 1415, wished to be able to trade for gold from West Africa without any intermediary role for the North African Muslims. Enslaved people were useful as a commodity to sell in exchange for gold. At first, the Portuguese tried to obtain slaves from West Africa by seizing people in raids, but they found Atlantic Africa a formidable obstacle in both physical and human terms. Prevailing wind and ocean conditions limited access to the African coast south of the Gulf of Guinea, while the extensive coastal lagoons and swamps of West

Africa made approaching the coastline difficult, and notably so for the Portuguese deep-draught ships. Penetration inland was variously hindered by dense tropical rainforest and, to the north and south on the coasts of modern Mauritania and Namibia, by vast deserts and heavy breakers hindering approach to them.

Once ashore in West Africa, the Portuguese faced deadly diseases. They also found the rulers south of the River Senegal too powerful to overawe, with the Malinké on the Gambia River seeking to use canoes to trap two Portuguese ships in 1455. The strength of the ruler helped ensure that there was a dependence on local cooperation in order to pursue the slave trade. Indeed, the Portuguese in Atlantic Africa generally followed a process of joint activity, one that contrasted with the control offered by their colonial position on Madeira.

Ships and Navigation

Significant improvements in the capability of shipping were crucial to the ability of Portugal and Spain to become the first transoceanic Atlantic powers. Drawing on recent developments in ship construction and navigation – specifically the fusion of Atlantic and Mediterranean techniques of hull construction and lateen and square rigging, the spread of the sternpost rudder, as well as advances in location-finding at sea – the Portuguese and Spanish were sailing better ships than hitherto. Carvel building, in which hull planks are fitted flush together over a frame, replaced the clinker method employed by the Vikings, one of shipbuilding using overlapping planks. This change contributed significantly to the development of stronger and larger hulls and, therefore, the bigger ships necessary for large-scale trade across the Atlantic, which prefigured the impact of using iron for ship-building in the nineteenth century.

The increase in the number of masts on large ships expanded the range of choices for rigging and provided a crucial margin of safety in the event of damage to one mast. In turn, developments in rigging, including an increase in the number of sails per mast and in the variety of sail shapes, permitted greater speed, a better ability to sail close to the wind, and improved manoeuvrability.

The increase in navigational expertise was also important in itself and contrasted with the situation in other Atlantic societies. The use of the magnetic compass was matched by the spread from the Mediterranean to Atlantic Europe of astrolabes, cross-staffs and quadrants (which made it possible to assess the angle in the sky of heavenly bodies), as well as other developments in navigation, such as the solution in 1484 to the problem of measuring latitude south of the Equator. As a result of all of these, it became possible to chart the Atlantic Ocean and to assemble knowledge about it. This helped ensure that the information brought by individual voyages into, and across, the Atlantic became a knowledge system that could be readily used, with new information slotted in, and notably so in maps and charts. Indeed, the Atlantic as a series of coasts and a number of islands was to be filled in surprisingly rapidly: the mid-Atlantic between 1440 and 1540, the South Atlantic between 1480 and 1580, and much of the North Atlantic between 1490 and 1590. At the same time, uncertainties continued, notably over the routes from the North Atlantic into the Arctic.

At the level of individual voyages, exploration was far from easy, with very many ships sunk and navigators disappearing, for example John Cabot on his second voyage to North American waters. One of Ferdinand Magellan's five ships was lost in the (southern) winter of 1520 in a storm off the Patagonian coast. Furthermore, as with the English party left in North Carolina in 1585, some of those landed on the coasts disappeared, possibly killed by Native Americans or dying from disease or famine. The French settlers from Charlesfort, South Carolina, who tried to sail home in 1563 in an open boat without a compass turned to cannibalism before some reached English waters. The next settlement there, in 1577, was stranded by the loss of its ship and wiped out by Native American opposition.

However, alongside these and many other failures came the steady expansion of knowledge seen with the maps of coastlines and the ability of navigators to take ships to specific destinations: return voyages in both senses were the key to success in crossing the Atlantic. Navigational equipment included the thirty-two-point compass, log and line (for speed and distance measurement), the traverse board (for recording the ship's movement), the sandglass (for timing), and lead and line (to identify location and establish safety by depth of water and the nature of the seabed).

PORTUGAL

Centred on Christopher Columbus, who, sailing from Palos de la Frontera near Huelva, reached the southern Bahamas in 1492, the standard impression is of a Spanish Caribbean. On the Old World side of the ocean, Gran Canaria was finally subdued by Castile (which with Aragon became Spain) in 1483 and Tenerife in 1496. However, the centre of attention was now on the prospects offered by Columbus. Taking forward the division of the 'known' Atlantic world by Portugal and Spain, the Treaty of Alcáçovas of 1479, a key step was the prompt Papal division of the New World in 1493 by Pope Alexander VI, followed by the Treaty of Tordesillas in 1494, a step that allocated to Spain what was then understood as the New World, or likely to be; with the African side of the Atlantic conversely given to Portugal. The division was along a meridian 370 leagues west of the Cape Verde Islands, whereas the 1493 one, 270 leagues west, had been more favourable to Castile. John II of Portugal used the threat of force to secure this alteration, which may have reflected secret knowledge of the Brazilian coast.

The eye of history then gazes westward to Spain's rapid expansion in the Caribbean, principally the conquest of Cuba, and then the invasion of Meso-America (modern Mexico and Central

America) with the overthrow of the Aztec empire by Hernán Cortés in 1519–21 and subsequent swift expansion, not only in that region, but also southwards, notably with the overthrow of the Inca empire of the Andean chain in 1531–6.

These were impressive as well as deadly feats, and the resulting Spanish empire was to be articulated by regular transatlantic links, but it can drown out attention to the even greater mastery of the ocean shown by the Portuguese. It was they who sailed more of the Atlantic than the Spaniards, explored more of its coasts, established bases on the distant, facing shores of the South Atlantic, and used the ocean as a means to sail on to another ocean in the shape of the Indian. Moreover, Ferdinand Magellan, a Portuguese explorer, entered the Pacific in 1520, albeit in Spanish service as, with a route to the East Indies via the Indian Ocean already established, King Manuel I of Portugal had refused support.

Taking many forms, Portuguese activity reflected a long engagement with the Atlantic, notably because of the importance of fishing. Thanks indeed to its position and this history, it was to be Portugal, and not Spain, that most fully took forward the Atlantic potential of the Iberian peninsula. A key figure, Henry the Navigator (1394–1460), the third son of John I, did not actually sail forth further than the capture of Ceuta in Morocco in 1415, and 'the Navigator' was a later title. In order to pursue conflict with the Moors and free the Holy Land, Henry exploited his control over the Order of Christ, as its lay governor, to finance exploration, much of it by Italians, and also tried to focus on navigational expertise to aid that goal. The navigation school Henry reputably founded at Sagres may be a myth, in as much as no evidence of a physical building or teaching staff has been found, but there was a school in the sense of a collected body of navigational knowledge, and, under Henry, the Portuguese discovered the pattern of Atlantic trade winds, a crucial knowledge enabler.

The latter was important in the discovery by the Portuguese of Atlantic islands. Madeira, the Azores and the Cape Verde Islands, all uninhabited, were discovered in 1419, around 1427 and 1456, respectively; and their settlement began in about 1420, 1439 and 1462. Henry the Navigator was responsible for the introduction of wheat, vines and sugar cane to well-watered and heavily wooded Madeira, which was particularly suited for sugar as wood was needed to power the boiling of the cane. Sugar was exported not only to Portugal but also elsewhere in Europe, notably the Low Countries and Venice, thus providing more finance for the industry.

Henry also organised the settlement of the cooler Azores, which were used for cattle raising and for the cultivation of woad, a key source of textile colour and one that reflected the absence of synthetic dyes. The arid Cape Verde Islands were less attractive, not least as a result of the environmental damage done by the sheep and goats introduced by the Portuguese, which was also to be a problem on the drier of the Canary Islands seized by Spain. The Cape Verde Islands would not be another Madeira, but became a major centre for the organisation of the slave trade from Africa.

On the African mainland, a key 'join' between north and south was made in 1434 when Gil Eanes, who had failed the previous year, rounded the stormy Cape Bojador (a headland on the northern coast of what is now Western Sahara), proving it was safe to do so, as had been doubted. Tales of monsters and of a burning sea were a reflection of the difficulties passing Cape Bojador, caused by a strong north-east wind, an underwater reef that extends the Cape and shallow coastal waters, as well as the impression of a bubbling sea caused by fish rising to the surface.

Then, in a spurt of activity not matched by local rulers, the Portuguese reached Cape Blanco in 1441 and rounded Cape Verde in modern Senegal in 1444. Cape Blanco (White Headland), or Ras Nouadhibou in Arabic, is at the tip of a peninsula now divided between Western Sahara and Mauritania. Rounding Cape Verde, the westernmost point of the African continent and the site of the modern city of Dakar, its greenness was very different to the sand dunes to the north, which marked an achievement overland as well as by sea, as the Portuguese had now got past the Sahara, which to the north reaches the ocean near Cape Bojador, and had reached West Africa. Trade links were actively pursued and, in 1452, the gold from West Africa meant that it was possible to mint the first gold *cruzado* coins.

Afonso V (r. 1438–81) was known in Portugal as 'the African' because of his expansionism in Morocco where Alcácer was captured in 1458, and Arzila, Larache and Tangier in 1471. That year, he became the first Portuguese king to call himself 'King of Portugal and the Algarves' as the territories added in Africa came to be regarded as possessions of the kingdom of the Algarve, and the Algarves were thought of as the southern Portuguese territories, whether in Europe or in Africa.

Moreover, in 1479 by the Treaty of Alcáçovas, in an agreement confirmed by Papal bull in 1481, Castile surrendered its claims to trading rights in Guinea and the Gold Coast to Portugal. In part, this reflected the extent to which the Portuguese, unlike the Spaniards, had developed the expertise, infrastructure and financing to make a success of the slave trade and, with Madeira, had a key offshore market. The Portuguese also benefited from the experience gained in long-distance, deep-sea commerce and voyaging. Nevertheless, Spain retained the Canaries. There were no opportunities for the Italian mercantile republics, Genoa and Venice, and no prefiguring of the later attempts by England, France and the Dutch to break into the Iberian Atlantic. In large part, this reflected the need by these Italian republics for Spanish support, their commitment to trade to the eastern Mediterranean, and the impact of the Ottoman (Turkish) advance; but there were also the opportunities, especially for Genoa, to be gained by financing the Iberian powers.

Due to the *Reconquista*, the driving back of Moorish invaders, the Portuguese and Spaniards had a long tradition of enslaving captured people. The initial sub-Saharan Africans the Portuguese encountered were Muslims but, unlike the Moors, these victims, let alone enslaved non-Muslims from further south, were peoples with whom there was no traditional antipathy. Nevertheless, the Portuguese were to import up to 170,000 enslaved people by 1505. Most worked on Madeira or in Portugal, but some were re-exported to Mediterranean slave markets.

Afonso did not really pursue Henry the Navigator's work after the death of his uncle in 1460, focusing instead on Morocco, which was the dominant African consideration for the Portuguese Crown until the 1480s; but, after Afonso's death, there was not a comparable effort in Morocco until the 1500s. Instead, John II (r. 1481–95) drove forward a consolidation of the Portuguese position in Atlantic West Africa, followed by a move into the South Atlantic. The profits, notably in gold trading, from the West African trading base of São Jorge da Mina (Elmina) on the Gold Coast, founded in 1482, financed later voyages, such as those of Diogo Cão and Bartolomeu Dias. Elmina itself was a logistical achievement, prefabricated with stones, timbers and tiles all prepared in Portugal. The islands of Fernando Póo, Príncipe, São Tomé and Annobón were discovered in the 1470s and settlements founded there, Fernando Póo and São Tomé becoming major sugar producers, although the sugar was regarded as of poor quality. Further south, a presence was established on the coast of what became Angola.

The initial steps in the creation of the sub-Saharan Portuguese Atlantic involved not only conflict and trade, but also proselytism. In 1483, Diogo Cão became the first European to set foot in the kingdom of Kongo. Peaceful relations were established and, in 1491, the king was baptised as John I. A blend of Christianity and local religious elements spread readily, and this was a key step in the eventual development of creole societies in many parts of the Atlantic world, one taken forward by the movement of enslaved people from this area to the New World.

By 1491, a Portuguese voyage had entered the Indian Ocean. Bartolomeu Dias, a squire of the royal court who had been instructed to find the dominions of Prester John, the mythical Christian ruler in East Africa and a much-sought ally against Islam, had rounded the Cape of Good Hope in January 1488, without seeing it, and entered that ocean. Reaching the mouth of the Boesmans River, his crew forced him to abandon his plan to sail to India. Indeed, Dias was sunk in 1500, probably off the Cape, in a storm on his second voyage, under the command of Pedro Álvares Cabral.

Meanwhile, in 1498, another expedition, that under Vasco da Gama, had dropped anchor near the Indian port of Calicut, thus establishing a route that was not dependent on Islamic powers, although he brought little of interest to India, which already had a flourishing trade with South-west Asia and East Africa. Indeed, the Portuguese had to use force to establish their commercial position. This route to India made the South Atlantic more significant. Hopeful of its potential, John II had already renamed Dias's Cape of Storms the Cape of Good Hope.

Moreover, the route to India led to Portuguese knowledge of the other shore of the ocean. An expedition under Cabral 'discovered' Brazil in 1500, although, in 1497, da Gama's expedition had observed indications of land. Cabral, who, having already lost a ship near the Cape Verde Islands, went on to lose four more in a South Atlantic storm, at first thought that he had found an island, initially called *Vera Cruz* (True Cross) or *Terra dos Papagaios* (Parrot-land), and, under the Portuguese–Spanish Treaty of Tordesillas of 1494, this was therefore Portuguese.

Brazil rapidly entered the European imagination. It was represented with colourful tree parrots in the *Cantino Planisphere* (1502), a map that was commissioned for Ercole d'Este, Duke of Ferrara, by Alberto Cantino, his envoy in Lisbon. The map accompanied an account of the second voyage of Gaspar Corte-Real to American waters in 1501, a voyage on which he and his ship disappeared. The coast of Brazil stops abruptly and uncertainly to the south on this map, whereas the Atlantic African coast is revealed in far greater detail. In *The Adoration of the Magi*, painted around 1503–5 by the Portuguese painter Vasco Fernandes (known as Grão Vasco, the Great Vasco) and held in the museum of his work in Viseu, a Brazilian Indian is depicted as one of the three kings. The Tupiniquim whom Cabral had met were friendly.

There was no comparable Portuguese territorial claim and presence elsewhere in the New World Atlantic; notably there were no island possessions in the Caribbean, which remained the case, whereas the list of those with a presence there by 1700 included Spain, England, France, the Netherlands, Denmark, Courland and Brandenburg, by 1800 Sweden, and by 1900 the United States. Farther north, the coast, especially of Labrador, was explored by João Fernandes Lavrador and Pêro de Barcelos in 1498, but Portugal did not establish a territorial presence, although its fishing ensured that it was important, and particularly so on the Grand Banks off Newfoundland where Portuguese fishermen found cod in great quantities and salted it for sale in Portugal. This brought prosperity to a number of Portuguese ports, especially Aveiro, where there were important salt pans. Fishing off North America continued and was a background factor in the large Portuguese communities on the east coast, notably in Rhode Island and New Jersey; adding to cod, the Portuguese ventured into whale catching, with many expeditions departing from the Azores. The cod fisheries showed how a model of economic activity could be expanded in a new context, rather as the Portuguese were to take their slave–sugar system from Madeira to Brazil. Lavrador had set sail again in 1501 with a patent for exploration from Henry VII of England but was never heard of again.

Under Manuel I (r. 1495–1521), the new and rapidly expanding territorial and commercial spread of Portuguese power was greeted as a sign of providential purpose and divine support, and both wealth and role were expressed in the Manueline art and architecture of the period, notably in the Jerónimos monastery at Belém, west of Lisbon, built from 1502. Its exotic cloisters present the symbolism of the Age of Discovery, with the armillary sphere, a navigational device associated with Manuel, and the cross of the Order of Christ, the military order that financed some of the voyages.

Yet, the route to India meant that distant Portuguese maritime and military activity focused on the Indian Ocean and not the Atlantic. Saint Helena was developed as a point of call for Portuguese ships en route to or from India, as the island had fresh water and timber. There was no permanent settlement, but fruit trees were planted.

As far as the Atlantic was concerned, it was Morocco's Atlantic coast that was the prime target for Europeans, with the seizures of Agadir in 1505, Aguz and Mogador in 1506, Safi in 1508, and Azamor, São João da Mamora and Anfa in 1515. In contrast, Brazil, where, as yet, there were no bullion finds to exploit, was not actively developed until the 1530s, and there was no attempt to challenge Spain in Central and North America. There was opportunity when Charles I of Spain (Holy Roman Emperor Charles V) faced major rebellions there in 1519–20, but Manuel did not pursue this. Instead, his son John III (r. 1521–57) married Catherine of Austria, Charles's sister, in 1525; his daughter Isabella married Charles in 1526; and the two agreed, by the Treaty of Saragossa with Spain of 1529, to provide a corresponding line of delimitation in East Asia to that of Tordesillas. Agreement dramatically reduced the potential, risk and cost of Portuguese and Spanish activity, and there was no need to challenge that situation in Atlantic America.

The Atlantic became more challenging for Portugal from the 1530s. Given the dominance of hindsight, it is the situation in Brazil (rather than Africa) that arouses most interest, and incursions by French seamen led to greater Portuguese attention to Brazil. The Portuguese could repel them, but made only slow progress at the expense of the Tupinambá (who were ready to ally with the French) and Tapuya, with their muskets of little value against mobile warriors who were expert archers and well adapted to forest warfare. In 1532, the colony was organised into captain-cies (provinces), with each of twelve hereditary captains receiving a grant of 50 leagues of coastline in an attempt to encourage settlement, which only some did effectively. However, port-cities were developed, Recife being founded in 1535, São Vicente in 1534, Ilhéus in 1534 and Santos in 1545. Bahia became the capital in 1549 when a governor-general was sent out, and Rio de Janeiro was founded in 1565. Coastal Brazil became of much greater interest as sugar production was developed there. It enjoyed an advantage from a lengthy harvest season, comparatively mild weather, relatively fresh soil in plentiful quantities and slave labour, and the number of sugar mills rose from 60 in 1570 to 192 in 1600.

The initial emphasis in Brazil was on the native slave popula-tion, one based on slave raiding into the interior, but resistance limited this, while a smallpox epidemic in 1560–3 and a measles one in 1563 hit Native American numbers. As a result, the Portuguese turned to importing enslaved people from Africa, which helped ensure that the slave trade became more important than obtaining gold. A reminder of the role of the Atlantic as link-ing, not separating, this trade was made easier by the closeness to Africa of north-east Brazil, the centre of sugar production and its ports, especially Bahia and Recife. Relatively short voyages cut death rates and the need for credit between the purchase and sale of enslaved people. In the 1570s, the number of Africans among the enslaved people in north-east Brazil increased so that, by the mid-1580s, about one-third of enslaved people there were Africans, and, by 1600, they were in a majority. In the last quarter of the sixteenth century, about 40,000 African enslaved people entered Brazil in a trade that provided revenues to the Crown as, aside from enslaved people moved on the royal account, private slave traders were taxed. Hacking down sugar cane was backbreaking work and even worse under a hot sun. The bulky and fibrous cane is not easy to work.

'Blackness' had proved a slippery concept for Europeans, who tended to see some of their own number as dark-skinned. Yet there was a racial typecasting of Africans that drew on a Western tradition of presenting the inhabitants of tropical lands as strange creatures, including humans with different characteristics. This rested on Greek accounts of mythical peoples in distant areas, not least Aristotle's erroneous claim that it would be too hot for humans to live in the tropics. Strange races were depicted in Africa and Asia on medieval Christian maps, such as the Hereford *Mappa Mundi* of the 1290s, and a one-eyed 'Monoculi' was still depicted in West Africa in Sebastian Münster's *Geographia Universalis* (1540). The very humanity of the inhabitants of these regions was at stake in such depictions and, at best, there was a sense of disturbing strangeness.

Racial typecasting, moreover, was linked to the treatment of those who were non-Christian and they were regarded as inherently less worthy because the Christian message had not historically been offered to them or accepted by them. As a result, slavery was justified by commentators as it also was based on Aristotle's argument that enslavement was not a treatment of equals but of those who inherently should be slaves. However, there was Christian proselytisation in West Africa from the late fifteenth century, notably in Kongo, and enslaved people from there offered a different Catholic heritage to those European Christians, one that contributed to the creole culture of the New World.

As a result of the slave trade, black Africans were further stereotyped and many African cultural practices were misunderstood and recast in a negative light. Denigration as inferior and uncivilised was related to pigeonholing in occupations linked to physical prowess and thus to slavery. Racism became a much stronger element.

In sub-Saharan Atlantic Africa, meanwhile, the Portuguese founded more bases, notably Fort Saint Anthony in 1515 in modern Axim, Ghana (captured by the Dutch in 1642), and Luanda in

1576. The latter was founded by Paulo Dias de Novais, a member of the royal household and a grandson of Bartolomeu Dias. Arriving in Angola in 1575, he was, from that year until his death in 1589, the first Captain-Governor of Angola, and arrived with both soldiers and settlers. Expansion, however, was thwarted by local resistance, notably from the inland kingdom of Ndongo, and disease, and a peace negotiated in 1599 left the Portuguese largely confined to the coast, which is where, despite efforts the following century, they essentially remained until the mid-nineteenth century. To the south, Benguela was founded in 1617, but also did not become the basis of a colony reaching far into the interior.

The Portuguese believed their firearms were important, as in going to the aid of the king of Kongo in 1571, about which Filippo Pigafetta reported: 'the king was restored to his throne, triumphing more by the noise and power of his guns, than by numbers'. However, in practice, victory required a year and a half of fighting the spear-wielding Jagas. Furthermore, an understanding of the limitations of the early-modern European military model, notably gunpowder weapons fired in volleys, has been part of a reconsideration of the sub-Saharan Atlantic in which the weakness of European powers prior to the mid-nineteenth century emerges. Related to that comes an appreciation of the linked European and African interests involved in the misery of the slave trade.

Brazil had great potential for the Portuguese Atlantic, not least when linked with the slave trade from Africa, but it was Morocco that was the centre of attention. It also deserves more attention now. There is an understandable tendency to present Atlantic history, notably over the last 600 years, in terms of the European powers, and, during that period, they and their sequels, principally the United States, were the sole ones with navies and merchant marines in the Atlantic. Nevertheless, that did not mean that only these powers were powerful on the coasts of the Atlantic: that was not the case of sub-Saharan Africa nor with the Saharan coast of the Atlantic in the shape of Morocco. There, the dynamic power from the 1460s to 1500s had been Portugal, with its clear military superiority at sea and on land. The fall of the Marinid sultanate in 1465, and its replacement by the Wattasids, had not ended the challenge from Portugal, toward which, as a result, conciliation replaced unsuccessful conflict. In turn, the overextended Portuguese had abandoned both Mogador and Aguz in 1525 and had only held São João da Mamora for a brief time in 1515.

Wattasid weakness ensured that the Saadian dynasty, which had ruled all of southern Morocco from 1511, overthrew them in 1549 and, definitively, 1554. Prior to that, the Saadians had already pushed back against Portugal, capturing the fortress of Santa Cruz in Agadir in 1541, their first artillery victory in a siege. In turn, Mohammad al-Sheikh, the first sultan of the Saadian dynasty, benefited from the Portuguese abandoning Azamor and Safi in 1541, while that of Arzila followed in 1549. Only Ceuta, Tangier, Anfa and Mazagan were left in Portuguese hands, the last now the most southerly possession. Morocco thereby largely ceased to be an arena of contest with Portugal and, instead, became a significant power. As such, Mohammad al-Sheikh was one of the makers of the modern Atlantic.

His success brought him into conflict with the Ottomans who had backed the Wattasids, helping them briefly regain power in Fez in 1554. Mohammed al-Sheikh refused to pay the Ottomans homage as other distant rulers, such as the Khan of the Crimean Tatars, did. The Ottomans had him assassinated in 1557 and invaded Morocco in 1558, leading, however, to an inconclusive battle at Wadi al-Laban and the withdrawal of the Ottomans in the face of Spanish preparations for intervention.

The Spanish–Moroccan alignment and long-standing Moroccan–Ottoman enmity are reminders of the mistake in thinking in terms of wars of civilisations, in this case Christendom and Islam: conflict between Christian powers, and also between Islamic counterparts, was frequent, as were alignments across this divide. In geopolitical terms, the frequency of warfare with the Ottomans helped distract Moroccan attention from what otherwise might have been more of an effort against Atlantic rivals. The second Saadian sultan, Abdallah al-Ghalib (r. 1557–74), suffered from the failure in 1558 of the large-scale Spanish expedition against Mostaganem, which was intended as a step in the conquest of Algiers. Thereafter, nevertheless, the sultan was able to keep the Ottomans at bay, although they gave shelter to his rebellious brothers. He unsuccessfully besieged Portuguese-controlled Mazagan in 1562, and was sympathetic to the Morisco revolt in Granada, southern Spain, in 1568–71, but did not intervene there, nor seek to provide help as the Ottomans considered doing. After Abdallah al-Chalib died, his son, Abdallah Mohammed, was over-thrown by his Ottoman-backed uncle, Abd al-Malik I, in 1576, and turned to Portugal for help.

In 1578, the young King Sebastian of Portugal hoped to benefit from divisions within the Saadian ruling house in order to establish a client ruler in Morocco, as well as to stop Ottoman influence there. Landing in Arzila, he sought a decisive clash. The resulting battle of al-Qasr-al-Kabir/Alcácer-Quibir was a complete defeat for the Portuguese, with Sebastian, Abd al-Malik and Abdallah al-Ghalib all dying. It was fought in the interior, but helped to determine the fate of the coast, and was one of the most important battles for the history of the Atlantic. Thereafter, the Portuguese did not try anew to expand in Morocco, which, instead, remained the most significant part of the North Atlantic under non-European rule.

The battle, in addition, led to the creation of a Portuguese–Spanish dual monarchy two years later, as the unmarried and childless Sebastian was succeeded by Henry, his clerical and childless great-uncle, the last of the Aviz dynasty. This left rival claimants, but Philip II of Spain (r. 1556–98) had the great advan-tage of power and wealth and, in 1580, his forces rapidly conquered Portugal, which provides the conclusion to Donizetti's opera *Dom Sébastien* (1843).

In turn, a short Atlantic war began. A rival claimant, António, Prior of Crato, had fled to Philip's rival France. In return for the promise to cede Brazil, the French provided support for him, including about 6,000 to 7,000 troops, to establish himself in the Azores, which held a strategic position athwart transatlantic maritime routes. However, after failure in 1581, Spanish expeditions in 1582 and 1583, under Don Álvaro de Bazán, Marquis of Santa Cruz, brought this to an end. The Spaniards intercepted and defeated a larger French fleet off San Miguel in the battle of Punta Delgada in 1582. One of the major sea battles of the century, involving ninety sailing ships, the Spaniards used Mediterranean naval tactics, with a reliance on troops to board opposing ships rather than cannon fire to sink them. The following year, the Spaniards successfully made an opposed landing on Terceira in 1583. A significant element of the landing force was made up of galleys, and for them to tackle the Atlantic was a mark of the confidence of the galley commander.

António fled to France again. This was the end of one of the Atlantic might-have-beens, that of a Franco-Portuguese cooperation at sea against a Spain that dominated Portugal on land. As with many hypotheticals, the possibilities can be variously debated. France was weakened by its civil conflicts, the Wars of Religion, but they were not at one of their most acute stages. However, Spain, with its new naval base at Lisbon, was militarily powerful and better placed to be the Atlantic naval power. At any rate, Philip II, crowned Philip I of Portugal in 1581, established a dual monarchy that lasted until 1640 with two states under one king. The Atlantic was now more under one power than it had ever been before. Philip ruled the New World Atlantic seaboard from Florida to the Plate estuary, as well as controlling the Western presence in Africa. Britain, however, was to be more powerful at sea from 1695 to the Second World War, being succeeded by the United States, although, to a degree, they had to share this position earlier in the twentieth century.

The Spanish Atlantic

It was because of Columbus that the Atlantic was redefined by Europeans from the 1490s. News of the exploration rapidly spread, so that the Saint Thomas Altarpiece in Cologne, by the Master of Bartholomew's Altar, which dates from 1495–1500, portrays the 'wild' Mary the Egyptian, as well as three ships sailing towards the otherwise uninhabited coast where she lives.

Rather differently, the accuracy of mapping the Atlantic coasts increased quickly. Columbus's pilot on his second voyage, Juan de la Cosa, is usually held to have produced the first map to show the discoveries, although it is possibly later than the traditional date given for it, 1500. This second voyage, that of 1493, was significant as it helped establish a viable and repeatable route. In 1506, a map by the Italian Giovanni Contarini had a significant impact because it was printed: Cuba and Hispaniola were shown, but Newfoundland and Greenland were inaccurately presented as parts of a peninsula stretching north-east from China. Between them and the West Indies on this map lay a large body of water giving access between Europe and China, with South America depicted as a separate continent, as was also the case with a map published by Johannes Ruysch in 1507 or 1508 and with Johannes Schöner's map of the world in 1520.

That year, the Magellan expedition, sailing through what was to be called the Strait of Magellan, was the first to round South America, thus showing that the Atlantic and Pacific were linked there and not as an extension of the Caribbean. Named the Strait of All Saints by Magellan, this route between mainland South America and Tierra del Fuego is difficult to navigate but less stormy than the open seas of the Drake Passage south of Tierra del Fuego. However, the Strait of Magellan was also difficult to enter in high winds as the next Spanish expedition, the García Jofre de Loaísa one, discovered in 1526 with two ships wrecked in the process.

Established through conquests – those in the Caribbean, Mexico and Central America, and, later, that of the Portuguese empire – the Spanish empire dominated the Atlantic, but the measure of its power was very different to that suggested by a small-scale map. In practice, ships, inherently vulnerable to the sea and to storms, made lonely tracks across the ocean (and even more rarely the Pacific), or pooled their risk and increased their security against human attack by sailing in a group.

The Spaniards tended to be less bold Atlantic sailors than the Portuguese as they generally needed to range less far, and certainly not to sail into the Pacific round Cape Horn as the Portuguese did round the Cape of Good Hope. Nevertheless, the Spaniards were also concerned to acquire information about navigation. Indeed, the problem that a straight line on a plane chart was not a straight course because of the curvature of the Earth was highlighted by the Portuguese mathematician Pedro Nunes in his 1537 *Tratado da Sphera* (*Treatise of the Sphere*), a work that introduced new methods and instruments in navigation. It was not possible to provide both accurate bearing and equal-area mapping.

The geographical department of the *Casa de la Contratación de las Indias*, the Crown agency for the Spanish empire established at Seville in 1503, was instructed by the Spanish government to create a *Padrón Real* (official royal chart), a work that was frequently updated to take note of new reports from navigators; the Portuguese equivalent was the *Padreo Real*. A manuscript map of the world produced in 1526 by Amerigo Vespucci's nephew, Juan, survives and shows how Spanish knowledge of coastal waters rapidly increased. The successive estuaries on the coast of North America were recorded, while the outline of some of the American islands was considerably more accurate than on earlier maps, particularly Cuba and Hispaniola, but not Jamaica. Diego Gutiérrez's 1562 map of South and Central America offered a complete account of the coastline, which captured the general configuration, but the interior was only poorly covered. The

Padrón Real, however, was a portolan chart, essentially a directional guide, without projection, grid of latitude and longitude or common scale. Disputes over how to correct the *Padrón Real* led to its slipping into disuse in the 1560s.

By then, Philip II of Spain was having to confront growing problems in the shape of French and English ships challenging Spanish territorial and commercial interests in the New World. At the same time, other issues were more to the fore, notably the Turkish challenge in the Mediterranean until 1574 and, more clearly, the battle of Lepanto in 1571, and the Dutch revolt against Spanish rule that became serious from 1566 and, even more, 1572. With time, Dutch naval forces became significant in the Atlantic, surprising and destroying a Spanish fleet off Gibraltar in 1607.

Given this context, it is not surprising that the New World was not to the fore in Spanish concerns. In so far as it was, the yield from the colonies was the prime issue, particularly of bullion, and their expansion, notably in Mexico and Chile, was on land. There was no significant Spanish attempt to use maritime power projection up the east coast of North America beyond Saint Augustine, the main base in Florida, nor along the coast of South America east of Venezuela.

War Over Florida

In some respects, Florida was an equivalent to the major islands of the Caribbean and, in many respects, an outlier of the Caribbean. Huguenots (French Protestants) founded Fort Caroline on the banks of the Saint Johns River in present-day Jacksonville County in 1564, in part in order to threaten the route back to Europe taken by the Spanish treasure ships from Veracruz in Mexico, and in part as a consequence of the French Wars of Religion: Philip II was a key supporter of the Guise faction, the main opponent of

---

the Huguenots. Florida also represented significant French attempts to benefit from the Atlantic, at least in the shape of the entrepreneurial energy of Atlantic and Channel ports such as La Rochelle and Dieppe, the key Huguenot strongholds.

Just as the French in the 1550s failed to challenge the Portuguese in Brazil successfully, however, so French Florida (which included Charlesfort in modern South Carolina) rapidly fell victim to Spanish counter-attack, and, in particular, to the greater ability of Spain to deploy power from nearby Cuba. Fort Caroline was captured in 1565 in a surprise dawn attack in which the defenders were massacred. The National Park Service has built a nearly full-size replica.

The Spaniards established their first fort at Saint Augustine in 1565 but it was precarious, not least due to hostility by the Timucua. Indeed, after the 1560s, Florida, despite a major Spanish effort at proselytism among the native population, was very much a marginal colony and, as such, not an effective base for power projection further north, nor a source of profit or lobbying that provided an encouragement for such action. Sir Francis Drake attacked St Augustine in 1586 and burned it down as a punishment for the killing of a member of his expedition.

There was some Spanish activity further north, including the short-lived base of San Miguel de Gualdape in Georgia in 1526, a base until 1587 at what had been Charlesfort, and the Ajacán Mission of Jesuits in Virginia, who landed in 1570 but were massacred in 1571. In 1572 and 1573, Spanish explorers visited the Chesapeake. No more colonisation was pursued in Virginia, but in Georgia's coastland there were Franciscan missions from the 1580s to 1706.

As opposed to Florida, the other extent of Spain's Caribbean Atlantic at this stage was set by Venezuela, but the coastal regions did not yet attract the extent of interest and settlement that was to be seen in the eighteenth century. So also with the islands to the north of Venezuela, which were not settled by Spain. As such, there was no basis for Spanish expansion into the Guianas.

Beyond that, in 1500 Vicente Yáñez Pinzón, a Spanish explorer who had already sailed along the northern Brazilian coast, became the first European to discover an estuary of the Amazon. Respecting the Tordesillas division, Brazil was not sought by Spain through conquest but, further south, Spain did establish a colony on the wide estuary of the River Plate. However, this again was marginal, and certainly not the basis for a Spanish South Atlantic either there or on the Atlantic coast of Southern Africa, which would otherwise have been a possibility had there been a willingness to break the division. Juan Díaz de Solis was in 1516 the first Spaniard to reach the mouth of the River Plate, only to be killed there by Native Americans. Buenos Aires was founded in 1536 by Pedro de Mendoza, a Spanish noble, who had set sail in 1534 with the support of the Crown. It was defended by a quickly assembled 1-metre (3-foot) thick wall made of mud, although that did not prove resistant to the rain. Attacks by the indigenous people forced the settlers away. Abandoned in 1542, the site was re-established only in 1580.

Wherever the Spaniards settled, they founded towns and, even more, churches, the latter crucial to their mission of Christianisation. The religious architecture is still very much obvious in the old centres of towns such as La Laguna on Tenerife, once the island's capital. Founded in 1496, it holds, in the *Plaza del Adelantado*, the Saint Catalina Convent while the city has old churches, notably that of the Conception built at the start of the fifteenth century. On La Palma, Santa Cruz has the church of El Salvador on the central square with an impressive sixteenth-century wooden ceiling in the Islamic-style Mudéjar. On

Fuerteventura, Béthencourt founded Betancuria as the capital, with the cathedral church of Saint Mary. The ruins of a monastery built in 1496 can also be seen. In 1544, the cathedral of *Santa Maria le Menor* was completed at the heart of Santo Domingo, the capital of Hispaniola, the oldest European city in the New World, which had been founded by Columbus's brother Bartholomew in 1496.

Linked to Spain from 1580 to 1640, the Portuguese world faced pressure from its opponents, and that encouraged attempts to consolidate the Portuguese position. Thus, in response to French interest in northern Brazil, the captaincy of Maranhão was founded in 1615, that of Pará, with its centre at Belém do Pará, was established in 1616, and a separate *Estado do Maranhão*, with its own governor-general, created in 1621. The last was part of a pattern that was to be long-standing in which northern Brazil was seen in Lisbon as being a different entity to the rest of the colony, which was understandable given both the scale of Brazil and the issues involved in navigating its coast.

The Spanish Atlantic of the late sixteenth and seventeenth centuries was largely not a means to expand power along its shores but, instead, a conduit between the most important and wealth-producing parts of the Spanish American world – Mexico and Peru – and Spain itself. Fleets with New World goods sailed from Veracruz and Portobello, in modern Mexico and Panama respectively, to Cádiz, providing an intensity of activity, but one that covered only a portion of the ocean. Purpose-built warships, including fast *fragatas* to carry gold and silver, helped protect these sailings in the 1590s, and it is to the challenge that the Spanish Atlantic now faced that we shall turn in the next chapter.

Yet, as a reminder that more important developments were also underway, maize, now Africa's leading cereal crop, was introduced there by the Portuguese from the 1490s. The plant had been domesticated in Mexico about 7000 BCE, spreading thereafter across much of the New World before being brought to the

Old World by the Spaniards after 1492. Cassava (manioc) was another American crop that succeeded in Atlantic Africa, while potatoes did well in northern Europe. Far less success was had with tobacco in Europe, but in Africa it became significant. The tomato also spread from America, being introduced into European cultivation in the 1540s, but not initially in Africa being affected by diseases and insect pests. Nevertheless, the tomato was to become a significant vegetable crop in Africa. More generally, the Atlantic world saw movements of people, animals, products and diseases that helped lessen biological and human differences between its four continents, often though to deadly effect, as with the arrival of smallpox in the New World with Europeans.

Pursuing Freedom

Born in the Bissagos Islands off West Africa, Benkos Biohó was seized by a Portuguese slave trader and sold to a Spaniard at Cartagena, Colombia. He escaped in 1599 into the nearby marches and came with other Maroons (escaped enslaved people) to dominate the nearby Montes de María. The encouragement of other escapes posed a threat to Spain but, after a failed attempt to defeat the Maroons, peace was negotiated in 1612, only to be treacherously broken in 1619 when Biohó was seized. He was executed in 1621, but the Maroons in the Montes de María continued their defiance. There is a statue to Biohó in San Basilio de Palenque, a village founded by him as the first free African town in the Americas. It is the only one of these walled settlements founded by escaped enslaved people to survive in modern Colombia. The present inhabitants are the descendants of the enslaved people and preserve Palenquero, a creole language, as well as African customs.

4

New Atlantics, 1569–1678

Gonzalo: We split, we split! ... Now would I give a thousand furlongs of sea for an acre of barren ground – long heath, brown furze, anything. The wills above be done, but I would fain die a dry death.

...

Miranda: The sky, it seems, would pour down stinking
    pitch
But that the sea, mounting to th' welkin's cheek,
Dashes the fire out. O, I have suffered
With those that I saw suffer! A brave vessel

...

Dash'd all to pieces! O, the cry did knock
Against my very heart.

The vivid account of the shipwreck at the beginning of William Shakespeare's *Tempest* (1611) was set in the Mediterranean, sailing from Tunis to Naples but with a magical element to it, making the location somewhat mystical. The account was probably based on that of an Atlantic storm in 1609, which led to the deliberate beaching on Bermuda of the *Sea Venture* en route to resupply Jamestown, Virginia. Shakespeare apparently drew on accounts of the storm. Indeed, in the play, Ariel refers to the 'still-vex'd Bermoothes'. At the same time, other sources for the description have been given, including a passage in Erasmus's writings. The scene depicts the professionalism of the crew and the fear of the passengers, but all are cast into the raging and apparently deadly ocean, and are only saved as a result of sorcery.

SEEING THE OCEAN

Navigation demands precision, especially if planning to reach a specific destination on the other side of the ocean, and this was provided thanks to the Fleming Gerhardus Kramer (1512–94), Latinised as Mercator, who, in 1569, produced a projection that treated the world as a cylinder so that the meridians were parallel, rather than converging on the poles. Taking into account the curvature of the Earth's surface, and that any attempt to represent a sphere on a flat surface will result in distortion of either size or shape, and using the grid of latitude and longitude in order to create practical navigation charts, Mercator's projection kept angles, and thus bearings, accurate in every part of the map. A course of constant bearing, or loxodrome, could thus be charted as a straight line across the plane surface of the map, a crucial tool for compass work and navigation, and an achievement unmatched by other societies.

To achieve the navigational goal, the scale was varied in the Mercator projection, but this distortion assisted in the understanding and overcoming of distance. Indeed, Mercator's work was part of the process by which maps provided essential conceptual information to help Westerners cope with the new shape of their known world, taking forward the use of the globe, and the graticule (grid) that covered it, as intellectual and practical tools.

Psychologically there were key dynamics in the reimagining and new way of seeing the Atlantic. Firstly, the projection underlay the idea of the entire Earth as habitable and open to travel; as opposed to the classical idea of four continents, the inhabitants of which could not communicate with each other. Secondly, a Mercator projection need not necessarily include more of the northern hemisphere than the southern, nor place Europe at the top centre, and the Atlantic therefore to the fore. However, Mercator did all three, and this choice helped make the projection one about the Atlantic and, more particularly, how to cross it. This impression was later taken forward in the Western imagination by the strength and position of Western European empires, notably that of Britain, and by the extent to which America was for long dominated by its east coast cities, a situation satirised on 29 March 1976 in a famous *New Yorker* magazine cover looking west across the Hudson River, with the land beyond vague.

The ability of explorers to provide new information helped to enhance a sense that the Western world view was correct and should shape the world. Maps indeed fixed knowledge of exploration and came to make shapes, such as that of the Atlantic, normative. Maps also were the background to an assertion not only of the potential of, and for, new discoveries, but also of a sense of maritime destiny. However, the ability to provide new information also created problems about how best to integrate this information with existing material. Furthermore, many of the additions were inaccurate, sometimes because they included material from explorers who had not understood what they saw. For example, in 1524, Giovanni da Verrazzano, a Florentine-born explorer who was sailing North Carolina's Outer Banks in the service of Francis I of France, reported to the king that he had seen a long isthmus between the Atlantic and the Pacific, with Pamlico Sound marking the start of the Pacific. This was shown in Visconte Maggiolo's 1527 map of these travels, and then adopted by other map-makers.

Verrazzano had already explored Newfoundland and was sent by Francis to find a sea route between there and Florida to the Pacific, and thus help France compete globally with its rival Spain. In 1523, four ships were sent due west toward Newfoundland, only for two to be storm-sunk and the other two to return to Brittany. Repaired, these two sailed westward by a more southerly route via Madeira, one reaching North Carolina in March 1524. After North Carolina, Verrazzano entered New York Bay, sailed along Long Island, entered Narragansett Bay, discovered Cape Cod Bay, and followed the coast as far as Nova Scotia before sailing back to France via Newfoundland. He termed the new lands Francesca, a reference to Francis. In 1527, Verrazzano sailed from Dieppe to Brazil, bringing back Brazilwood: as for other voyages, specific benefit, and not the quest of discovery, was the purpose. In 1528, he set off anew but did not return, possibly being executed for piracy by the Spaniards, and possibly eaten by Caribs on Guadeloupe. Bridges are named after him in New York Bay (until 2018 spelled with only one z), Narragansett Bay and Maryland.

Ignorance About Africa

of the Cannibals that each other eat,
The Anthropophagi, and men whose heads
Do grow beneath their shoulders. (Act I, Scene 3)

Othello's description of Africa, provided to Venetians, captured a sense of strangeness, but also significant ignorance.

ENGLISH EXPLORATION

The first precise information about English transatlantic navigation relates to the Italian John Cabot, who, having had his requests for help rejected by Portugal and Spain, but met with backing by Henry VII, sailed west from Bristol in 1496 only to turn back due to bad weather and supply issues. In 1497, he sailed anew from Bristol in the *Matthew* with a crew of eighteen to twenty, hoping to reach the wealth of East Asia reported by Marco Polo and others, and, instead, probably, sailing to Newfoundland, his 'new found land'. Cabot was convinced that it would be easier to sail to Asia in higher latitudes, and claimed to have found both mainland and plentiful cod.

In 1498, Cabot set out on another voyage, again with backing from Henry VII (who regretted his failure to heed Columbus's request for support), but, this time, with five ships in order to enable him to find Cathay (China) and trade on the Asian coastline he claimed to have discovered the previous year. Little is known of this expedition, and it is probable that the fleet, including Cabot, fell victim to a savage storm with the exception of a ship that had earlier been forced by another storm to take shelter in Ireland.

Other English expeditions were mounted in 1501-5, in order both to explore and to trade. They led to knowledge of parts of the North American coastline from Labrador probably to Cape Cod, but made it clear that China had not been reached. In 1508, Cabot's son Sebastian set out to find a passage to Asia around the new continent and may have reached Hudson Strait, before wintering further south, possibly in Chesapeake Bay, and returning to find Henry VII dead, his pension (salary) revoked, and Henry VIII uninterested in supporting transatlantic voyages. Instead, Henry focused his glory on Continental power politics, rapidly going to war with France, with a strong additional interest in expanding his power and authority in Ireland and, in the 1540s, trying, without success, to subjugate Scotland.

Despite the fishing wealth of Newfoundland's waters, Cabot's voyages were very much on the margins of profitable activity and came to be seen in that light. English expeditions failed to discover a direct route across the Atlantic to Cathay or, subsequently, a Northwest or a Northeast Passage – a route to the wealth of East Asia round North America or North Asia. They also missed out on the compensation of American bullion that was to bring such wealth to the Crown of Spain and help finance its policies in Europe, not least by providing a basis for plentiful credit.

THE NEWFOUNDLAND FISHERIES

By spreading knowledge of the Newfoundland fisheries, voyages of exploration contributed to England's interest in the region, and the route was soon followed by numerous English fishermen. The role and impact of the fishermen who sailed to Newfoundland have not received adequate attention in general surveys of the development of the Atlantic. Building on the methods of the Icelandic fishery, which continued strong into the seventeenth century, the Newfoundland fisheries eventually led large numbers of ships and men to cross the Atlantic and return each year. This resulted in two important foundations for future activity: firstly, knowledge about Atlantic navigation, specifically the currents, winds and coastlines of the North Atlantic, and, secondly, a sense that sailing across the Atlantic was normal. The Portuguese, French and Basques were initially most active in the Newfoundland fisheries but the English, who had very much focused long-distance fishing on Iceland, came to play a more prominent role from the 1570s and, by the end of the century, several hundred English ships were sailing there each year. The conflict between England and Philip II of Spain (from 1580 also Philip I of Portugal) was also played out in these distant Newfoundland waters, with the English and French winning.

Cod was the principal target, and was brought back in sufficient quantities both to hit the North Sea cod fishery and to strengthen the role of sea fish in the Western European diet. The Newfoundland fisheries involved not only fishing but also activity on land, especially the salting and drying necessary to preserve it. This led to the development of a coastal infrastructure, with wharves, washing cages, drying platforms and vats for cod liver oil. Salting and drying also increased the labour demand of the fishery and, as this would not be fully met by the native Beothuks, who were few in number and in competition with the Europeans for the fish, there was a reliance on labour from south-west

England. This helped spread the impact of maritime activity because, aside from experienced or 'specialised' fishermen, there was also a tapping of the general labour market that took advantage of the widespread need for money and of the extent to which fishing was also part of a less specialised labour world. Thus, farmers and tradesmen turned to the sea in order to supplement their income, and the Newfoundland fisheries helped to introduce the seasonal migration of labour, which was so important to English labour, to the transoceanic world, although the lengths of the voyages ensured that the ships and seamen were less available for other activities than was generally the case with fishing. The labour needs of the fisheries and the length of the voyages also increased the requirement for capital. In Newfoundland, salt cod was to be a form of currency from the seventeenth century to the early twentieth.

The Beothuk

The indigenous population of Newfoundland, after those of the Dorset culture died off or left, the Beothuk were hunter-gatherers who took salmon and seals from the ocean, using canoes made of wood and caribou or seal skin. Relations with Europeans were generally poor and, affected by loss of access to food sources and by infectious diseases, the people were officially declared extinct in 1829.

With time, the fisheries became more complex, as sources for fish and technical and market possibilities were probed, and investment was directed to what was proving an important source of profit. Initially, boats sailed from England, moored in harbours and then sent out shallops (7.5–9-metre/25–30-foot boats that had been transported in sections) to fish, while, once caught, the cod was salted lightly, washed and dried. Some ships, however, came to sail to the offshore banks where they preserved the cod in the hold by heavily salting it; the 'wet' or 'green' fishery led to a more perishable product, but required less labour.

The need for salt, which was obtained from Iberia or the Mediterranean, increased the diverse sailing patterns to which the fisheries gave rise, as well as underlining the capital needs of the industry, which extended the impact of the fisheries within Britain: although boats and men came often from small ports, merchants in larger ones, especially and increasingly London, were important in financing and marketing the trade. This was to look towards a degree of specialisation in the late seventeenth century, with the use of larger ships based in a smaller number of larger ports.

The fish trade was not simply bilateral as, benefiting greatly from the injunctions on Catholics not to eat meat on Fridays and in particular seasons, fish was also exported to Spain, Portugal and Italy, playing an important role in English trade. Moreover, the supply of salt was an aspect of the multilateral character of the trade, which thereby anticipated that of the Atlantic slave trade.

Furthermore, the Newfoundland fisheries were seen as important to the strategic strength of the country, as a 'nursery' of sailors, for war and peace, an idea still frequently expressed in the eighteenth century, while the caught fish provided food not only for the fishermen but also for the navy. The Newfoundland fisheries also helped establish methods of organisation, particularly capital support, that were to be important to other Atlantic trades.

A Wider English Engagement

Irrespective of England's diplomatic position, there was growing interest in distant prospects, and clashes occurred in the 1550s and 1560s as merchants unsuccessfully attempted to break into Portugal's trade with West Africa. The range of commodities sought and sold by the English in West Africa indicated the varied search for opportunities that was so important to the quest for profit, and that reflected the absence of specialisation in trade. The goods imported were in part designed to contribute to English industry: the cloth industry, the most important in England, benefited from gum arabic, used for sizing cloth, and, from the 1600s, redwood, employed for dyeing it. Such imports contributed to the diversity of commercial links with the outer world, the growing interdependence that trade brought, and the proportion of the population affected, at least indirectly, by transoceanic activity.

Naval officers invested in the West African voyages dispatched in 1562 and 1563, and the merchants involved probably hired the warships that helped provide protection. This close relationship between public and private, official and unofficial, was important to English transoceanic activity, partly because an unwillingness by the Crown to confront directly the imperial interests of Portugal and Spain encouraged a reliance on unofficial or semi-official action such as privateering, but also due to the weakness of state finances. From the 1540s, cheap cast-iron cannon able to fire iron shot with a high muzzle velocity were produced in England, although bronze cannon remained dominant.

In the 1560s, the attempt to take a share in the profitable slave trade between Africa and the Spanish New World was an important aspect of an English search for overseas opportunities that in part reflected difficulties with trade to the Low Countries. Trade with West Africa and the search for bullion took precedence over interest in settlement in the New World. The prime area of competition over Spanish claims in North America occurred in Florida, but the principals there were France and Spain and, although an English expedition to Florida was mounted in 1565, the lack of bullion led to a failure to establish a settlement. Again, no fort was built in West Africa, where most English voyages in this period were for pepper, hides, wax, ivory and in search of gold, rather than for enslaved people. Nevertheless, John Hawkins sold enslaved people to the Spanish West Indies until, at San Juan de Ulúa (near Veracruz in modern Mexico), in 1568 on his third voyage, the presence of the Viceroy of New Spain led to a Spanish attack on what was, in the official view, an unwelcome interloper, helping ensure that the venture made a large loss. Francis Drake's role helped spark his lifelong desire for revenge against the Spaniards.

Privateering also led the Scots and English to more distant waters. As associates of the French (and thus opposed to England), Scottish ships had taken part in attacks on the Spanish New World from at least 1547; while privateering voyages led the English into waters that were new to them, including, in 1555, the earliest recorded occasion of an English voyage into the southern hemisphere.

In turn, mercantile horizons expanded as did advocacy for an English Atlantic destiny. A sense of maritime destiny was pressed in England by a number of writers, including John Dee, whose *General and Rare Memorials Pertaining to the Perfect Art of Navigation* (1577) argued for England's position as an Atlantic power, and Richard Hakluyt in his *Principal Navigations, Voyages, Traffiques and Discoveries of the English Nation* (1598–1600). Linking exploration and mathematics, Edward Wright (d. 1615) produced a mathematical rendering of Mercator's projection, calculating the position of parallels, and helped to disseminate the necessary information by publishing a table of meridian parts for each degree.

As tension between England and Spain rose in the 1570s, privateering attacks on Spanish trade and settlements in the New World became more common, helping in turn to increase tension, while greater lawlessness at sea affected those who tried to maintain a peaceful trade. Francis Drake attacked the Spanish silver route across the Panama isthmus in 1573, although he encountered serious difficulties, including yellow fever and a stronger resistance than had been anticipated. In the 1940 American blockbuster *The Sea Hawk*, part of the action includes a planned attack on a Spanish gold caravan on that isthmus.

At this stage, however, as England and Spain were not at war, Elizabeth I (r. 1558–1603) was hesitant about overly offending Spain, especially as relations improved in the mid-1570s. For example, Sir Richard Grenville's attempt to mount an expedition in 1574–5, in order to establish a colony in the southern reaches of South America and raid into the Pacific, was unwelcome to the government, which retracted its initial permission.

An English landowner, Grenville (1542–91) was typical of interest in a new Atlantic of apparent expansion. A Member of Parliament, he killed someone in a brawl in London while aged twenty, and fought the Turks in Hungary in 1566 before becoming involved in 1569 in taking over land in Ireland, which helped lead to the first of the Desmond rebellions. In 1575, Grenville developed Bideford in north Devon, in which he had an interest, as a port trading to the North Atlantic. In 1585 and 1586, Grenville commanded the squadrons that sailed to Roanoke, North Carolina; in 1588–90, he sought to develop his Irish landholding; and, in 1591, he died fighting the Spaniards off the Azores.

Full-scale conflict with Spain broke out in 1585, lasting until 1604, and produced an Atlantic of war that was different to the briefer episodes hitherto. The major campaigns were in European waters, with Spanish fleets sent to the British Isles and English ones to Iberia, notably Cádiz, Lisbon and Corunna, but there was also conflict in the New World. The English, however, found success there, as opposed to fame, elusive.

Richard Grenville and the *Revenge*

A larger Spanish fleet put a surprised English counterpart to flight off Flores in the Azores in 1591, with Sir Richard Grenville staging a rear-guard action that held off Spanish ships for a day and a night, sinking and damaging several. Badly damaged, the *Revenge* fought on until the badly injured Grenville surrendered. He died two days later, while the *Revenge* and fifteen Spanish ships sank soon after off the Azores in a lengthy storm.

The battle became an epic of British heroism, with Alfred, Lord Tennyson (1809–92) producing 'The Revenge: A Ballad of the Fleet'. The long battle section is the most famous, not least the depiction of Grenville's grim defiance and his willingness to see the *Revenge* sink rather than be captured:

'Sink me the ship, Master Gunner – sink her, split her in twain!
Fall into the hands of God, not into the hands of Spain!'

However, the close of the poem captured the Atlantic storms:

And the water began to heave and the weather to moan,
And or ever that evening ended a great gale blew,
And a wave like the wave that is raised by an earthquake grew,
Till it smote on their hulls and their sails and their masts and their flags,
And the whole sea plunged and fell on the shot-shatter'd navy of Spain,
And the little Revenge herself went down by the island crags
To be lost evermore in the main.

English attention focused on the Caribbean, the site of Francis Drake's failure and death in 1595–6, while there was also fighting in and around the Atlantic islands where Drake failed to capture Las Palmas in 1595 due to the well-handled Spanish artillery.

ENGLISH NORTH AMERICA

It was elsewhere, however, that an impact was to be made in the more mundane form of settlements lacking bullion, although not initially. The English made efforts to establish a colony on the eastern seaboard of the North American mainland, which was called Virginia in honour of the unmarried Elizabeth. In 1585, 108 colonists were landed on Roanoke Island, in what is now North Carolina, far enough from Saint Augustine not to prove too easy a target for Spain. However, the colonists found it difficult to feed themselves, had tense relations with the native population, and were taken off the following year. Another attempt was made in 1587 but, when a relief ship arrived in 1590, it found the village deserted: disease, starvation or Native Americans may have wiped out the colonists. Nevertheless, the positive impression created by Thomas Hariot's *A Brief and True Report of the New Found Land of Virginia* (1588) and other reports encouraged fresh efforts to establish a colony.

It was not until a base was established by the Virginia Company at Jamestown in the Chesapeake area in 1607 that a permanent English colony was founded on the eastern seaboard. Spain regarded this colony as an invasion of its rights and protested about its foundation, but, although the defences at Jamestown, the vulnerability of which is apparent to the modern visitor, were prepared to resist Spanish attack, it did not come: Virginia was too distant from the centres of Spanish power, Jamestown upriver inside the Chesapeake was a relatively secure location, and the Spaniards were to put more effort into preventing Sir Walter Raleigh from establishing himself in Guiana. Jamestown was thought to be a good location for inland exploration and for acquiring furs.

Despite heavy initial losses of settlers, largely due to the impact of disease in a unfamiliar environment, the Virginia colony expanded as a result of the continued arrival of new settlers and the willingness to put an emphasis on growing food, and, after much bloodshed, native resistance was overcome in 1622–4 and again in 1644. Disappointingly, no gold or silver was found there. Nor was it possible to trade with the Spanish colonies in order to obtain sugar and tobacco that could be profitably sold in England, as Spain was determined to exclude foreign traders. The bankrupt Virginia Company failed in 1624, but not all of its investors wanted to surrender the charter which had to be taken away, the native uprising providing the excuse. The colony was continued with a royal governor.

A key opportunity for profit arose when tobacco became the major crop in both Virginia and Maryland. Tobacco's limited capital requirements and high profitability fostered investment and settlement, while, because tobacco was an export crop, the links with England were underlined.

In 1602, Bartholomew Gosnold, who had sailed from Falmouth with thirty-two on board, established a settlement further north on an island near what he had named Cape Cod. The settlement was rendered redundant by Gosnold's failure to develop initial trading contacts with the natives and, in the face of the latter's hostility, it had to be abandoned. Gosnold went on to play a major role in founding the Virginia Company and died in Jamestown in 1607. Off Maine, he had encountered a boat with eight 'savages' on board.

In 1620, the Pilgrim Fathers, a group of Protestant nonconformist separatists or 'saints', as well as 'strangers' who had been recruited by Thomas Weston or his agents, left Plymouth. The group, who had leased a concession from the New England Company, sailed on the *Mayflower*, made a landing at Cape Cod, and established a settlement at New Plymouth, beginning the development of a colony in New England, a term first used in 1614 by Captain John Smith when he described the coastline north of the Hudson, and popularised by his *Description of New England* (1616). The settlers sought to create a Godly agrarian world, and believed their righteousness made them more entitled to the land than the natives, although it was not only Protestant nonconformist settlers who saw natives as savages. The settlers were greatly helped by the impact on the latter of (probably) a plague in 1616–18 and of smallpox in 1634.

The separatists were followed by other settlers who were not separatists but who were also zealous for a Godly commonwealth, and these more mainstream Protestants, sponsored by the Massachusetts Bay Company established in 1629, founded Boston in 1630. This colony expanded rapidly, and the natives were unable to confront the growth of the English presence. The settlers' brutal defeat of the Pequots in a brief war in 1637 confirmed the Puritans' position and their conviction of divine support. The settlement spread, for example in the Connecticut River Valley from 1634, and, with it, a new landscape was created. By 1642 there were over 15,000 English settlers in New England, and by 1650 nearly 23,000. An emphasis on spreading settlement can lead to an underrating of the role of ports, especially Boston, and, more particularly, the importance of the beginning of the annual sailing season and the arrival of ships that brought immigrants, products, money and news: their likely arrival was the focus of continual discussion and concern.

The English also colonised Newfoundland: Humphrey Gilbert, Raleigh's half-brother, had claimed it for Elizabeth I in 1583, but was essentially laughed off by the English, French and Portuguese fishermen, and it proved difficult to develop the English presence from fishing stations to a settlement colony. In 1610, the new Newfoundland Company established a settlement at Cuper's Cove in Conception Bay, and, thereafter, the Company granted land to settlers on the Avalon peninsula, but it proved difficult to make such settlements a success. The hopes outlined in *Brief Discourse of the New-found-land with the Situation, Temperature, and Commodities thereof inciting our Nation to go forward in that hopeful plantation begun* (1620), a pamphlet by John Mason, the governor of the Conception Bay settlement, proved deceptive, as the climate was too harsh for farming. By 1630, the colony at Cuper's Cove contained only a few settlers, while George, 1st Lord Baltimore, who came to Newfoundland in 1627 to help the colony he had established at Ferryland in 1621, found the climate unpleasant and became more interested in more clement climes further south, ultimately obtaining a charter for Maryland. Nevertheless, the seaborne empire relied on flexibility and probing limits, and the Newfoundland settlements showed that it was possible to overwinter there, which provided the basis for a strengthening of the fisheries, as the fishing season was extended.

The bleaker environment of eastern Canada, however, proved unpropitious for Sir William Alexander who, in 1621, was granted a charter giving him and his heirs a claim to what are now the Maritime Provinces of Canada. The charter was renewed by Charles I in 1625, but it proved impossible to establish a successful settlement on the south shore of the Bay of Fundy. A ship sent in 1622 left the colonists in Newfoundland, and by 1623 only ten of them were willing to continue. Their experience of Nova Scotia did not persuade them to stay. Alexander's son established a colony at Port Royal in the Bay of Fundy in 1629 but, like Québec, which had been captured from France, it was handed over to France in 1632 as part of the peace agreement. Although, in 1633, he gained the title Viscount Canada, Alexander died bankrupt in 1640, and it was the French who founded a settlement at Port Royal that lasted.

The English Atlantic

Bermuda, an uninhabited island remote from all others, was discovered but not settled, probably in 1505, by Juan Bermúdez, a Spanish navigator returning from Hispaniola. An English shipwreck in 1609 was followed from 1612 by the arrival of settlers. Tobacco cultivation was swiftly established and ambergris, a product of sperm whales used for flavouring, was exported. The first enslaved people were imported in 1616. The island was rapidly fortified in order to provide protection against possible attack, whether by Spain, France or pirates, and John Smith's map of 1624 showed numerous forts. However, the small size of the island and the far more abundant possibilities in North America restricted the size of the population.

In contrast, the inherent difficulties of the task, notably disease, but also Spanish opposition, bore the major responsibility for the failure of the schemes for a colony on the Amazon, as well as of Sir Walter Raleigh's better-known plans for Guiana.

Sir Walter Raleigh (c. 1552–1618)

Having fought in France and Ireland, and been given, like Grenville, land in the latter, Raleigh, in 1584, was granted a royal charter to establish colonies in the New World. This was the basis for the Roanoke, North Carolina, expeditions of 1585 and 1587. In turn, in 1594, Raleigh became interested in accounts of gold in what is now Venezuela and Guyana, exploring the area in 1595 and publishing *The Discovery of Guiana* (1596), which asserted the existence of El Dorado. In 1597, Raleigh was a commander in the unsuccessful Anglo-Dutch attempt to occupy the Azores and intercept the Spanish treasure fleet. In 1617, Raleigh was given permission by James I to find El Dorado. A detachment of his men attacked a Spanish outpost on the Orinoco River in breach of the 1604 peace treaty with Spain, and against James and Raleigh's instructions. In addition, no gold mines were found. Raleigh was beheaded on his return.

The English developed a significant presence in the Caribbean from the 1620s but, largely, by means of establishing colonies on islands hitherto without European settlement. Lasting colonies were founded on Saint Christopher (usually known as Saint Kitts, 1624), Barbados (1627), Nevis (1628), Antigua and Montserrat (both 1632), but there was competition with the Caribs, French and Spaniards.

There was also a presence in West Africa, where, after the trade to the Gambia in 1618–21 launched by the Guinea Company had failed, success was won in the 1630s with the establishment of positions on the Gold Coast. By the start of the English Civil War in 1642, there was an English Atlantic on both sides of the ocean. This English Atlantic was less extensive than many writers and projections had predicted and, in contrast to later memorialisation, was the product of the reigns of the first two Stuarts, rather than Elizabeth I, but the basis had been laid for a significant presence in the North and Central, but not the South, Atlantic. The last is downplayed in English accounts of the history of the ocean.

The 1650s and 1660s brought renewed expansion. Jamaica was conquered from Spain in the late 1650s, while Carolina was established as a separate colony in 1663, leading to a marked rise in the slave economy of the English Atlantic, with the new colony owing much to Barbados interests and providing land for younger sons.

The French Atlantic

The timing of the establishment of the French Atlantic was similar. Efforts in the sixteenth century, notably in Brazil and Florida, had not led to success. The French founded Henriville (named after Henry II who had provided the two ships) on the site of present-day Rio in 1555, and Fort Coligny nearby, and tried to colonise São Luís (Maranhão), which they termed *France Équinoxiale*, in 1612, but all without success. The French had traded on the Brazil coast from the 1500s, particularly for Brazilwood, which yielded a red dye. Additional colonists arrived in 1557, but the divisions between Protestants and Catholics and among the former, led to weakness, and Portuguese attacks in 1560 and, finally 1567, defeated and expelled the French. The colony was known as France Antarctique. A Portuguese expedition from Pernambuco defeated and expelled the São Luís colony in 1615. Other French efforts on the Brazilian coast, in alliance with local Native Americans, notably on the northern coast of Brazil, also eventually failed.

Exploration in North America had also not delivered on French hopes of finding commodities, routes and places for settlement. Yet, in the first half of the seventeenth century, the French, while convulsed by civil war and also committed to a seemingly intractable struggle with the Habsburgs and war with Spain in 1628–31 and 1635–59, had, nevertheless, established positions in modern-day Canada, notably the Saint Lawrence Valley and Nova Scotia, as well as in the West Indies. They were then obliged to organise voyages in order to sustain and develop the colonies.

There was also an interest in creating links between the colonies, although the difficulty of the task helped limit peacetime prospects. The Saint Lawrence Valley was seen as a source of food and industry that would complement the fishing off Newfoundland and the colonial goods from the West Indies, producing mutually supportive and profitable interactions in the French New World. Grain, fish and timber were exported from New France and Newfoundland to the West Indies. Named in 1682 and settled by the French from 1699, Louisiana was subsequently proposed and then developed as another source for food and plantation goods.

Cayenne, the basis of French Guiana, was founded as a colony in 1643, but abandoned due to Native American attacks and only finally established in 1664. French efforts to control the coast to the east failed. In 1558 and 1612, the French made unsuccessful attempts to colonise São Luís to the east of the Amazon, while, in 1688, Louis XIV claimed much of the coastline to the Amazon as part of Cayenne, arguing that the French had been continually trading there since 1596. As an instance of the dependence, at least at the diplomatic level, of Atlantic affairs on European power politics, Louis's priority was not shared by all, as the support for it from the Ministry of the Marine was not backed by the Marquis de Torcy, the foreign minister, who did not wish to lose Portugal's support over the contested Spanish succession. The Portuguese envoy in Paris was convinced that Torcy lacked the authority to prevail, but the claim was abandoned in order to win Portuguese support in European power politics.

In West Africa, the French established slave trading bases: Saint Louis on Bocos Island, at the mouth of the River Senegal in 1638 (relocated due to flooding to the island of N'dar in 1659), Gorée near Cape Verde in 1677, and Assinie on the Ivory Coast in 1687, although the last was abandoned in 1705, the French not building a post on that coast again until Fort Joinville in Grand-Bassam in 1843. The precarious profitability of Atlantic commerce, not least the vulnerability to rival European powers, was shown in 1674 when the French West India Company, which had been founded in 1644, was dissolved, in part due to wartime losses. The company had created bases in Dahomey at Savi and Ouidah, and controlled France's slave trade. The successive French Senegal companies that administered Saint Louis and Gorée reflected the same problems.

Attractive to Navigators

Long days eking out supplies made the arrival at islands with fresh water and farmland particularly welcome. In 1669, Captain John Wood commented on Madeira: 'The fruit of this island is sweet and sour oranges, lemons, dates, figs, walnuts, chestnuts, pomegranates, plantains, bananas, onions, but the chief is the grapes ... fishing and a little

---

cotton.' Two years later, Captain John Narbrough wrote of São Miguel, 'above the cliffs is all planted fields of corn . . . the island looks very green and is divided into fields', and of the Azores as a whole: 'wheat and beef and pork and other provisions . . . all provision for the life of man is plentiful'.

Moroccan Ambitions

Ahmad al-Mansur, Sultan of Morocco from 1578 to 1603, had bold plans for expansion not only to gain West African gold and for alliance with Queen Elizabeth I of England against Spain, but also of colonising the New World with Moroccans, and thus having Islam proclaimed on both sides of the Atlantic. In practice, this was part of the rhetoric of Atlantic aspiration so frequently voiced in this period by European powers, and, more specifically, a reflection of the ability of Atlantic hopes to substantiate other aspirations, in this case the Moroccan desire to counter the rival Ottomans. The sultan might have sought this Atlantic goal, but nothing was done to give force to it. Nevertheless, 'Barbary Corsairs', Berber raiders, were able to inflict considerable damage, as in 1593 on the island of Fuerteventura in the Canaries, the cathedral in Betancuria being destroyed. Yet, it is indicative that no effort was made to conquer the Canaries. In the 1660s, the difficulties the English encountered in opposing Moroccan corsairs off Tangier led to English interest in the use there of Mediterranean galleys, which were more manoeuvrable in inshore waters.

The Dutch Atlantic

The United Provinces (modern Netherlands; colloquially known by the leading province, Holland) was an unexpected player in Atlantic power politics as it had gone from the Burgundian to the Habsburg inheritance. As part of the latter, there was a major engagement with the sea, but this was focused on North Sea fishing and Baltic trade, and the further seas that were explored were those to the north of Europe. The situation changed, however, as a result of the Dutch revolt that began in the 1560s and made the Spanish world, which, from 1580, included the Portuguese empire, the target for this maritime energy. Attacks were widely mounted, not least in Asian waters, but the Atlantic and, more particularly, its shores became a battleground, and notably after the hostilities that had ceased with a truce in 1609 recommenced in 1621. For the Dutch, power, profit, and Providence were to be pursued by seizing Spanish and Portuguese colonies and trade. This was the major Atlantic war of the seventeenth century, but it is one that is seriously underplayed in most accounts due to its not involving England or France.

Despite significant and, often successful, resistance, the Dutch conquered the northern provinces of Brazil from the 1620s, capturing in 1630 the major port of Recife which, under the governorship of Count Maurits of Nassau from 1636 to 1644, became Mauritsstad. He was defeated when he attacked Salvador da Bahia in 1638, but took it in 1640, and Dutch control was extended from Sergipe to São Luís.

Moreover, in Atlantic Africa, the Dutch captured the Portuguese slaving bases of Luanda, Benguela and São Tomé in 1641, which encouraged the Portuguese in Brazil to turn to slave hunting in the interior. The Dutch claimed Saint Helena in 1633 but did not occupy it and, instead, focused on their colony at the Cape of Good Hope, founded in 1652, a colony better situated for supporting ships en route to or from the Indian Ocean.

The Dutch South Atlantic appeared matched to a Dutch Central Atlantic, with slaving bases on the West African coast, where São Jorge da Mina, captured from the Portuguese in 1637, was renamed Elmina, and Axim was captured in 1642. In addition, the Dutch had colonies in the Caribbean, notably Curaçao and Saint Eustatius. In the Guianas, the Dutch established colonies: Demerara, where a New Amsterdam was founded in 1627, and Surinam, where Paramaribo was founded in 1613. Dutch Brazil was primarily a continuance of this settlement pattern, but also part of the South Atlantic.

In addition, the Dutch North Atlantic saw the Dutch as the leading naval power in European waters, able to inflict a major defeat on the Spanish fleet in the English Channel in the battle of the Downs in 1639. In North America, the Dutch had a base on Manhattan Island at another New Amsterdam, and their power had spread up the Hudson Valley. As a result, the English colonies in New England and the Chesapeake were divided. Moreover, the Dutch strengthened their position by seizing the Swedish colony along the Delaware Valley in North America in 1655, while, in 1658, the Danes captured the Swedish positions in West Africa, which were then sold to the Dutch West Africa Company. Meanwhile, in 1643, the crew of a Dutch East India Company ship made the first definite landing on Tristan da Cunha, four more landings occurring over the following twenty-five years, and, in 1656, the Dutch produced the first charts of the archipelago.

The mid-century high point of Dutch power was linked not only to commercial enterprise, naval strength and a determination to focus on imperial expansion, but also to the civil wars affecting the Spanish empire in 1640–52, the British Isles in 1639–51 and France in 1648–52. Moreover, Portugal was involved in a lengthy war of independence from Spain in 1640–68. Spain itself negotiated peace with the Dutch in 1648. The Dutch benefited from this situation to make permanent gains from the

Portuguese empire in modern Malaysia and Sri Lanka, but did not have the same success in the Atlantic world. In part, this was because the Dutch West India Company was weaker than its East India counterpart, but the strength of resistance was also significant.

This resistance was both international, with the English a major challenge to the Dutch in the Atlantic world in three wars fought between 1652 and 1674, but also from within the Portuguese world. In Brazil, from the 1630s, the Neapolitan troops in Spanish/ Portuguese service proved better able than their Dutch opponents to adapt to the possibilities of the terrain, adopting far more open formations as well as using frequent ambushes. From 1644, when they withdrew from São Luís, the Dutch were on a downward trajectory in Brazil, from where, in 1648, a Portuguese fleet recaptured Luanda, Benguela and São Tomé. Finally, the Dutch were driven out of Brazil in 1654 when Recife was recaptured.

The Dutch, like the English and the French, were to retain a stake on the Guiana coast further north, but were to make no further effort to take Brazil. Portugal had regained Brazil in its entirety, and this provided the basis for a marked revival of the integrated Portuguese slave and sugar economy in the South Atlantic, one that was never again to be seriously attacked by another power. By 1680, the enslaved population was about 150,000. This economy was to be greatly strengthened by the discovery of large-scale gold deposits in the early eighteenth century. As a result, the Portuguese Atlantic empire did not suffer from the lack of capital and relative uncompetitiveness seen in Portuguese Asia. Brazil became a viceroyalty in 1663, and southward expansion led to the foundation of Laguna in 1654 and the establishment of the Colônia do Sacramento on the north bank of the Plate estuary in 1680.

The Portuguese Atlantic also involved creolisation, the role of black freemen and enslaved people in creating New World culture, including creole languages, religious syncretism, transatlantic musical culture and maroon communities. For example, associational networks and values maintained African or African-style practices and beliefs while others related more directly to the New World. In particular, lay brotherhoods linked to the Catholic Church developed, so that ancestor worship became an aspect of Catholic devotion. The deculturation and depersonalisation inflicted by the slave trade did not completely define the people's experience. For many a sense of self was maintained and, albeit in probably far more difficult circumstances than for enslaved people within Africa, those transported to the Americas were able to rebuild their lives by using and also adapting their own experiences and beliefs, thus helping them survive in a harsh environment. Participation in the informal economy was an element, one that reflected the importance of slave energy and skills, for example cultivation in provision grounds.

THE ANGLO-DUTCH WARS

While the Dutch–Portuguese conflict determined the fate of the South Atlantic until the early nineteenth century, the three Anglo-Dutch wars of 1652–4, 1665–7 and 1672–4 were very important in the North Atlantic, although they left unclear what might happen if France and England fought each other. The First War was largely waged in European waters, and the major Atlantic expedition of the English in the 1650s was against Spanish-held Hispaniola in 1651–5. Well-protected Hispaniola was not captured but, despite Spanish opposition, relatively unpopulated Jamaica was. Earlier, the Parliamentary victors in the English Civil War had sent a fleet of seven ships under Sir George Ayscue that blockaded Barbados into compliance.

In the 1660s, in contrast, the valuable slave trade from West Africa led to conflict there from 1661, with the seizure of bases and ships. That year, the Dutch fort on what is now Kunta Kinteh

Island, 33 kilometres (21 miles) from the mouth of the River Gambia, was recaptured and named James Fort after James, Duke of York, later James II. The link between the two sides of the Atlantic was demonstrated in 1664 when Captain Robert Holmes, having seized the Dutch bases on the Gold Coast, sailed to North America, capturing New Amsterdam and renaming it New York in honour of his patron, James, Duke of York. Full-scale war broke out in 1665, although, again, large-scale operations were focused in European waters. The Treaty of Breda of 1667 confirmed English possession of New York, but left Essequibo and Surinam in the Guianas with the Dutch, and acknowledged French control of Acadia, later Nova Scotia. In the Third War, France allied with the English, not, as in the Second, the Dutch. The Dutch attacked English shipping in the Caribbean and off North America, and also recaptured New York in 1673, but battles were restricted to European waters and New York was returned by the Peace of Westminster of 1674 in which Charles II abandoned his alliance with France.

The Dutch and the French fought on until 1678, with significant operations in the Atlantic, notably off West Africa and in the Caribbean. In the first, the French captured the slave trade bases of Gorée in 1677 and Arguin in 1678, ruining the Dutch trade. In 1676, the Dutch captured Cayenne from the French, only for it to be retaken that year. In the West Indies, Saint Martin and Tobago were recaptured by the French, but, in 1678, their squadron ran aground on the Isle of Aves off the coast of Venezuela in an unsuccessful attempt to capture Curaçao; seven ships of the line were lost.

Understandably, as they were naval powers, the struggle between European powers dominates attention in Atlantic history of this period. Moreover, European power expanded in the Atlantic, with the English settling Saint Helena from 1659 and building a fort there. The Dutch captured the island in 1673, but were driven off by the English the same year. It became a key port of call, as with Cape Town for the Dutch from 1652. The latter became a settler colony and had to face native peoples. Neither the problems of managing a settler colony nor those of native resistance were issues for the English on Saint Helena, but both of which were for them in the New World. In King Philip's War in New England in 1675–8, the English, after defeats including the burning of Providence in 1676, prevailed over the Wampanoags and Narragansetts thanks to local allies, and the impact of disease, starvation, lack of ammunition and relentless English pressure.

ATLANTIC AFRICAN POLITICS

The discussion hitherto, although one that covers standard topics, would, however, be an inadequate account of Atlantic history, because most of Atlantic Africa remained in non-European hands; as did Patagonia. In Morocco, the Saadian dynasty had expanded after defeating the Portuguese in 1578, but not as an Atlantic power. Instead, the Tuat and Gourara oases of modern Algeria were taken in the mid-1580s, which expanded control over trans-Saharan trade, while the Songhai empire of the Niger Valley was captured in 1591. It was no wonder that Morocco appeared potent and fabulous to the audience of Shakespeare's *Merchant of Venice*, although, in practice, this conquest led to a long period of difficult sub-Saharan conflict. In *Titus Andronicus*, Aaron, 'that dam'd Moor', is a dangerous, vicious and crude villain.

Affected by civil war in 1603–27, and then by the autonomy of many of its more powerful figures, the Saadian dynasty ended in 1659. However, the European powers did not play a role in these civil wars, although Spain captured Larache on the coast in 1610. After another period of conflict, the Alaouite dynasty, the current Moroccan royal family, came to power, with Mulay al-Rashid proclaimed sultan at Fez in 1666. Again, no opportunity could be taken by the European powers. Indeed, as discussed in the next chapter, his successor, Ismail Ibn Sharif (r. 1672–1727), was to put pressure on them, as well as on the Ottomans in Algeria.

The Salé Rovers

A privateering republic was proclaimed at Salé in Morocco in 1619 by Moriscos who had fled from Spanish persecution. Its first president and grand admiral, Reis Mourad the Younger, was a Dutch privateer, born Jans Janszoon van Haarlem, who, seized in Lanzarote by Barbary corsairs in 1618, had converted to Islam in captivity and became one of the famous Salé Rovers. Their fleet was eighteen strong, but the ships were fairly small, the *polacca* type having twenty-four cannon and a crew of seventy-five. They journeyed far in search of slaves and loot. In 1622, Janszoon sailed into the English Channel and, in 1627, captured Lundy and raided Iceland, although with only limited success, and in 1631 raided Baltimore in Ireland. He also raided frequently in the Mediterranean. In 1669, Captain John Wood noted of the Portuguese-ruled island of Porto Santo, to the northeast of Madeira, that it was very exposed to Salé Rovers. The previous year, however, the Moroccan sultan, Mulay al-Rashid, seized Salé and ended its independence.

Further south, in West Africa, the Europeans were a marginal force other than the Portuguese based in Angola. There was a number of states on the coast, including, in 1625, Great Fulo, Kayor, Sine, Kaabu, Kokoli, Mane, Asebu, the Akan state, Popo, Benin, Calabar, Loango, Kakongo, Ngoyo and Kongo. Most were relatively small, and those that were more extensive, notably Great Fulo, Loango and Kongo, were not in a position to develop a maritime force beyond the canoes that were successfully used for river, lagoon and inshore activity, all of which were important. Benin used wood for boat building and benefited from fishing and from troop movements by canoe, but, although the city state was impressive and it controlled trade along the Bight of Benin (now Togo, Benin and western Nigeria), it suffered from a scarcity of metals and sought trade with Europeans. Politically less powerful, Sine, on the north bank of the Saloum River delta, was another society for which fishing was important. There was no need for deep-draught shipping, and most of the coast was totally inappropriate for it. Instead, fishing boats were run on to the beach and launched from there.

In West Africa, warfare was changed by the spread of missile weapons, first archers and then firearms, which led to an increasing preponderance of firepower over hand-to-hand combat. On the coast, the Asebu army of the 1620s was the first to include a corps of musketeers, their guns being supplied by the Dutch as a means to advance commercial interests. The two had allied in 1612, with the Dutch allowed to found Fort Nassau near Moree; the Portuguese had destroyed the Dutch trading base there in 1610. Muskets replaced bows on the coast from the 1650s to the 1670s. The emphasis on missile weapons, bows and, later, muskets interacted with the transformation of peasants into mass armies. The replacement of shock by missile tactics was linked to a shift from élite forces reliant on individual prowess to larger units reliant on conscription. Larger armies increased the numbers that could be captured in conflicts, which took place over much wider areas and could yield large numbers of captives, helping fuel the slave trade.

These military changes were related to the rise of the states of Akwamu and Asante on the Gold Coast and Dahomey on the Slave Coast. These powerful states had a very great impact on European options in West Africa and serve as a reminder that the Atlantic was not simply an ocean bounded by European power. Any discussion of the relationships, and specifically military balance, between Western and non-Western powers should not centre simply on initiatives by the former and, unlike Portugal, other Western powers did not try to make conquests in sub-Saharan Africa, other than of other European bases. Thus, the European presence in West Africa was anchored by coastal forts that served as protected bases for trade. For example, on the Bight of Benin, Anecho (now Aného) became a Portuguese base in 1645 and Whydah (now Ouidah) had an English one in 1672. In some areas, however, there were no settlements and the traders operated from their ships. This also saved on the cost of forts.

The garrisons of the European forts were very small and badly affected by disease; and they relied upon the forces of African allies, both for their own security and for their capacity to intervene in local conflicts. The emphasis therefore was on cooperation, not conquest. For example, the Swedish African Company was able to play a role on the Gold Coast in the 1650s, with Fort Carlsborg founded in 1652, because the Futu wanted to balance the influence of the Dutch. More generally, this cooperation was crucial to the establishment of new trading posts, although the Swedish Gold Coast was conquered by the Danes in 1658 and 1663. In 1694, Denmark had to buy back Fort Christianborg from the Akwamu tribe.

The key European advantage rested not on force or superior military capability, but on a purchasing power that derived from the prosperity of plantation economies in the Americas shipping goods back to Europe, and thus on the integrated nature of the Atlantic economy. In contrast, African economies were undercapitalised. Purchasing was crucial because, whereas warfare between African powers provided large numbers of enslaved people, European powers were not able to seize significant numbers. Some African states became centralised, while others were decentralised and governed by coalitions of autonomous interests. Each process could owe much to the slave trade, in part depending on how the resulting profit was controlled and distributed. On the Gold Coast,

the slave trade encouraged the disintegration of the small, centralised Fante kingdoms on the coast into a decentralised federation.
In 1673–7, Abd al-Kadir led Muslims in a jihad along the River
Senegal, in part expressing hostility to the sale of enslaved people
to Christians, but this had no lasting effect.

In Angola, the part of Africa with the largest European presence (although one that was far smaller and more restricted to the
coast than present-day Angola), the Portuguese were effective
only in combination with African soldiers. Unlike the nineteenth-
century pattern of European-organised units filled with African
recruits, the Portuguese in seventeenth-century Angola were all
organised together into a single unit with its own command
structure, while the Africans, either mercenaries, subject rulers
or allies, were separately organised in their own units with their
own command structure. It was only at the level of the army as a
whole that Portuguese officers had command, providing control
for entire operations. The Portuguese found the Africans well-
armed and formidable opponents.

The Atlantics of the 1670s

The links across the Atlantic were stronger by the 1670s than a
century earlier, and that despite there being more powers competing there for power and profit. These links could be seen in terms
of transatlantic trade, migration and power projection, and the
rise and fall of particular states were thereby registered. The fall
of the Dutch Atlantic seemed most apparent, with the Dutch
losing their territorial presence in Angola and São Tomé in 1648,
Brazil in 1654, Cayenne (where they had established a presence in
1658) in 1664 and North America (finally) in 1674.

Yet, there were also separate Atlantics, that, while linked in,
were distinctive. A key example was that of fishing, the longest
lasting human interaction with the Atlantic and the one that had
been continually underplayed. English, French, Portuguese and

Spanish, mostly Basque, ships fished off North America, especially Newfoundland, and heavily salted the cod they caught, taking it to European markets; although the number of Portuguese and Basque ships declined in the late sixteenth century. The numbers involved in fishing were considerable: in 1664 alone, three French ports, Le Havre, Les Sables-d'Olonne and Saint-Malo, sent 231 fishing boats to Newfoundland. This trade had a number of permutations, with ships in the eighteenth century increasingly based in Newfoundland. Already in 1675, about 1,700 English fishermen overwintered there, while New Englanders came to play a bigger role in the fishing.

The number of workers involved in processing the cod, including collecting the oil from the livers, was large; but the absence of a significant native population, and the unsuitability of the climate for enslaved people, led to a reliance on Europeans. The Newfoundland trade involved a number of flows, including salt from western France and Setúbal in Portugal. Most of the cod caught by English fishing boats was sent directly to Spain, Portugal and Italy, some salted fish went to the West Indies, not least to feed the enslaved people, and cod liver oil went to England.

MIGRATION

Voluntary and involuntary migration was across the Atlantic from east to west. There was a reverse flow, but it was small-scale, voluntary and restricted, for example of Puritans back to England in the 1650s. The number of European emigrants to the New World far outnumbered those to Asia and Africa, and increased the number and percentage of non-natives there, a process that owed much to the impact of disease on the native population. This was a continuing process. Thus, smallpox wiped out half of the Cherokee in the late 1730s.

The enslavement of Africans, in large part a substitute labour supply given the failure to enslave sufficient natives, was the principal cause of compulsory migration, although not the sole one, as convicts could be sent for example to Barbados, Bermuda and Virginia. In 1618, street children in London were seized for work in Virginia. The largest individual market for African enslaved people was Brazil, which received 42 per cent of the enslaved people imported into the Americas during the seventeenth century. This was a reflection of the 'white gold' economy of sugar, but also of the harsh nature of work and life on the sugar estates in Brazil: enslaved people had a life expectancy of fewer than eight years. The high death and low fertility rate of African enslaved people once arrived in Brazil reflected the cruel hardships and disorientation of enslavement, transport and labour. These rates ensured that it was necessary, in order to sustain the numbers needed for work, to import freshly enslaved people, and this continued import affected the nature of slave society, sustaining its African character, as in the traditional pattern of marriage customs, religious beliefs and related ideas about kin and family, and thus its difference to native societies. As with other European slave trades, the enslaved people were supplied not by the Portuguese government but by Afro-Portuguese slaving networks which linked the African interior to the Atlantic, provided the capital, dominated the supply and took the profit. The brutality of the slave trade was matched by the ferocity of the fighting against slave rebellions, as in 1694 when the Maroons of Palmares (near Pernambuco in Brazil) were defeated.

In the second half of the century, the relative significance of the West Indies as a market for enslaved people increased, and this market was largely met by Dutch, English and French traders, although others sought a role, including Danes, Brandenburgers, Courlanders and Swedes. The individual and collective misery involved at every stage was a growing part of Atlantic history. Coercion, prejudice and racism were all central parts of the fabric of life and of the experience of blacks, both enslaved and free.

5

Atlantic Struggles, 1679–1774

MOROCCO

Ismail Ibn Sharif is not a name that trips off the tongue when thinking of the Atlantic in the late seventeenth and early eighteenth centuries, but he testifies both to the marked diversity of the societies on the shores of the ocean, and to the need to avoid any tendency to focus on the Europeans, or to present non-Europeans essentially as victims, notably in the case of enslaved people. Born around 1645, Ismail was the seventh of the fifteen sons of Mulay Sharif, a key figure in the rise of what became the Alaouite dynasty of Morocco. Mulay Sharif's eldest son, Muhammad Ibn Sharif, succeeded, only to be killed in 1664 in battle by the troops of his half-brother, al-Rashid, who overran much of Morocco in the late 1660s, becoming the first Alaouite sultan in 1664. The polygamous nature of Islamic ruling houses and the absence of primogeniture contributed greatly to the instability of their dynastic histories.

Al-Rashid died in 1672 after a fall from his horse, a frequent problem in a horsed society, and was succeeded by his half-brother Ismail, although the latter had to fight his nephew and brothers, as well as Berber rebels, until 1679. Marrakesh proved a particular centre of opposition. Meanwhile, in 1678, Ismail, a determined, cruel and wilful man, who was reputed to have eventually had over 1,000 children, enforced his control over the tribes in the Saharan provinces to the Senegal River, and also reimposed his control over the Pashalik of Timbuktu.

Driving the Christians from their Atlantic positions was to Ismail but part of the process of re-establishing the Moroccan state. Tangier, Portuguese from 1471, had been part of the dowry of Catherine of Braganza when she married Charles II in 1662. The fortifications of the city had been much improved by the English and a mole to protect the harbour was constructed, and they held off the siege in 1680, but the cost to the English of maintaining the garrison led them to abandon it, and the Moroccan army entered the city in 1684. Occupied by the Spaniards from 1614, La Mamora was successfully besieged by Ismail in 1681, and renamed al-Mahdiyah. The statue of Jesus in the church was taken as loot, as were the Spanish captives, including women and girls, and the Spanish cannon and arms. In opposition to the commonplace consequences of Christianisation, a mosque, madrasa and traditional inn were constructed as part of the restoration of the twelfth-century kasbah.

Rather than pursuing Atlantic power politics, Ismail had to deal again with the Ottoman forces in Algiers and, until 1687, with rebels. Then, he turned on the city of Larache, near Tangier, which Spain had held since 1610. It fell in 1689, and the garrison was enslaved. Azila, besieged soon after, was evacuated by the Spaniards and occupied by the Moroccans in 1691. The last unconquered Berber tribes were subjugated in 1692–3, which brought all of Morocco under Ismail's control.

With his substantial and experienced army, notably the Black Guard, a large, professional force, many of whom, as with the Ottoman janissaries, were enslaved people, Ismail was one of the strongest rulers in the Atlantic world, but his was very much a land power. There was no naval equivalent to the Black Guard, and no opportunity for Morocco to reshape the larger Atlantic world by sea power. Moreover, he was not capable of extending his control south of the Senegal River, nor of invading Spain, nor of allying with rulers in sub-Saharan Africa. Instead, Ismail unsuccessfully fought the Ottomans in 1692–3, being heavily defeated in 1701 when he attacked anew. Ismail also besieged Spanish-held

Ceuta (1694–1727) and Melilla (1694–6), but without success and with his weak artillery inviting derision.

In turn, rebellion by his sons created serious problems in the 1700s and divisions within the royal family caused serious civil war between 1727 and 1757. Under Mulay Ahmad Adh-Dhahabi (r. 1727–8, 1728–9), the Black Guard became a force for chaos, trying like the Praetorian Guard of Imperial Rome to sell its political support. The weak sultan was deposed in 1728 by his half-brother Abdalmalik, but the latter then fell out with the Black Guard who turned to Ahmad Adh-Dhahabi, leading to a civil war, the division of the country into two states, a failed attempt by Abdalmalik to kill his half-brother, and the arrest and, in 1729, murder of Abdalmalik. As a result of struggles between Ismail's sons, Mulay Abdallah was sultan in 1729–34, 1736, 1740–1, 1741–2, 1743–7 and from 1748 until his death in 1757.

Morocco had control over ports, and not only those seized from the Europeans. In 1668, al-Rashid had seized Rabat and Salé, ending the independence of the Salé Rovers who were not employed in order to develop naval strength that could be used for political purpose, or even to blockade European cities. Nor did the Moroccans match the naval strength and activity of the Barbary states in North Africa: Algiers, Tunis and Tripoli, notably the first.

Conflict between Morocco and European powers arose from privateering by the former, although there were also attempts to redeem captives by means of negotiations, Britain and Morocco reaching agreements accordingly in 1700, 1713 and 1751. The Moroccans used the *chebeck*, a light sailing vessel with auxiliary oars. The economics of privateering ensured that the ships were employed for commerce raiding, not fleet engagements, and attempts were made to avoid clashes with other warships. The crew of a Dutch frigate was captured in 1751, but only after it had been driven ashore during a storm. The Dutch were formally at war with Morocco in 1751–2 and 1774–7, while the French had a naval show of force in 1765–6. However, conflict was generally fruitless other than in encouraging the Moroccans to show restraint. Privateering bases were difficult targets, not least because deep-draught warships risked running aground on uncharted rocks off their approaches. The French bombardment of Larache and Salé in 1765 achieved little and a French attempt to land at Larache failed in the face of heavy fire. There was no comparable conflict with any of the states in West Africa.

Elizabeth I of England had sought to align with Morocco, with the export of naval-grade timber to Morocco in exchange for saltpetre, a key constituent in gunpowder, authorised in 1581, the English Barbary Company established in 1585, privileges given to English merchants, and cooperation discussed against Spain. In contrast, when James O'Hara, Lord Tyrawley, the martial envoy in Lisbon, suggested in 1738 that the Royal Navy be used to back a Moroccan invasion of southern Spain, this was clearly ridiculous as Morocco was no longer in a shape to play a significant role in power politics. However, under Mohammed ben Abdellah al-Khatib, Mohammad III (r. 1757–90), there was a revival, a process continued, after he won a civil war for control, by Slimane (r. 1792–1822).

West Africa

In West Africa, the local rulers, although they had coastal-operating ships, did not develop a long-range force to match that of the Barbary corsairs. Among the states that had a coastline were Walo, Benin, Loango, Kongo and Mbailundu. On land, however, the West African rulers became more powerful, not least as flintlock muskets superseded the less reliable matchlocks. European positions could be under pressure. Although the English base at Cape Coast Castle was successfully defended in 1688, bases were taken, including Offra (Dutch) and Glenhue (French) in 1692, Christianborg (Danish) in 1693, Sekondi

(English) in 1694, Glenhue (Portuguese) in 1727, and Hueda/
Whydah (Portuguese) in 1729 and 1743. The last fell to Dahomey
which, under Agaja (*c.* 1716–40), became more powerful, in part
due to an effective use of European firearms combined with
standards of training and discipline that impressed European
observers. Europeans on the Slave Coast had to take careful note
of Dahomey views, not least in ensuring that their quarrels did
not disrupt relations with that kingdom: Dahomey supplied the
enslaved people exported from the Bight of Benin. Moreover, the
widespread availability of firearms in Dahomey facilitated the
slave trade by contributing to its aggression.

THE SLAVE TRADE

The slave trade was only possible thanks to the active cooperation
of African rulers for whom slave taking was a long-established
practice, as was the sale of enslaved people to Islamic societies in
North Africa and South-west Africa. This cooperation included,
on the part of Agaja of Dahomey, an interest in permitting the
establishment of European plantations. If African traders and
rulers served the needs of a European-dominated Atlantic economy, the Europeans needed the slaves and, as with the British
base on Bunce Island near the mouth of the Sierra Leone River
from 1748 to 1779, were in a system in which the Africans were
able in large part to structure the system. Guns, money and
enslaved people proved interchangeable elements of trade and
force. There was a prominent role for private enterprise, as well
as an overlap between it and state authority. This process was
seen in the European–native networks of trade that brought
enslaved people to the coast, as well as the chartered trading
companies, such as Britain's Royal African Company that ran the
coastal forts.

At the individual level, the reality of slavery was of the trauma
of capture by African chieftains, sale to European merchants,

often after passing through African networks, and transportation: violence, shock, hardship and disruption. These factors need emphasising throughout this book, as they are a continual reality alongside the changes that are charted. Individuals were taken from their families and communities. Many died in the process of capture, although the number is very obscure. Others died in the drive to the coast, in which they were force-marched, and joined by coffles which secured them by the neck while leaving their legs free for walking. Again death rates in this stage are very obscure. Yet more died in the port towns where they were crowded together in hazardous circumstances while awaiting shipment. At Cape Coast Castle, the enslaved people were confined in the vaulted brick slave hole, a crowded, infectious, twilight existence where they were chained round the clock apart from when they were driven to the Atlantic coast twice daily in order to be washed. Others died on the ships that transported them across the Atlantic, the stage for which death rates have been calculated, and, also, soon after arrival, as the entire process exposed enslaved people to unaccustomed levels and types of disease. In the process of capture, transportation and sale, the enslaved people were also intimidated, humiliated and exposed to terrifyingly unfamiliar circumstances.

Racism played a role, and a racism that drew on a feeling of superiority and a degree of fear. This was linked to intellectual views. Thus, there are statements in the writings of David Hume and others that can be read as racist, in the sense of believing that 'Negroes' were intellectually inferior. This was a widespread view, and, if not necessarily a programme of proposed mistreatment, certainly one that was conducive to it.

The slave trade increased in scale in the eighteenth century, especially in the years of peace between the major European powers: Britain and France did not fight in 1714–42, Britain and the Dutch in 1689–1779, and France and the Dutch in 1714–43 and 1749–92. In wartime, slaving stations were captured, as were slave-plantation colonies. For example, James Fort, which protected the British in the local slave trade and contested the French position in Senegal, was captured by the French in 1695, 1702, 1704, 1708 and 1779, while Howell Davis, a pirate, captured the French fort in 1719, but was killed later that year. The 1755 plan of the fort by Justly Watson shows men and women's slave houses and yards. In 1775, in a report to the Admiralty, Captain William Cornwallis captured the precariousness of the European presence in his account of a voyage up the River Gambia:

> I thought the appearance of a man of war might be of service. I therefore went up the river in the *Pallas* to James Fort, which I found in great distress for want of stores, and particularly gun-carriages, not having above three or four serviceable ones in the fort, and most of their guns rendered totally useless for want of them . . . I stayed in the river eight days, during which time we got the king of the country on board, and showed him all the civility we could; he seemed very well pleased; so I hope all will go on well again.

Britain was the leading slave trader and notably so in the second half of the eighteenth century, with the slave economy in the West Indies increasingly supplemented by the spread of slavery in British North America. Alongside the determination to control slaving bases in West Africa, garrisons were maintained in the West Indies to suppress slave conspiracies and rebellions that occurred with some frequency, as on Jamaica in 1760, 1765 and 1776, Montserrat in 1768, and Tobago in 1770, 1771 and 1775. There were specific slave flows in response to supply and demand. The Igbo shipped from the Bight of Biafra were favoured by Virginia planters, but were seen as insufficiently strong by Carolina and Georgia planters, who preferred Bambara and Malinké from Senegambia, or Angolans. Enslaved people in

Virginia and Maryland benefited from the relatively more benign, or at least less deadly, conditions of working with tobacco, and approached demographic self-sufficiency as early as the 1720s. In contrast, work was harsher in the rice lands of South Carolina and the sugar plantations of the Caribbean, the percentage of enslaved people was greater, death rates were higher, and more enslaved people were imported.

The second biggest slave shipper was Portugal, which continued to dominate the South Atlantic and responded firmly to competition, destroying the British trading settlement at Cabinda in 1723. In contrast to the conflict between Britain and France, the Portuguese slave trade did not face a challenge comparable to that mounted by the Dutch in the seventeenth century. Angola supplied about 2 million enslaved people during the eighteenth century, mostly to Brazil, but the Portuguese had more bases further north, notably at Cacheu, and also traded along coasts where they did not have any bases. It took about forty to forty-five days to sail from West Africa to Salvador (Bahia), the capital of Brazil until 1763, and about fifty to sail from Luanda to Rio, its replacement; and this difference explained the particular linkages of the Portuguese transatlantic slave trade.

France and the Netherlands were the next major slave traders in that order. France focused on its West India colonies, although Cayenne and Louisiana were also significant. In 1719, the French fortified Fort Saint Joseph to protect their trade along the Senegal River. Gifts of guns were used to expand French influence, which depended on local cooperation.

The Dutch had more of an entrepôt trade to the colonies of other states, a situation also seen with the Danes and Brandenburg-Prussia, the latter of which sold its two forts on the Gold Coast to the Dutch in 1717. However, the Dutch began slave-based coffee production in Surinam in 1712 and, by 1772, were producing over 12 million pounds per annum there, being noted for a harshness discussed by Voltaire in *Candide* (1759) where an enslaved person tells Candide:

'Those of us who work in the factories and happen to catch a finger in the grindstone have a hand chopped off; if we try to escape, they cut off one leg. Both accidents happened to me. That's the price of your eating sugar in Europe ... Dogs, monkeys, and parrots are much less miserable than we are. The Dutch ... who converted me, tell me every Sunday that we are all children of Adam.'

From 1722, the French also produced coffee in Cayenne. In turn, the large-scale cultivation of rice in the coastal regions of the British colonies of South Carolina and Georgia stemmed from the movement from West Africa of rice plants and of enslaved people used to cultivating them.

This was a harsh and brutal Atlantic, one of cruelty and dehumanising conduct. Whipping for offences was commonplace, as in Bermuda regulations of 1674, not least for wandering at night without permission, which was seen as a prelude to possible revolt, as had been attempted in 1664, 1673 and 1681. The 1696 Carolina Slave Code decreed that for the second offence a male runaway was to be castrated and a woman to lose her ear, and that, if an owner refused to inflict these punishments, he could lose the slave to an informer, while the death of slaves as a result of such treatment was to be compensated, thus encouraging it. These provisions were maintained in the 1712 Act. Accordingly escapees were castrated, as if animals. Visiting Charleston in 1736, Charles Wesley noted in his journal, 'It was endless to recount all the shocking instances of diabolical cruelty which these men (as they call themselves) daily practice upon their fellow-creatures; and that on the most trivial of occasions.' He commented on a slave woman beaten unconscious and revived, before being beaten again, and having hot candle wax poured on her skin. Her offence was overfilling a teacup. Aside from often routine physical violence, there was considerable verbal abuse as well as the contempt of gesture. Government regulation of treatment, for example as introduced by the Dutch in Surinam in 1772, was generally limited, infrequent and remote.

Slave Ships

The Atlantic crossing was dangerous and harsh. There are no precise figures for overall deaths, but many enslaved people died on the Atlantic crossing where they were crowded together and held in poor, especially insanitary, conditions, with holds proving both fetid and crowded. Furthermore, the enslaved people had already been weakened by their generally long journey to the Atlantic coast, while there was also an unwillingness on the part of their captors to spend much on provisions. This situation exacerbated the serious health problems already caused by the severe impact of malnutrition, disease and conflict among those who became enslaved. As a result, they were more vulnerable in their journeys. Most died from gastrointestinal illnesses, such as dysentery, which were a reflection of the very crowded nature of the ships and the dirty conditions in the holds. In order to prevent rebellion, enslaved people were generally shackled, usually at wrist and ankle, and lay in their excrement which contributed greatly to the pungent atmosphere in the holds. Ventilation panels were closed in bad weather and high seas.

The percentage of deaths on a crossing clearly varied, not least because, if the crossing was delayed, casualty rates rose; but the average percentage was grim. An average loss of 17.9 per cent on Dutch ships between 1637 and 1645 has been calculated, and the losses for the British Royal African Company between 1680 and 1688 were about 23.5 per cent. Statistics record these experiences of brutal custody, for the vast majority of those involved are now nameless.

Suicide was one response, with some enslaved people jumping overboard, while the melancholia noted by ship surgeons was also conducive to high rates of illness. There are 493 known risings on slave ships, especially in the late eighteenth century, and the threat ensured that the crew was considerably larger than on merchant ships of a similar size, thus increasing the cost. Disease hit the crew, and the harsh treatment of the enslaved people may have been a consequence of the unpopularity of the work. James Field Stanfield, who had worked as a sailor on a slaver from Liverpool to Benin and then Jamaica in 1774–6, argued in the *Observations on a Guinea Voyage* (1788) that brutality, shortage of water and disease were the lot of the crew, with the harsh beating of the cooper by one of the mates described, as was frequent flogging. Unsurprisingly, the enslaved people were also very poorly treated.

The requirements of the Dolben Act of 1788 regulating British slave ships, notably the limitation on the number of enslaved people according to the tonnage and the requirement for each voyage of the presence of a doctor, encouraged the use of larger ships. In 1789, a less rigorous, but similar, Act was passed by the Dutch, and in 1799 British restrictions were strengthened.

EUROPEAN MIGRATION

At the same time, the scale of European transatlantic emigration rose. Convicts, vagrants and prostitutes could be sent, the first notably by Britain after the Transportation Act of 1718. The pace of voluntary emigration was particularly high from the British Isles, and this, as much as conquest and trade, helped to make the North Atlantic increasingly British. The French tried to develop a system linking the Saint Lawrence Valley, Cape Breton Island (a substitute for Nova Scotia), fishing off Newfoundland, the French

West Indies, Cayenne and the French African slaving bases. A major military base founded at Louisbourg on Cape Breton Island in 1720 was designed to protect both Canada and the Newfoundland fisheries. This system, however, lacked people, in part due to a limited desire to emigrate and in part due to a drive for Catholic colonists. Only about 11,370 French people settled in Canada between 1608 and 1759. The climate was discouraging, as was the shortage of readily cultivable land.

In contrast, the less populous British Isles sent more migrants, encouraged by the more liberal attitude of successive governments to the religious and national character of emigrants, as with the Plantation Act of 1740. In the seventeenth century, English migrants dominated emigration from the British Isles to the New World, but, in the eighteenth, there was also extensive emigration from Scotland and Ireland. Many were indentured servants who, in return for their passage, bound themselves to service for a number of years. Demand for these servants reflected economic demand, for example the rising price of tobacco. Disease had a major impact on migration. There would have been a British New World dominated by the West Indies, with nearly 3 million people in 1760, compared to only 1.7 million in British North America, but disease, notably yellow fever, prevented that, as well as hitting enslaved people harder in the Caribbean.

Most European migration to the colonies was within individual imperial systems, with particular characteristics. Whereas enslaved people had no choice, the British, in large part due to the degree of religious freedom they accepted and the availability of cultivable land, were uniquely successful in attracting settlers from areas that did not have transatlantic imperial systems, notably subjects of the German states. The expansion of the colonial imprint encouraged this process, notably the establishment of Georgia in 1732, Savannah being founded the following year. Initially, Georgia, very differently to South Carolina, where by 1740 two-thirds of the population were enslaved people, was not a slave colony according to the London-based trustees; but, under pressure from the settlers, that situation did not last.

This migration of white people (not the enforced one of enslaved Africans) was to be important to the British victory over France in the struggle for North America. The British outnumbered the French, not only in regular troops sent from Britain but also in local militia, and, supported by naval dominance, the local logistical base for their operations to conquer Canada was stronger; whereas the Americans in the War of 1812 lacked that dominance. Conversely, the French, who had the second largest fleet in the world, did much better in 1778–83 when allied with a large North American population in the shape of the American Patriots who had already rebelled against Britain. To a degree, the movement of people was destiny but, in the Atlantic world, a key element was that much of the movement was of enslaved people who were then kept in enslavement, such that, although there was the alternative, and notably in the cities, of a freed black population, it was not the opportunity for most enslaved people.

Most migration was from the Old World to the New, but there was reverse migration, as with the Acadians, French settlers in Nova Scotia, expelled by the British in 1755–64, some of whom settled in Belle Île in 1766, occupying land abandoned during the British occupation of the island in 1761–3.

Ships

Meanwhile, navigation developed during this period. There is an understandable tendency to focus on the major changes that were to come in the nineteenth century, those to steam and to iron ships, and, as a result, to regard the Age of Sail as a unity with wooden ships operating in a consistent fashion. In relative terms, that was the case but, nevertheless, there were changes of significance and, combined with organisational developments, these ensured that navigation altered. Moreover, change encompassed warships as well as merchantmen. The net effect was to make the Atlantic less unpredictable, both as a series of routes and for navigation as a whole.

There was indeed what has been referred to as the shrinking of the British Atlantic. The introduction of the helm or ship's wheel soon after 1700 dramatically increased rudder control on large ships by removing the need to steer with the tiller by means of a bar fitted to the rudder post.

In addition, the average annual number of transatlantic British voyages doubled between 1675 and 1740, and the number of ships that extended or ignored the 'optimum' shipping seasons also increased on several major routes. Links became more frequent and easier, and average peacetime passages from England to Newfoundland were five weeks, from the eastern Caribbean colonies to England eight weeks, and from Jamaica to England fourteen; although any concept of the average concealed a wide variety that was largely dependent on the weather, but also affected by the seaworthiness of the ships.

More frequent links helped in the development of postal services by 'ship letter', with captains charging a fee. In addition, the British government began its first contract postal service in 1702, between Falmouth and the West Indies. The government contract service expanded in 1710 to include a route from Bristol to New York, but this ended in 1712. Instead, a monthly service between Falmouth and New York started in 1755. In contrast, the voyage round the Cape of Good Hope between Lisbon and Goa usually took six to eight months in either direction, as did the Pacific crossing from Manila to Acapulco.

TRADE AND SHIPPING

In the British Atlantic, and far more than its French, Portuguese and Spanish counterparts, sailings largely reflected commercial opportunity, not government permission, although the ability of the navy to ensure the peacetime safety of the seas, particularly by banishing or at least containing piracy, enabled ships to sail with fewer cannon and thus to need a smaller crew, a measure that greatly helped the profitability of shipping, not least by permitting a larger cargo as opposed to supplies for the crew. A reduction in the time ships spent in harbour, and a fall in the cost of credit and insurance, as well as the costs of packaging and storing goods, were also important to greater profitability. Improved transatlantic passages benefited the fisheries, trade and the navy, and, in particular, the growing complexity of trading relationships that criss-crossed the ocean. Average annual British exports to North America rose from £0.27 million in 1701–5 to £1.3 million in 1751–5, and that in a period of very low inflation. Shipping tonnage rose greatly, with the increased focus on transatlantic trade playing a major role in this expansion and in that of the maritime labour force which, in turn, helped in the wartime manning of the navy.

Losses to storm, shipwreck and privateers encouraged insurance and ensured that it was necessary to build, if only to maintain shipping capacity, but greater demand meant that shipbuilding was far more than just for replacement. The need for ships was not met by imports, and the Navigation Acts dating from the 1650s ensured that it had to be met by British and not foreign carriers. Furthermore, long-distance trade entailed particular requirements for shipbuilding. In Britain, most large ships were built on the Thames. However, the Union of England and Scotland in 1707 opened up the English commercial world to Scottish enterprise, not least creating opportunities for Scottish shipbuilding, the number of ships from Glasgow, the key centre, rising from thirty in the late 1680s to seventy by the 1730s. In the colonies, shipbuilding began in North America, notably Boston, and, to a lesser extent, Bermuda, Barbados and Jamaica. Bermuda and Jamaica developed particular types of sloops. These were usually built of cedar, which was resistant to rot, and were designed for agility, speed and relatively shallow waters, which helped make them suitable for privateering.

The increase in the range, as well as the volume, of Atlantic trade helped spread the benefit of empire through different areas of British industry, notably the iron and textile industries. Aside from significant qualitative changes that flowed from the economics of scale made possible by export, production and trade, the turnover produced the profit necessary for reinvestment.

BRITISH COMMITMENT

Comparable benefits were seen with other Atlantic powers, but none had the naval heft enjoyed by Britain, and this dramatically reduced their wartime trade and increased their costs, not least with reference to insurance. Britain's allies, the Dutch from 1689 to 1780 and the Portuguese from 1703, were able to benefit, while their liquidity helped finance the large credit needs of Britain's expanding Atlantic economy, creating in a way an Anglo-Dutch-Portuguese world that was to remain important into the twentieth century. Dutch holdings were very significant for the financing of the British national debt, while Britain's success in gaining access to Brazilian gold was crucial in developing the finance and infrastructure for credit and in letting Britain fight its wars, not least pay subsidies to Continental allies providing troops.

The foundation of the Bank of England in 1694 was part of the process as it greatly assisted in the stabilisation of financial markets in London. By providing the funds and instruments for long-term credit, the so-called Financial Revolution underwrote British participation in an Atlantic economy that ran on borrowed capital. This process was important to the growth of shipping, as well as to the development of tobacco production round the Chesapeake, sugar production in the West Indies, and the slave trade that provided the manpower necessary for both.

The Royal Navy in turn configured itself for long-distance operations. The emphasis in the seventeenth century had been on ships designed for operations in the English Channel and the southern North Sea against the Dutch, but war with France meant the need to engage with greater distances, and this increased with the growing concern with transatlantic power projection. In place of a focus on carrying large numbers of cannon came that on ships as being better sailers. In addition, transatlantic bases developed to support the warships, while the emphasis shifted to Atlantic-facing dockyards. The workforce at Plymouth, where in 1691 contracts for work on a drydock were changed so that it would be able to take the biggest ships of the line, becoming a front-line operational facility, rose from 54 in 1691 to 1,837 in 1759.

In France and Spain, there was also an emphasis on Atlantic dockyards, notably Brest, Lorient, Ferrol and Cádiz, alongside the continual role for Mediterranean ones, especially Toulon and Cartagena. Britain itself was a Mediterranean power, with control of Gibraltar and Minorca from 1704 and 1708 respectively. However, the British commitment to the Mediterranean was less than that of the other two powers, in part because of the latter's commitment to Italian power politics but also due to the Mediterranean not yet being seen by Britain in terms of a route to India, let alone *the* route. Indeed, in so far as the route to India was concerned, it was the Atlantic that provided that route, and for the navy as well as for trade. The other powers did not have the same focus on the Atlantic as Britain did in this period. This is surprising given the significance of New World bullion to Spain, but Spain was also a Mediterranean imperial system with the routes there dependent on naval power.

Britain's naval predominance helped ensure its leading role in the campaign against Atlantic piracy that was successfully pursued in the late 1710s and 1720s, one that spanned West Africa, the Caribbean and North American waters.

The Atlantic had been largely explored prior to this period, but there were large areas in the far north and far south that were poorly understood. In this period, this situation was improved more in the latter area, not least as a result of voyages by William Dampier and Edmond Halley. The former was famous for his exploration of Australia, but circumnavigated the world three times, and published a very successful *New Voyage Round the World* (1697) and *A Discourse of Trade Winds* (1705). In 1701, Dampier's ship HMS *Roebuck* foundered at Ascension Island, being run aground to cope with the consequences of its taking on water through the planks, which were riddled by seaworms. Fortunately, the crew were brought back by an East-Indiaman on its return from India.

Halley, an astronomer, explored the South Atlantic in the *Paramore* and produced his chart of trade winds in 1689, the first scientific astronomical tables in 1693, and his 'General Chart' of compass variations in 1701, all important tools for navigators.

Greater British interest in the Pacific, an interest seen in a series of books, helped also increase that in the South Atlantic, which was the general route thither for Britain, as with two of Dampier's circumnavigations and with George Anson's circumnavigation of the world in 1740–4. Indeed, in 1749, Spain objected to the establishment of a British base in the Falkland Islands that was considered as a way to support future British activity on that route. The British were also interested in the other extreme of the Atlantic in order to discover a navigable Northwest Passage to the Pacific, but attempts in the 1710s and 1740s failed.

Until the eighteenth century, there were no clocks accurate enough to give a ship's meridian position, and longitudinal mapping faced problems. Many islands were placed too far to the west or the east; combined with the failure of captains to know where their ships were, this caused shipwrecks. Indeed, in 1741,

Anson nearly ran aground on Tierra del Fuego: dead reckoning had put his position more than 480 kilometres (300 miles) out to sea. In 1714, Parliament established a Board of Longitude and offered a substantial reward for the discovery of such a method, with France copying this move the following year.

Easy to offer, difficult to fulfil, but in 1761–2, at variance with the Royal Society's emphasis on astronomical tables as the solution to the problems of longitude, John Harrison, a clockmaker, devised a chronometer. Its timekeeping was so accurate that, on a return journey from Jamaica, the ship carrying it found her distance run erred by only 30 kilometres (18 miles) on the anticipated position. Such calculations depended on the precise measurement of local time in reaction to the time at the Greenwich meridian. Elizabeth Montagu reflected on an advance made in wartime: 'I imagine the French themselves would have been sorry if they had destroyed this fine instrument, for the realms of science, and the acquisition of invention are open to all, and they will share with us the improvements of navigation and the ascertainment of geography.'

As a result of Harrison's chronometer, navigators were able to calculate their positions far more accurately, which made it easier for map-makers to understand, assess and reconcile the work of their predecessors. Initially chronometers supplemented the earlier practices of dead reckoning and lunar observation, rather than immediately driving them out, but they were swiftly used, including by James Cook, as well as by Captain Constantine Phipps on his failed voyage towards the North Pole in 1773, a voyage that disproved the idea that the sea did not freeze because of its salt content. This voyage was another instance of the unsuccessful attempt to match for the North Atlantic the routes to other oceans offered by the South Atlantic. There were also improvements in the method for finding latitude more precisely.

Aside from charts of the ocean, maps of its coastline also improved during the period. Indeed, the coastline of the South

Atlantic was increasingly explored. In particular, there was a search for Pepys Island, which was alleged in 1683 by William Crowley, a privateer, to lie about 230 nautical miles (420 kilometres/260 miles) north of the Falkland Islands, and was probably a misidentified account of the latter, one that found its way into travel accounts, such as William Hacke's *Collection of Original Voyages* (1699) and maps. It may have been Puig, a phantom island that the French believed to exist.

In 1764, Captain John Byron, who had sailed on Anson's voyage, being shipwrecked off Chile, was sent to find Pepys Island, which was seen as a potential base on the route to the Pacific. There was no island, but Byron in 1765 explored the coast of Patagonia, an area well to the south of the Spanish settlements in the Plate estuary, and also sailed to the Falkland Islands before going on into the Pacific. On his return in 1766, there were reports that the crew had met 3-metre (nine-foot) giants in Patagonia, and this led to the frontispiece illustration in the 1767 published account of the circumnavigation. Earlier voyages, including those of Magellan, Drake and Cavendish, had also claimed to encounter such giants. The reports were countered by the official account of Byron's voyage, which appeared in 1773. The year 1767 had also seen a French corvette make the first full survey of the Tristan da Cunha archipelago.

Meanwhile, information on the region increased, notably with *A Description of Patagonia and the adjoining parts of South America* (1774), based on the papers of the English Jesuit missionary Thomas Falkner (1707–84). Falkner's life was typical of those that criss-crossed the Atlantic, eroding national boundaries, although the harsh treatment of non-Europeans frequently limited this process. Brought up as a Calvinist in Manchester and trained as a surgeon, Falkner took a post as a surgeon on a ship taking enslaved people to Buenos Aires where, falling ill, he was cared for by the Jesuits and then became a Jesuit missionary to the native peoples in Patagonia. In 1768, the Jesuits were expelled from the Spanish empire, and Falkner returned to England to minister as a Catholic priest. In Argentina, he had been employed by the Spanish government in 1750 to draw a map of the coast from south of Brazil to Tierra del Fuego, which was printed in 1761. His 1774 book was translated into French, German and Spanish.

At this stage, knowledge of Namibia was also increasing, in part due to the British interest in the 1780s in establishing a convict colony there as a substitute for sending convicts to North America. The inhospitable nature of the dry coast, the Namib Desert, helped lead to the decision, instead, to focus on Australia. Even though Walvis Bay, the natural harbour in Namibia, had been 'discovered' by Bartolomeu Dias in 1487, there was no claim to it, or settlement there, until the 1790s, and it was not annexed (by Britain) until 1884.

Conflict 1688–97

It is readily possible to provide an account of warfare between the European powers that emphasises conflict in the West Indies and on the Atlantic shores of Africa and the New World. That, however, would be to underplay the significance of fighting in the British Isles, Continental Europe and European waters. Nevertheless, the first and last of those had a clear Atlantic dimension, with French and Spanish intervention in the British Isles a matter not only of cross-Channel schemes, but also those in north-east Atlantic waters. So, moreover, with British power projection into the Mediterranean, which could only be achieved through Atlantic waters.

The tasks pursued as well as the nature of navigation were such that naval conflict throughout the period focused on waters near coasts and, in particular, near or approaching ports. This was the case for example with the two battles off Cape Finisterre in 1747, with the battles of Lagos (Portugal) and Quiberon Bay, both in 1759, with Ushant in 1778, Virginia Capes in 1781, the Saintes in 1782 and the Glorious First of June west of Ushant in 1794. All of these were battles between the British and the French. In 1689–97, the comparable battles, Beachy Head (1690) and Barfleur (1692), were in the Channel, although, in the battle of Bantry Bay in 1689, the English failed to defeat a French fleet covering a landing of troops in Ireland. Thereafter, the English had to return to Portsmouth for repairs because as yet there was no drydocking in the Channel further west. This gave the French a major advantage, as Brest was a better port as far as access to the Atlantic was concerned, although westerly winds posed a major problem there. After heavy defeat at Barfleur, the French devoted far less attention to their navy, focusing their resources instead on war on the Continent.

Trade War in the Atlantic, 1693

The role of Atlantic waters as a key conduit for trade within Europe was captured in 1693 in the battle of Lagos, off the Algarve. A convoy of over 200 merchantmen bound for the Mediterranean, the Smyrna Convoy, under the escort of thirteen English and Dutch warships, was stopped by a French fleet of seventy warships. Two Dutch warships in the rear put up a ferocious resistance, enabling much of the Allied fleet to escape to Madeira, and from there return to Ireland, but about ninety merchantmen had been captured, with France making a major economic gain. There was a political stink in Parliament about the failure of naval protection. Several admirals were dismissed.

Both England and France fought in the Caribbean and in Canada, but the key Atlantic war was that for Ireland, which was totally won by William III in 1691. Disease hit English operations in the Caribbean, notably in 1692–3, but the English were usually able to take the initiative, although attacks on Guadeloupe (1691) and Martinique (1693) failed. Separately, the French took most of the English bases in Newfoundland in 1696, including Saint John's, which was burnt, but an English expedition in 1697 rebuilt the latter, adding barracks and defences. This was not yet an Atlantic where the British were clearly the most potent naval power not least because, as with the battle of Lagos in 1693, much of the fleet had to stay in home waters to protect against invasion.

CONFLICT, 1702–13

War for England and France resumed in 1702 with the War of the Spanish Succession, with Spain's colonial position ensuring that transoceanic concerns played a major role, which they had not done in 1689. England was troubled by French commercial opportunities in the Spanish empire.

Although in 1712 a French squadron raided Rio, the concentration of French expenditure on the army strengthened the position of the Royal Navy which was successful in attacking a Spanish squadron at Vigo in 1702, in leading Portugal to abandon its French alliance in 1703, and in seizing and retaining Gibraltar in 1704, providing England with another naval base on the Atlantic. A large fleet was sent to the Caribbean, but in 1702 a separate attempt to capture Saint Augustine failed when Spanish warships from Cuba relieved the garrison. There was bitter fighting in Newfoundland in which, from 1706, the French largely took the initiative, but neither side there won lasting success nor received adequate support from regular forces. In 1704–10, Nova Scotia was captured by New England and British forces, but in 1711 an expedition sent against Québec failed.

The Peace of Utrecht of 1713 left Britain much stronger in the Atlantic, with the gains of Gibraltar, Saint Kitts, Nova Scotia and

Newfoundland. However, there were still unsettled issues, as well as a French presence that provided opportunities to weaken Britain. The French settlers in Nova Scotia, the Acadians, maintained a French interest in the colony, while, in Newfoundland, in order to support their fisheries, the French retained (until they were exchanged for concessions in Africa in 1904) seasonal shore rights from Port Riche to Cape Bonavista. In addition, the peace left Britain for thirty years with the *asiento*, the right to supply enslaved people to the Spanish empire, and also with a limited, although potentially profitable, right to trade there.

PIRATES IN THE ATLANTIC

Pirates brought complexity, disruption and energy to the Atlantic world and its maritime systems of trade and ports, and were particularly active in the late seventeenth and early eighteenth centuries. Piracy was an essential part of the lifestyle of the sea: the sea was both less policeable than land and it spanned claims to state authority. The inherent attraction of piracy, as a means, however precarious, to adventure, livelihood and wealth, was enhanced by the role of war in the definition of English, French and Dutch views of the Caribbean. Overlapping with this came the economic rationale: piracy could be a rejection of society, but also part of the varied processes of creating and mediating economic links, and in a governmental and legal contest where the established official position did not meet the varied needs and expectations of much of the population. Alongside plundering others, not least by seizing enslaved people who could be readily resold, pirates provided fledgling communities with supplies, protection, loot, and commercial and fiscal opportunities. Maritime predation became a means to safety and financial viability, which helped make it acceptable, and notably so in colonies where there was a shortage of both force and liquidity, which was generally the case.

Thus, pirates became privateers in acceptance, if not law, and this was the case for all of the powers. Just as imperial forces were inserted into local patterns of opportunity and need, both exploiting them and being exploited by them, so also with piracy. Local politicians were calculating pragmatists, willing to turn a blind eye to criminal behaviour, while popular support rested in similar patterns, as well as traditions of self-reliance and autonomy that rejected metropolitan attempts to control the situation. Rulers and officials were willing to have peace in Europe but war 'beyond the line', as with the English at the expense of Spain in the 1660s. This practice, orally agreed between the English and Spanish negotiators of the Treaty of Cambrésis in 1559, meant that whatever happened in the Caribbean would not lead to war in Europe.

Moreover, that ambiguity was the practice for many in the region. Pirates were not a counterculture or criminal culture in their home territories, but part of a continuum with privateering and one that was highly fluid in its context, contours and circumstances, again contributing to the nature of the Caribbean as a frontier zone. Thus, pirates could be integral members of coastal communities that were more than simply lawless or at least disorderly. Indeed, piracy, like privateering, was a product of liquidity in the shape of investment, and in turn enhanced by it.

Nearly everyone who plundered in the Caribbean during these decades had paperwork of some sort, for example from the Danes in Saint Thomas or the French in Petit-Goâve, Saint-Domingue, and the degree to which these men called themselves privateers, a term coined in 1661, is instructive, not least because it underlines the fluid nature of war, commerce and sovereignty in the Caribbean. Buccaneers were initially French cattle rustlers who turned to plunder on occasion. The English soon anglicised *boucanier* into buccaneer, and simply forgot or ignored the original meaning of the term.

Most men made their way to the Caribbean with few prospects or by force, for example criminals sent there to make up numbers or Irish compelled to go to Barbados as a result of the Cromwellian conquest. These men had no means of purchasing a plantation or enslaved people to work those plantations, and did not intend to toil like slaves. This was the origin of logwood cutting, cattle raising and, eventually, piracy.

Even though piracy is usually associated with the Caribbean, the North American coast as well as West Africa saw much pirate activity. Pirates came from many backgrounds, but a disproportionate number were British, and from a seafaring background. Many were from captured merchant vessels, and some were free or escaped African Americans. Pirate ships were typically relatively small, and therefore easier to conceal in shallow water and careen (repair), while also being quicker than large warships over short distances. However, large vessels could carry more firepower, although pirates preferred to capture ships by intimidation rather than the risks and costs of conflict. There are many indications that pirate crews were more equal than those of other vessels, but there can be a misleading tendency to romanticise piracy.

However, a combination of peace from 1713 and the threat from buccaneering to trade changed attitudes: attacks were no longer legalised or accepted by governments as with privateering. Anti-piracy legislation was accompanied by harsh legal retribution for captured pirates and by the large-scale use of the Royal Navy against pirates, notably the killing of Edward Thatch (Blackbeard) in the Ocracoke Inlet on the North Carolina coast in 1718, and of Bartholomew Roberts at Cape Lopez, Gabon in West Africa, in 1722. Fifty-two of Roberts's captured crew were hanged. Earlier that year, Roberts had captured slave ships in Whydah and made the owners pay ransom. In 1720, operating far afield, he had raided Newfoundland. In 1718, Woodes Rogers, a privateer-turned-governor, brought the pirate base in New Providence in the Bahamas under control, with mass executions of pirates there in 1718 and 1720. In 1723, Thomas Anstis, a former colleague of

Roberts, was surprised by a British warship off Tobago and, once defeated, murdered by his crew. The idea of pirates in British waters was fantastical by the time of Gilbert and Sullivan's comic operetta *The Pirates of Penzance* (1879).

WAR, 1739–48

War with Spain in 1718–20 had largely been waged in Europe, but in 1726–7 there was a blockade of the Spanish Caribbean port of Porto Bello and in 1739, when war with Spain resumed, operations focused in the Caribbean. This was in part a consequence of the development of British capability there. A naval base was established at English Harbour, Antigua, from 1728, and others at Port Antonio (from 1729) and Port Royal (from 1735) on Jamaica.

Success in taking Porto Bello in 1739 was followed by abject failure against Cartagena on the coast of modern Colombia in 1741. In contrast, success in capturing Louisbourg on Cape Breton Island in 1745 was followed by two striking victories off Cape Finisterre in 1747: the French could not keep their fleet in Brest safe (but also a threat to the British) if they wished to maintain an imperial commercial system, but attempts to escort trade exposed them to attack. On 3 May, Anson defeated an outnumbered French fleet. Rather than fight in line, Anson ordered his captains to close with the French as rapidly as possible, and thereby fight a series of individual actions in order to prevent the French from escaping under cover of darkness. On 14 October, Edward Hawke followed Anson's tactics and, although the French fought well, the British benefited from having taken the initiative and from abandoning the rigid tactics of a line in order to direct heavier concentrations of gunfire on individual French ships. This led to the surrender of six of the French ships and to the French loss of 4,000 sailors, a crucial limitation of their maritime strength. As the French fleet thereafter could no longer escort major convoys bound for French colonies, the logic of the French Atlantic system had been destroyed and the British victories contributed both to a serious crisis in French finances and to a sense that the war should be brought to an end.

WAR WITH FRANCE AGAIN, 1754–63

Although the Seven Years War is dated 1756–63, that reflects the formal declaration of war rather than the outbreak of hostilities in North America in 1754. Neither side wanted war but once fighting had broken out in the Ohio Valley, on the margins of empire, it spread because neither side was willing to compromise sufficiently. Fortunately for Britain, Spain did not enter the war until 1762 and by then France had been defeated at sea and most of its colonies taken, Canada falling in 1758–60 and most of the French West Indies in 1759–62. The navy provided not only crucial 'lift' or power projection, but also cannon and gunners, which were of particular significance because so many colonial bases were located at the crucial interchange of transoceanic routes with local land and sea ones, as with Havana, captured in 1762.

As in other wars, the Royal Navy did badly in the initial stages and then improved. From 1758, its ability to act as an offensive strategic force and as a restraint on French trade was fully demonstrated. This was a cumulative process, as French effectiveness declined with the capture of sailors, leading to strains in its smaller maritime labour pool. The quality of British warships also improved. Naval success owed less to any bold new strategic conception than to the ability of the administration to keep a large number of ships at sea and to the quality of the commanders, the captains and the crews. Bases were also significant. The harbour facilities at Halifax were able to support the overwintering of a substantial squadron in 1758–9. This was a key instance of the combination of local and distant resources, one differently seen with the development of colonies able to produce militia and supplies. Whereas the French force that temporarily captured Saint John's, Newfoundland, in 1762 had to come from France, the British force that drove it out came from North America.

The key naval victories occurred in 1759. Edward Boscawen defeated one French fleet near Lagos on the Portuguese coast and Edward Hawke the Brest fleet in Quiberon Bay on the Breton coast. As a result, political and financial support for the navy ebbed in France, the French plan for a joint Franco-Spanish invasion of Ireland in 1762 did not get off the ground, and the British navy was left to take the initiative at sea, launching successful expeditions without hindrance, for example in the Caribbean in 1762. Already, the French bases in West Africa had been easily taken in 1758. They were poorly fortified and inadequately garrisoned, lacked hinterlands that could provide support, and were particularly exposed to naval attack.

The Peace of Paris of 1763 recorded Britain's triumph as an Atlantic power. It returned gains, including Guadeloupe, Martinique, Cuba and Gorée, but retained others, including Canada, Florida, several Caribbean islands and Senegal. Sir Ellis Cunliffe, MP for the major slave-trading city of Liverpool, had pressed the government hard over Senegal. There was a feeling of ambitious new opportunities, as in the *Briton*, a prominent London newspaper, on 27 November 1762: 'The possession of Senegal opens us an avenue to the inland parts of Africa, to regions hitherto unexplored by European merchants, abounding with gold, ivory and ... in all probability with many other rich sources of commerce which industry and adventure will discover.'

The paper also offered a sense of strategic gain, as in the issue of 11 December: 'The possession of Saint Augustine stops an ugly gap in our southern colonies, prevents the desertion of our negro slaves, and by the help of row galleys ... enables us in a great measure to command the Channel of the gulph through which every Spanish ship must pass from the Havana in her return to Europe.'

Transatlantic Linkage

The vitals of our West Indian islands are our African settlements ... though we have been possessed of trade, particularly on the Gold Coast, Whydah, and Gambia, upwards of eighty years, the French are daily undermining us there, so that if by open force they do not exclude us from all trade to Africa, they will at least by degrees worm us out of it, as they have already done upon the Gum Coast; if we do not immediately take such salutary measures as may effectually frustrate this long and deep-laid design of the French.

Anon, 'A Letter from a Merchant of
the City of London to William Pitt' (1757)

The Gum Coast refers to the exports of gum arabic for textile printing from Senegal.

THE DUTCH ATLANTIC

Alongside the struggles between Britain and both France and Spain, other Atlantics continued and developed. The Dutch Atlantic saw the development of Surinam where Fort Amsterdam was built at the confluence of the Surinam and Commewijne rivers from 1734 to 1747 to protect the capital, Paramaribo. Relative naval weakness made the Dutch less consequential, but neutrality offered protection during the Seven Years War, although privateering was always a problem, as with the French privateers who held Curaçao to ransom in 1713. The poor financial state of the Dutch West India Company and the heavy cost of its West African operations led it to depend on government subsidies. The Dutch East India Company did not develop its colony at the Cape of Good Hope, but the settlers did, attracted by well-watered lands, a temperate climate and the inability of the few Khoikhoi to mount much of a resistance. They did not feel a need to rebel comparable to that of Britain's North American settlers.

THE PORTUGUESE AND SPANISH ATLANTICS

The strengthening of the Portuguese economy and state under the administration of the Marquis of Pombal saw a major enhancement of the Portuguese Atlantic, in part as a result of the development of gold and diamond production in Minas Gerais. Portugal and Brazil took significant quantities of British products, particularly textiles, paying for them with Brazilian gold, which helped to keep the British financial system buoyant and to finance British trades that showed a negative balance, although Portugal put a major effort into preserving from Britain its position at Ambriz at the northern coastal end of Angola. French, or French-supported Spanish, invasions of Portugal in 1762, 1801 and 1807 were in large part directed against Britain, and the first and last led to the dispatch of British forces. Brazil was also a key source for diamonds, sugar, tobacco, coffee and cotton.

A Bourbon on the thrones of both France and Spain in 1700–92 meant that French opportunities in Latin America were largely restricted to the Portuguese world. There was a series of long quarrels between Portugal and Spain over the southern boundary of Brazil. The Portuguese established themselves in Rio Grande do Sul, but, in the face of large-scale Spanish naval action in 1777, and without British support, could not sustain their position at Sacramento on the northern shore of the Plate estuary where Spain had itself founded Montevideo in 1726. Off West Africa, Portugal under the Treaty of 1778 ceded Fernando Póo and Annobón to Spain, as well as Río Muni on the coast, as part of an agreement over the borders of Brazil and the Río de la Plata region. The new Spanish possessions were administered by the viceroyalty of the Río de la Plata based in Buenos Aires, an aspect of the South Atlantic as a unit.

Having lost Havana and ten ships of the line to Britain in 1762, Spain regained Cuba in the post-war peace. Spain, in turn, took Port Egmont, the British base on the Falkland Islands, in 1770, but British naval pressure forced the Spaniards to return their gain, albeit declaring that this concession did not affect their claim to sovereignty. In turn, the British gave a secret, verbal assurance that they would evacuate the Falklands, although, in the event, they did not do so until 1775, and then on the grounds of economy. Given the secret agreement, it was as well for the ministry that opposition demands in 1771 for the communication of more papers to Parliament were thwarted.

The Lisbon Earthquake

With its epicentre in the Atlantic at 36°N 11°W, about 200 kilometres (120 miles) south-west of Cape Saint Vincent in the Algarve, the earthquake of 1 November 1755 was responsible for a tsunami that completed the destruction of much of Lisbon by the earthquake, as well as hitting hard Cádiz, Ceuta, the Moroccan coastal cities, and the ports in the Azores and the Algarve. High winds also hit the Caribbean and Brazil.

BRITAIN AS THE DOMINANT POWER

Naval dominance was the background to the varied activity of the 1760s, whether Harrison's chronometer or Byron's Patagonian giants. It was also the background to a more integrated transatlantic knowledge and commercial economy. The former included the charting of coastal waters, notably of North America, and the publication of maps, for example Thomas Jefferys's *A General*

Topography of North America and the West Indies (1768). A wealth of information was offered to readers, for example the description of Cape Breton in *Owen's Weekly Chronicle* on 5 August 1758 and the account and map of the Falkland Islands in the *Gentleman's Magazine* of October 1770. The more integrated Atlantic economy included an expansion of trade, shipping and transatlantic industry. Thomas Pennant wrote of Kendal, which he visited in 1769: 'The number of inhabitants is about seven thousand; chiefly engaged in manufactures of ... a coarse sort of woollen cloth called cottons sent to Glasgow, and from thence to Virginia for the use of the Negroes ... the manufacturers employ great quantities of wool from Scotland and Durham.'

Exports produced by arduous slave labour brought profit and liquidity. In 1770, 513,581 hundredweight of sugar and 911,480 gallons of rum were exported from Jamaica to Britain.

Rapidly expanding Atlantic ports included Glasgow, Liverpool, the leading slave-trading port where new docks were added in 1753, 1771 and 1773, and Lancaster with new quays in 1755 and 1767. A sceptical Horace Walpole remarked with reference to the capture of Martinique, Grenada, Saint Lucia and Saint Vincent from France in 1762, 'I think we were full as happy when we were a peaceable quiet set of tradesfolks, as now we are heirs apparent to the Romans,' but that was not a majority view. Two years earlier, Elizabeth Montagu had captured the idea of an empire of trade:

> We often accuse the French of aiming at universal monarchy by endeavouring to extend their dominions, other powers may fear we should effect the same thing by extending our commerce, and in the present state of the world general commerce must give greatest power and strength. It seems to me a far more sure and lasting means of empire and superior rule, than extent of territory. Great tracts of land at distance from the seat of government, grow of little worth by the oppression of viceroys and deputies.

The British were vigilant about French and Spanish moves. Thus, in 1772, an explanation was demanded from the French ministry both of its plans for forming settlements to the north of the River Gambia, which would interfere with the British trade in gum arabic and its dispatch of warships to the area. Nevertheless, triumphalism was expressed after the Peace of Paris of 1763, in a Britain newly confident that its oceanic role had been fulfilled. That seems singularly inappropriate today given the human tragedy of slavery.

Pressure for War Over the Falklands, 1770

During the crisis of 1770, the *Westminster Journal*, in its issue of 1 December, printed a piece attacking popular prejudice and, in contrast to the general claim that the Bourbons could not be trusted, argued that their friendship should be cultivated, adding: 'We know very well that Jack Helter-Skelter says, "damn the Spaniards, we shall soon give them a belly-full, and bring home their treasure by ship-load after ship-load." Better to cultivate their friendship, and supply them with the manufactures of Great Britain.'

6

New 'Players', 1775–1825

We could see nothing of the ships except the flashes of their guns because of the smoke. The majesty of this sight can hardly be described.

> A Hessian quartermaster of a successful
> British attack on Charleston, 1780

The Atlantic changed greatly in the half century that began with the shots that rang out from Lexington in 1775. The new 'players' included the independent states of the New World: the United States, Haiti and the independent states of Latin America, beginning with Argentina. On the Old World side, territories of formerly enslaved people were established in Sierra Leone and Liberia, but most of Atlantic Africa remained under indigenous control. At the same time, the flux was shot through with war, both international and civil, migration, both free and enslaved, and a sense of new beginnings. The ocean itself continued both to link and to set obstacles.

Nelson in the Caribbean

The Caribbean was formative for the career of Horatio Nelson. As for so many, its waters offered career opportunities as well as the risk of death. There were also key personal events, notably his courtship and marriage with Frances Nisbet and his significant friendship with William, Duke of Clarence, George's III's naval son. Born in 1758, Nelson sailed first to the West Indies in 1771–2 on a merchantman

---

to Jamaica and Tobago. After seeing naval service in Indian waters in 1775–6, Nelson was promoted to lieutenant in 1777, and then made several cruises to the Caribbean. The hunt for prize money was a key goal, but he had time in 1777 to make notes on the wildlife of the Caicos Islands. Promoted to captain in 1779, he was placed in command of Fort Charles, Kingston, in the face of a French attack that did not in the event happen. Later that year, Nelson took American prizes in the Caribbean, but in 1780 fell seriously ill on an expedition to Central America. After recovery, a failed attack on a French position in the Turks Islands in 1783 was followed by the capture of French and Spanish prizes. Sent to the Caribbean in 1784 to enforce the Navigation Acts, Nelson married Frances 'Fanny' Nisbet, a Nevis widow, in 1787, the year in which he returned to Britain. He had met Clarence in 1782, and the latter served in the Caribbean in 1782–3 and 1786–9, giving away Fanny at Nelson's wedding which took place in the grounds of Montpelier House (now the Montpelier Plantation Inn), the property of John Herbert, president of Nevis and Fanny's uncle. A copy of the marriage licence is preserved at the nearby Fig Tree Church. In 1805, Nelson visited the Caribbean anew in an abortive pursuit of the French fleet he was subsequently to defeat at Trafalgar.

AMERICAN WAR OF INDEPENDENCE, 1775–83

War with France had broken out in 1754 as a struggle to control the North American interior. In contrast, the port cities, notably Boston, were the foci of division, with the revolt that erupted in 1775 leading to revolution in 1776. This reflected the more significant role of transoceanic trade than land in the geopolitics of the

British empire, one focused with the Boston Tea Party of 1773, when tea was seized and thrown into the harbour. Moreover, the Admiralty had used the navy to enforce imperial mercantilism – maximising profits for British and imperial trade by protectionist measures to restrict or prevent trade with other empires – which was repeatedly a cause of discontent among colonists who chafed at restrictions.

There were both parallels and contrasts in transatlantic politics, underlining the extent to which the Atlantic was regarded as a common political community. In 1772, General Thomas Gage, the commander-in-chief in North America, complained to William, 2nd Viscount Barrington, the Secretary at War, 'Your papers are stuffed with infamous paragraphs which the American printers, especially those of Boston, seldom fail to copy with American additions,' adding in 1774, 'The seditious here [Boston] have raised a flame in every colony which your speeches, writings, and protests in England have greatly encouraged.' Yet, there were also contrasts. The legislation of early 1774, the Coercive (or Intolerable) Acts, designed to punish Massachusetts, struck colonists, there and elsewhere, as an infringement of their charter rights; but the general election in Britain held later that year sustained the position of the ministry. Similarly, the French West Indian colonies were to see both parallels and contrasts with the developments in France during the French Revolution.

In the 1770s, both the supporters and the critics of government policy regarded American independence of action as a threat to the integrity of the British empire. The political, strategic and economic interdependencies of its constituent parts were taken as a given. It was widely accepted that the dominance of American trade supported British power, most crucially in any conflict with the Bourbons, and that, without political links, it would be impossible to maintain economic relationships. There was no actual monopoly on American trade, as not all goods were enumerated under the Navigation Acts.

The Atlantic as both link and obstacle was the case from the outset with the American War of Independence. Britain, France (from 1778) and Spain (from 1779) were all able to play a role in the fighting in North America. The last already had a colony in Louisiana (acquired from France after the Seven Years War) and only had to move troops from Cuba across the Gulf of Mexico, but both Britain and France had to send expeditionary forces and fleets across the Atlantic, and then had to sustain them with reinforcements and supplies. Furthermore, there was the movement for both powers of warships and troops in American waters and, most significantly, between them and the West Indies. In strategic terms, these tasks were possible, and in operational ones they were fulfilled. Repeatedly, these moves were carried out with considerable success, as when the British in 1778 seized Savannah and also moved troops to the Caribbean, or in 1779 when the American Patriots and French tried (albeit unsuccessfully) to regain Savannah.

Yet, there was also, for all powers, the strategic drag of the time taken to cross the Atlantic. This was important not only for warships and troops but also for messages, and the latter made the coordination of operations difficult, a factor that seriously affected the British in 1777 and 1781. As other structural (i.e. permanent) factors, there was the fear of hurricanes and the consequent wish to move ships north from the Caribbean, as well as the dislike of sailing in the gales that generally accompanied the equinox.

In addition to these strategic-level issues came the operational ones of crises for particular expeditions; the risk of which helped to create a strategic-level uncertainty. A classic instance of failure was the planned expedition to restore royal authority in the Carolinas in 1776, which was wrecked by administrative issues and bad weather. Due to sail from Cork on 1 December 1775, it did not do so until early February. Lieutenant-General Charles, Earl Cornwallis, who had sailed on 10 February, reported on 7 March:

'our voyage hitherto has been very unsuccessful; the wind has been almost always contrary, and, till the first of this month, constant and most violent gales of wind ... I fear there is no chance of our arrival on the American coast before the end of next month at soonest, and the assembling off Cape Fear, where there is no port, may be a work of some time.'

It had been planned that the expedition would reach Cape Fear by early February, but the first ships to reach the anchorage from Britain did not do so until 18 April, and Cornwallis until 3 May. Sailing thence at the end of May, the British did not attack Charleston until 28 June, and then unsuccessfully so; the North Carolina Loyalists had already been defeated. From there, the army sailed north to New York, not arriving until 2 August instead of the anticipated spring. Joined with the force from Halifax, it landed on Long Island on 22 August.

Charleston itself was captured in 1780, but British failure in North America was in large part a matter of being unable to suppress the revolution prior to French entry into the war in 1778, although the specific issue that led to a change in policy in Britain toward peace in 1782 arose from the surrender the previous October at Yorktown of a besieged British army that could not be withdrawn because the British had lost the local control of the sea. Thus, the ability of the French navy to avoid defeat was a key element. In 1778, General Sir Henry Clinton highlighted the risk of French warships capturing a British supply fleet; which, in the event, it never did.

The Anglo-French war had begun with a major naval battle, on 27 July, 160 kilometres (100 miles) west of Ushant. The French, with thirty ships of the line, were under instructions to avoid battle and thereby keep the fleet in being. The British were able to bring them to conflict but differences between the commanders compounded the French determination to keep the battle loose. There was an indecisive clash, with the French able to sail off after nightfall having handicapped British ships by firing into their rigging. Lieutenant John Blankett, on the flagship *Victory*, reported on the French keeping the advantage of the wind, adding:

> The French fired first and very effectually destroyed our rigging and sails, and very much damaged our masts and yards, ... our disabled ships formed [the line] very slowly ... In the night they [the French] bore away ... the forcing a fleet to action, equal in force, and with the advantage of the wind must always be done with great risk, and our fleet was not equal to that manoeuvre, but chance, which determines many events, put it out of the Admiral's power to choose his disposition, the eagerness of our van when fired on, putting all regularity out of the question. The French behaved more like seamen, and more officer-like than was imagined they would do, their ships were in very high order, well managed, well rigged ... Their fire was brisk and well directed, nor was there the least appearance of fear ... As our fire was directed low and was well kept up, I have reason to think it killed a great number of their men and did them great damage in their hulls. But the truth is, unless two fleets of equal force are equally determined for battle, whoever attacks must do it with infinite risk, but a fleet to leeward attacking one to windward [as the British had done] is a dangerous manoeuvre indeed.

There was no decisive battle in terms of ship losses until that of the Saintes in the West Indies on 12 April 1782, a British triumph. The battle of Virginia Capes on 5 September 1781, when nineteen British ships of the line fought twenty-four French, had been tactically indecisive, neither side having any ships sunk, but, as this had prevented the relief of the besieged British force in Yorktown, it had been operationally and strategically crucial. The wide-ranging war included conflict in the Caribbean, where Britain lost a series of sugar islands and West Florida, and West

Africa. There was also a long Spanish siege of Gibraltar in 1779–83, with the arrival of convoys there crucial to its survival. In the peace negotiations, the British argued that the Thirteen Colonies should be their main loss, but Spain also wanted Florida, Gibraltar and Minorca, and France gains in the West Indies, West Africa, the Newfoundland Fisheries and India. In the event, British agreement with the Americans encouraged France to press Spain to accept that it could not obtain Gibraltar, although Florida was regained by Spain in the 1783 Versailles peace settlement. France gained Tobago and Senegal.

America, meanwhile, had become an attractive 'other' for many European commentators critical of the ancien régime and no longer attracted to an image of the Orient. This response to the civilised, and yet reputedly free and egalitarian, American settlers was a reaction both to a general shift in sensibility and to the tyranny of fashion that influenced informal circles. As with Charles Dickens in the 1840s, those who had experience of America were not always sanguine. Thus, the Hessian soldiers sent to fight the Americans were not alone in their conviction that the American treatment of their slaves formed a hypocritical contrast with their claims of the equality of man.

Yet for many Europeans, America was a cause of hope, Christian Schubart writing in his *Deutsche Chronik* in 1777, 'Oh, you beloved America, you are still the hobbyhorse upon which we journalists can canter at ease.' American independence provided a concrete example of the possibility of a completely fresh start, a citizens' army and a written constitution, and offered an exciting perspective, bringing change and democracy from the realms of utopian fancy, revealing the weakness of the old order and showing that internal strife could produce radical reform, rather than simple anarchy. Independent America was not the equivalent of China in offering a contrast with European civilisation, but rather an alternative model that did not broaden the knowledge of other civilisations.

The *Zong*

Late 1781 is known mostly for the British surrender at Yorktown but, later that year, the *Zong* massacre threw appalling light on the cruelty of the slave trade. A Dutch slave ship based in Middelburg was captured with enslaved people on board by the British in February 1781 and sold the following month to a syndicate of Liverpool merchants. Sailing from Accra with 442 enslaved people on 18 August, the *Zong* had far more slaves than a British ship of that size would carry. The *Zong* reached the Caribbean but was affected by disease, short of water and poorly commanded. From 29 November, 142 enslaved people were killed by being thrown overboard. Their value was then claimed on the ship's insurance, which led to a legal controversy in 1783 over the insurer's liability, which was finally rejected by the courts. The episode was a long-standing *cause célèbre* for Abolitionists, and J. M. W. Turner produced a dramatic painting of the episode entitled *The Slave Ship* in 1840. It has also played a role more recently, as in Fred D'Aguiar's novel *Feeding the Ghosts* (1997).

New Players

The American Revolution created a new player in Atlantic power politics and trade, the first former colonial state of the modern era. Many predicted significant changes. Keen to suggest that Britain heed a French willingness to unite in 'some solid plan of permanent peace', William Eden, a British diplomat in Paris, wrote to the Foreign Secretary: 'Many of the most considerable and efficient people talk with little reserve of the dangers to be apprehended from the revolted colonies, if they should be encouraged to gain commercial strength and consistency of government.' Britain's surviving Atlantic colonies were particularly under threat and in the meantime its trade links to the former Thirteen Colonies were seriously disrupted.

However, America's naval potential was not rapidly developed, in large part because of political hostility toward the idea of a strong government, which was a requirement for such a force. The last ship in the Continental Navy was sold in 1785; there was no necessary infrastructure of bureaucracy and naval dockyards. Far from propounding a universal creed for change that it then sought to implement, the new American state did not prefigure nor face the challenges of its French Revolutionary counterpart in the 1790s. There was no earlier equivalent to the Monroe Doctrine of 1823, warning European states against further intervention in the New World, and nor was America in a position to give force to one. Indeed, quite the reverse. Moreover, any reading from the American Revolution to a wider crisis for European powers in the Americas, still less in the world as a whole, seemed alarmist in the late 1780s when the pieces apparently shattered by the American Revolution, notably Britain's empire, had been less damaged than had been feared.

As a result of their naval situation, the Americans found themselves vulnerable when clashing with France in the late 1790s in the 'Quasi War', having to finance naval construction by public subscription, and when at war with Britain in 1812–15. In 1812, the Americans had no ships of the line and their total navy, although including the most powerful frigates of the age, comprised only seventeen ships. America was to acquire Louisiana, but by purchase from France in 1803, not war, although force was used to gain Florida from Spain.

A lack of naval strength was an element of the successful revolution that led in 1804 to independence for Haiti (formerly Saint-Domingue), a struggle, begun in 1791 against French control, that was won on land. However, this struggle was also greatly assisted by the resumption of hostilities between Britain and France in 1803, a measure that meant that the French forces could be blockaded by the Royal Navy and certainly not reinforced from France. Due to a land frontier with the Dominican Republic, Haiti could spread its revolution there, but it was in no position to do so elsewhere. To do so would have brought Haiti into conflict with the European powers as only relatively few islands were under the control of the newly independent Latin American states, while Haiti was also unable to support the indigenous peoples, usually called Mosquito Indians, on the Caribbean coasts of Central America against these states.

The British navy was a key player in the Latin American Wars of Independence. It insulated Latin America from Napoleon's triumph in Iberia in 1807–8, and thus ensured that the local authorities in Spanish America could reject the claims of Joseph Bonaparte, Napoleon's king of Spain from 1808 to 1813. Moreover, the Portuguese empire was protected; notably the royal family took refuge in Brazil.

Iceland

Iceland was a semi-detached part of the European world, but one open to outside influences, in large part due to rule by Denmark. The royal commission sent there in 1770–1 received numerous complaints about the injustices of local officials and the burdens exacted by landlords. Icelandic officials guarded their own interests, especially their tax exemptions, held most Church and Crown lands as fiefs, and belonged to the families that possessed most of the privately owned land. They prevented the redress of peasant grievances.

When tourism began, John Stanley (1766–1850) visited in 1789, stopping en route at the Faroes. He knew a reasonable amount about Iceland's natural curiosities before he set off, and his learned party included the physicist and later astronomer Mark Beaufoy.

ANGLO-FRENCH NAVAL WARFARE, 1793–1815

Such protection was possible because of repeated British naval victories. Some, notably the battle of the Nile in 1798, were not in the Atlantic, but most were. At the Glorious First of June in 1794, Richard, Earl Howe, with twenty-five ships of the line, having gained the weather gauge as a result of skilful seamanship, attacked a French fleet of twenty-six ships of the line sent to escort a grain convoy from America into Brest. Although his plan for ships to cut the French line, so that each would pass under the stern of a French ship and engage it from leeward, could not be fully executed, sufficient ships succeeded, and British gunnery was superior and at close-range for long enough to cost the French six warships captured and one sunk. France also lost 5,000 sailors, a crucial number of skilled manpower, but the vital convoy reached France.

In the next major Atlantic clash, on 14 February 1797 off Cape Saint Vincent, Rear-Admiral Sir John Jervis and fifteen ships of the line attacked a superior and far more heavily gunned Spanish fleet of twenty-seven of the line. Thanks in part to Horatio Nelson, the British concentrated their attack on part of the Spanish fleet and, in the resulting mêlée of individual ship encounters, their greatly superior rate of fire had a deadly effect. Four Spanish ships of the line including two 112-gunners were captured, ten more ships badly damaged, and the fleet driven back into Cádiz, ending the plan for them to join the French at Brest. Nelson had lost his right arm in a mismanaged amphibious attack on a well-defended Santa Cruz on Tenerife the previous year, and the British were unable to gain the Canaries.

Another larger opposing fleet was defeated near Cádiz in a night-time action on 12–13 July 1801, with three of the eight Franco-Spanish ships of the line captured or destroyed by four British ships of the line. There were also many smaller-scale clashes, part of the bread and butter of naval warfare. For example, in 1798, the *Mars*, a seventy-four-gun ship that was part of the fleet blockading Brest, attacked the *Hercule*, a newly launched seventy-four-gunner en route from Lorient. The two ships came alongside, their bow anchors hooked, and the ships exchanged fire while touching, with many of the guns fired from inboard, which would have greatly increased the noise and stress for the sailors. After heavy casualties, including both captains, in the hour-long gunnery exchange which the British clearly won, the *Hercule* surrendered. There were also many clashes with smaller French warships and privateers, and British frigate squadrons harassed France's Atlantic coast, which was a proactive part of the blockade. Such successes helped to reduce the losses of British trade, and also maintained the sense of British naval power.

In 1805, bold French naval plans spanned the Atlantic, and to an unprecedented extent. Napoleon prepared an invasion of southern England for which he required naval superiority in the Channel and this seemed a prospect when Spain joined France. Napoleon planned for his squadrons to evade British blockaders, sail across the Atlantic, join at Martinique, and then return as a united force able to defeat the British. Arriving first, the Rochefort squadron captured Dominica, but then returned to Europe when no other squadron arrived within the prescribed time. The Toulon squadron under Villeneuve joined a Spanish squadron at Cádiz and, with the outnumbered British blockading squadron offering no hindrance, left again, reaching Martinique on 14 May, pursued by Nelson who arrived at Barbados on 4 June.

Evading the pursuit, Villeneuve sailed back for Europe, but had been unable to join the Brest fleet which, instead, had been kept in harbour by the British close blockade. In fog, west of Cape Finisterre on 22 July, Villeneuve fought an outnumbered British fleet under Vice-Admiral Sir Robert Calder, losing two Spanish warships. Villeneuve failed to renew the battle next day and, eventually, instead of trying to fight his way into the Channel, left harbour for Cádiz. Partly as a result of naval developments, but also in response to those in European power politics, Napoleon cancelled his invasion plans and turned against Austria, instructing Villeneuve to attack its ally Naples, which was an aspect of the degree to which Atlantic power could be deployed into European waters, an aspect that was to be speeded up and made easier when steam power replaced sail. Villeneuve was intercepted on 21 October by Nelson off Cape Trafalgar, a classic site where Europe's coastal waters were part of the Atlantic.

Trafalgar, the Epic Atlantic Battle, 1805

The fighting quality of individual British ships, which was based on seamanship and the rapid rate of close-range fire by trained crew, was combined with a bold command culture which emphasised manoeuvring and seizing the initiative in order to close with the opposing fleet and to defeat it in detail after it had been divided by intersecting the opposing line. Nelson's bold and well-executed plan and tactics provided the opportunity for British gunnery and seamanship to yield their results, and nineteen French and Spanish ships of the line were captured, including the four-deck, 136-gun Spanish flagship, the *Nuestra Señora de la Santísima Trinidad*. Launched at Havana in 1769 as a 4,950-ton ship with 112 guns, she was expanded from a three-decker to a four-decker in 1795. She was the largest eighteenth-century warship, and had served in the scheme to invade England in 1779, in the siege of Gibraltar in 1782 and in the battle of Cape Saint Vincent in 1797, where she lost her three masts to accurate British fire. After the battle of Trafalgar on 21 October 1805, storms then did their damage in sinking many of the captured ships, and the *Santísima Trinidad* was scuttled near Cádiz. Four of the French ships of the line that escaped the battle were attacked and captured off Cape Finisterre on 4 November.

After Trafalgar, the British enjoyed a clear superiority in ships of the line and, even more crucially, trained sailors. Subsequently, due to the Peninsular War, Napoleon lost the support of the Spanish navy, while six French ships of the line sheltering in Cádiz and Vigo surrendered to Spain in 1808.

There were also other important British naval victories. On 25 September 1805, Samuel Hood and the blockading squadron off Rochefort attacked a French frigate squadron bound for the West Indies with reinforcements: four of the five frigates were captured, although Hood had to have his arm amputated after his elbow was smashed by a musket shot. The following 6 February, in the last fleet engagement of ships of the line in open water during that war, a French squadron of five ships of the line, which had escaped Rochefort in order to raid British trade and influence the situation in the Caribbean, was destroyed off Santo Domingo, strengthening confidence in the British Atlantic. Santo Domingo fell to Anglo-Spanish forces in 1809. Meanwhile, on 11–12 April 1809, a French squadron of eleven ships of the line in Basque Roads at the mouth of the Charente River, intended to reinforce Martinique, was dispersed by fireships, partly ran aground and four warships were destroyed, while British warships took little damage. Thereafter there was no major French fleet sent into the Atlantic and the remaining French Caribbean colonies were left vulnerable.

Blockade was arduous, not least in bad weather or fog, and many British warships were driven aground, but blockade kept French warships from the Atlantic. Moreover, the successive capture of French overseas bases lessened their ability to challenge the British, as the *Junon* sailing from Halifax to the West Indies had successfully been by four French frigates near Guadeloupe in December 1809. The development of Bermuda and Barbados as naval bases helped the British position in the Atlantic, while signalling at sea improved, and the Admiralty Hydrographic Department was founded in 1795 to assemble and catalogue existing charts, followed in 1808 by the Admiralty Chart Committee. The first chart produced by Alexander Dalrymple, the hydrographer appointed in 1800, was that of Quiberon Bay. His successor from 1808 until 1823, Captain Thomas Hurd, had already surveyed Bermuda and the Breton coast, while Sir William Parry, who held the office from 1823 to 1829, was an Arctic explorer of note.

Across the Atlantic world, British naval dominance served as the support for successful amphibious operations. In 1795, an expeditionary force defeated the Dutch at Muizenberg near Cape Town, which surrendered three days later. The Dutch fleet sent in 1796 to regain the city was caught at anchor in Saldanha Bay by a larger British fleet and surrendered without fighting. Prior to the Peace of Amiens in 1802, Danish, Dutch, French (but not Saint-Domingue), Spanish and Swedish islands in the Caribbean were all captured, as were the Dutch colonies of Essequibo, Berbice and Demerara (from 1831 British Guiana), and Gorée in West Africa.

All bar Trinidad were restored under the peace, and then taken anew after war resumed in 1803: Fort Louis on the Senegal River, the last French base in Africa, in 1809, Martinique in 1809 and Guadeloupe in 1810. Cape Town had been captured after a brisk campaign in 1806: 5,000 troops, under Major-General Sir David Baird landed at Melkbosstrand on 5 January and won, in large part thanks to a bayonet charge, a conclusive victory over the outnumbered Dutch at Blaauwberg (Blouberg) on the 8th; they took the surrender of Cape Town on the 10th and that of the Dutch forces on the 18th.

Much of this force was then sent to Buenos Aires, capturing the city on 2 July 1809, only to surrender on 12 August in the face of a major popular rising. A larger British force successfully stormed Montevideo the following February, but an attempt to do the same at Buenos Aires in July was a total failure, and the British evacuated the Plate estuary. The local population did not wish to exchange Spanish rule for that of another group of foreigners, and one that was Protestant as well. There was also to be failure in North America, notably at New Orleans in 1815.

Overall, however, the Napoleonic Wars ended in a complete British success, and with Britain totally dominant in the Atlantic. The peace settlement awarded the Cape Colony, the future British Guiana, Tobago, Saint Lucia and Trinidad to Britain, Napoleon was imprisoned on Saint Helena, in 1815 the British annexed Ascension Island and, in 1816, Tristan da Cunha and Gough Island, in order to prevent them being used by France or the United States. There was concern that these islands might serve as a base for a rescue attempt for Napoleon, although none was made. There was also anxiety, in the aftermath of the War of 1812, about the Americans establishing bases, this anxiety looking toward Britain's acquisition of the Falkland Islands in 1833.

The War of 1812

The loss of the support of the Thirteen Colonies had not been significant for Britain in terms of the arithmetic of ships of the line, but it was important for the manpower that had been contributed to the Royal Navy, both directly and indirectly, through the role of the merchant marine of the colonies in British imperial trade, notably the supply of food to the West Indies. The Royal Navy struggled to meet its manpower needs, and its tactic of using press gangs, in the context of contrasting British and American legal and political assumptions, helped lead to the outbreak of the War of 1812, which lasted for three years.

In initial clashes in 1812, American frigates defeated less heavily gunned British counterparts. In addition, the Royal Navy's North American station was not a key one in the war with Napoleon and, consequently, had been starved of resources, and many of the ships were in bad condition. In February 1813, George Canning told the House of Commons that 'the sacred spell of the invincibility of the British Navy was broken'. It was only that June, when the American *Chesapeake* fought the *Shannon*, that two frigates of equal strength fought and the *Shannon* won.

The British reinforced their North American station, but were put under pressure by American privateering as well as the continuance of the war with France. Funding for the Royal Navy rose, reaching a peak of £20,096,709 in 1813, and Britain imposed a blockade of American ports. Nevertheless, some ships escaped the blockade and the British found themselves fighting American ships across the North and South Atlantic, the American *Argus* being captured off Wales in 1813 and the privateer *General Armstrong* forced to scuttle in the Azores the following year, but the *Constitution* capturing two outgunned British warships off Madeira in February 1815. Overall, American privateering could not prevent a rise in British trade, despite a loss of 1,175 merchantmen (of which only 373 were recaptured). At the same time, the protection cost of convoy escorts and blockaders was considerable.

The War of 1812 was no triumph for Britain's naval reputation, but it underlined the extent of Britain's naval power and indicated what this offered in terms of blockade and amphibious capability. Britain had 152 ships of the line and 183 frigates in 1810, and could afford to lose several of the latter.

The British had less success ashore. Their expedition to the Chesapeake in 1814, although initially successful, had to abandon a planned attack on Baltimore, while that on New Orleans in 1815 was a disaster. The difficulties of operating in the Atlantic were captured by Major Joseph Hutchinson of the 7th Regiment of Foot. Having been detained by contrary winds for nearly three weeks in Plymouth in October 1814, he noted later, 'After knocking about the Atlantic for two months we reached the West India Islands,' while disembarking off Louisiana, twenty soldiers died in a capsize. The others were to be exposed to deadly American fire in the battle of New Orleans. That campaign, however, indicated Britain's dominance of the Atlantic world and the capacity that offered for power projection. Earlier in 1814, units from the Duke of Wellington's army, victorious over the French, had been shipped direct, after Napoleon's first abdication, from southwest France to the New World.

THE LATIN AMERICAN WARS OF INDEPENDENCE

The Atlantic very much remained in the shadow of British power after the Napoleonic Wars and the War of 1812. As the level of naval threat diminished, the size of the navy fell rapidly from 1815, in part because some wartime launchings had been of ships rapidly built from unseasoned wood, and they swiftly deteriorated. Post-war debt and the ending of income tax forced retrenchment, but the reserve, eighty-four ships of the line in 1817, was potent, while the use now of seasoned timber meant that new ships were longer-lasting.

Unlike after both the Seven Years War (1756–63) and the American War of Independence (1775–83), neither France nor Spain launched a major programme of naval construction after 1815. Indeed, until the revival of French naval strength from the mid-1820s, the British Admiralty saw the American fleet as its most likely rival, not least because, in 1816, Congress agreed to finance a plan for nine new ships of the line and nine large frigates. However, only four and two respectively had been launched by 1826, while Britain and America essentially shared views, both wishing to stop Spain retaining control of its colonies in Latin America while neither seeking to take them themselves. Both also sought to suppress the slave trade and piracy.

Spain tried to build up a fleet to support its efforts to retain control of Latin America, not least by buying Russian warships in 1818–19, but it avoided conflict with Britain, which also dissuaded possible French intervention there on behalf of Spain, although the French did send troops into Spain on behalf of the monarch in 1823. British volunteers were important to the independence struggles in Latin America and, once independent, colonies that had been excluded by the colonial powers from direct trade with Britain developed close trading relations and became prime areas for British investment. The dispatch of British envoys to Latin America owed something to anxiety about American influence as the Americans had moved speedily in 1822 to recognise the new independent states. In response Woodbine Parish was sent to Argentina, negotiating a treaty of friendship and trade signed in 1825. The British played a major role in negotiating the independence of Brazil from Portugal and peace between Argentina and Brazil.

By the end of 1825, Spanish control of the mainland was at an end, and the Spanish Atlantic was reduced to Cuba, Puerto Rico, the Canary Islands, Ceuta, modern Equatorial Guinea, and a strong sense of defeat and loss.

With their recent history very different, Brazil declared its independence from Portugal in 1822, beginning a war that lasted until 1824. The success of the rebels in conquering the northern provinces and the coastal seas south of Rio in 1823 owed much to naval force, with British officers and men playing a major role. Thomas Cochrane was made the commander of the new navy, which was greatly increased in size. The navy helped to keep Brazil together, blockading Recife into surrender in 1824, and thus ending a rising in the province of Pernambuco. Portugal was obliged to recognise Brazil's independence in 1825. Two years later, the Brazilians defeated an Argentinian flotilla.

ATLANTIC AFRICA

The most important developments in Atlantic Africa were not set by the Europeans, but instead were a consequence of the jihads beginning in Futa Jalon in 1725 and culminating in a large-scale jihad of 1804-10 led by Shehu Ahmadu Lobbo that led to the establishment of the Sokoto sultanate that lasted until British occupation in 1903. These jihads aimed to create Islamic states. In part the reform movement was directed against European pressure, but the jihad states were inland, not coastal.

In the latter area, non-Islamic states remained dominant south of Senegal. While the brutality of the large-scale slave trade continued, the period was not one of Western conquest. Further south, the British presence was limited despite the publication in 1766 of a new version of Samuel Thornton's impressive map *Gabon, Loango, and Congo from Cape St John to the River Ambris*. The British were mindful of not wishing to anger their ally Portugal, for example by using force at the slaving port of Ambriz to the north of Angola in 1791 in order to protect British trade from a Portuguese attempt to create a commercial monopoly. Still further south, British interest in the development of a base on the south-west coast of Africa led to the *Nautilus* survey of the coast north of Saint Helena Bay in 1785, but, lacking water, it was found unsatisfactory as an area for colonisation, even for convicts.

A New Cast of States and Peoples

In 1816, Napoleon told Lieutenant-Colonel Mark Wilks, governor for the East India Company of Saint Helena, where he was being held prisoner: 'Your [British] coal gives you an advantage we cannot possess in France. But the high price of all articles of prime necessity is a great disadvantage in the export of your manufactures ... your manufacturers are emigrating fast to America ... In a century or perhaps half a century more, it will give a new character to the affairs of the world. It has thriven upon our follies.'

The new cast of states in 1775–1825 was the most dramatic change in a half-century on the shores of the Atlantic since that of 1492 onwards, and was not to be matched until rapid decolonisation from Morocco in 1956 to Namibia in 1990. At the same time, this new cast was even more dramatic in terms of peoples. By 1825, Abolitionism had scored its first major victories. There had been significant moves to abolish the slave trade, notably by Britain (1807), America (1808) and Denmark (1803). Britain put successful pressure on other states to stop the slave trade, which France did in 1815 and the Dutch in 1818. Sierra Leone was established by Britain in 1787 for freed slaves. Slavery itself had been destroyed through violence in Haiti, and was already under political pressure in the British Empire. As a result of a wider process, the number of free black people in the Atlantic colonial and ex-colonial world had greatly increased.

At the same time, the slave trade continued to flourish, notably in the South Atlantic to Brazil; and Brazil, Cuba and the American South all had expanding economic sectors heavily reliant on slavery. Cuba imported an annual average of 10,700 enslaved people in 1836–50, as the destruction of the slave economy on Saint-Domingue was followed by a transfer of expertise and capital to Cuba. Similarly, sugar production developed rapidly in Louisiana and also expanded in British Guiana. The arduous and often very brutal treatment of enslaved people is readily apparent from accounts of slave ships of the period, as well as of life on plantations, and contributed to opposition, as with the Georgetown rebellion in British Guiana in 1823. John Smith, an English church minister, complained that the enslaved people were overworked, neglected if ill, and frequently and severely punished. Death rates could also be high, as, for example, on Trinidad.

Alongside free blacks in Latin America came its more complex ethnic mix, with the status both of mestizos (mixed race people) and of descendants of the indigenous population unsettled but generally poor. Instead, power in the New World rested with the descendants of European colonists.

In Africa, such colonialism was still small-scale, being most developed by the Portuguese in Angola, and now by the British in the Cape Colony, in each case with officials from the metropole dependant on cooperation from the descendants of colonists. As in Britain's Caribbean colonies, where there was white opposition to pressure against slavery, this was an unstable political relationship, one of a number that was to add to the tensions of the Atlantic world.

The Reality of Power in the Atlantic World

Le Rodeur, a French slave ship, took on 160 enslaved individuals in April 1819 at Bonny to the east of the Niger delta, and, in the confined hold, infectious disease hit hard, first eye problems and then dysentery. Crowded in the noxious hold among their urine and excrement, the enslaved people found their water ration cut from eight ounces a day to half a wine glass. Allowed on deck for exercise, some threw themselves into the sea, which led to the others being continually confined. Contagion spread to the crew and by the time the boat had reached Guadeloupe many of the enslaved and crew had lost their sight in one or both eyes, and thirty-one enslaved people had been thrown into the Atlantic.

In Zachary Macaulay's *The Slave Colonies of Great Britain* (1826), he recorded the complaint of a slave in British Guiana: 'When the sun is down, if our row is not finished we get flogged. I received thirty lashes, as did Joe. We are taken to the stocks at night, and flogged next morning. We told the manager the work was too much, that we had no time to get our victuals, and begged him to lessen the task: this was the reason we were flogged.'

The Loss of the *Commerce*, 1815

An American merchantman sailing from Gibraltar to Cape Verde with twelve on board, the *Commerce* ran aground on a reef near Cape Bojador after sailing in dense fog. Going onshore they were attacked by the local population, and tried then to go by their longboat to the Cape Verde Islands, but after about 480 kilometres (300 miles) their food ran out. They landed and were enslaved, being brutally treated before release thanks to the American consul in Tangier. James Riley, the captain, published in 1817 a memoir now titled *Sufferings in Africa*, and the inspiration for Dean King's *Skeletons on the Zahara* (2004).

7

Steaming the Ocean,
1826–1913

A youngster is not always easily impressed, but I can still remember the power of the sight, and have the paltry postcard with which my centimes sought to recapture it. *The Raft of the Medusa* has drama and scale (4.91 x 7.16 metres/16 feet 1 inch x 23 feet 6 inches). Théodore Géricault's painting, first shown in the 1819 Paris Salon, now held in the stuffy splendour of the old galleries at the Louvre, captures the fate of a forty-gun, 1,080-tonne French frigate, launched in 1810, which served in the Atlantic and Indian oceans, before being sent in 1816 to take officials to Saint Louis, Senegal, to re-establish control after the end of British occupation in the Napoleonic Wars. An incompetent captain, a product of the appointment-by-patronage of Restoration France, took the *Méduse* too close to the shore and it ran aground on the Bank of Arguin, 50 kilometres (31 miles) off modern Mauritania. Most of the passengers survived, but 147 were put on an improvised raft that was to be towed by the frigate's launches, only to find themselves abandoned when the task proved too difficult. Cast adrift, with no means to navigate, those on the raft were exposed to a storm which swept many into the sea, leading to a struggle to get into the centre of the raft, and to inadequate supplies. Some rebelled and were killed, some committed suicide, some of the weak were thrown into the ocean, and others resorted to cannibalism. Only fifteen survived thirteen days at sea, and the episode became a *cause-célèbre*, not least due to the cannibalism. It was held up by some as an indictment of Restoration France and by others as a warning of humanity as being on the brink of barbarism.

Very differently, *Demologos* (Voice of the People) was the name of the first warship to be propelled by a steam engine. It was a wooden floating battery built to defend New York Harbour, laid down by Robert Fulton in 1814. Fulton's name for the boat reflected a view of America's role against Britain in the War of 1812. Steam power, in practice, was to increase the power of states at the same time that it also eased the passage of people and freight across the Atlantic.

Whereas the previous ninety years had seen frequent conflict in the waters and on the shores of the Atlantic, that was less the case in this period in part because Britain did not fight either France or the United States after 1815, while British imperialism focused on Asia, and the expansionist ambitions of the United States were trained first on other parts of North America and then on the Pacific. Nevertheless, the power politics of the Atlantic involved the reality or threat of conflict, and that helps explain the extent to which naval strength was developed and maintained in its waters and bases.

THE PORTUGUESE ATLANTIC

Portugal is generally treated as the sick man of Western Europe, its fall possibly a corollary of that of the Ottoman (Turkish) empire. There was interest in Portugal, however, in keeping the empire together, and notably in the shape of links between Portugal and Brazil. Peter, Emperor of Brazil from 1822, inherited the Portuguese throne as Peter IV in 1826 on the death of his father, John VI, creating the prospect of a dual monarchy. However, he abdicated in Portugal in favour of his daughter, Maria II, because he was aware that neither the Portuguese nor the Brazilians wanted a united kingdom. In turn, Maria was replaced in 1828 by Peter's brother, Miguel, launching a civil war. Peter was then busy in a conflict with Argentina over control of Uruguay, which had been part of Brazil from 1816. Reached in 1830, the settlement left Uruguay independent as a buffer state.

Peter then, in 1831, abdicated in Brazil in favour of his son, and sailed for Europe to challenge Miguel, first establishing a government on the liberal-run island of Terceira in the Azores. In 1832, Peter pressed on, capturing Oporto and in 1833 his navy, under Sir Charles Napier, defeated the larger Miguelist fleet off Cape Saint Vincent, the most important Atlantic battle that century between Trafalgar (1805) and Santiago de Cuba (1898). Also in 1833, Miguel was defeated in Oporto and Maria proclaimed queen anew. Miguel was finally defeated in 1834.

However, in a sign of the division of the Portuguese Atlantic, and of the degree to which South America and Africa now had decreasing links, Brazil played little role in the instability in Portugal, then or later, and did not try to gain Portugal's Atlantic islands and African possessions. Nor did Brazil seek to establish itself in those parts of Africa not ruled by Portugal, notably Cameroon, Gabon or Namibia, even though power projection across the South Atlantic would not have been too difficult, while the slave trade from Africa to Brazil remained important during the first half of the century and was financed by the shipping in return of textiles. Most of the annual revenue of Angola derived from export duties on enslaved people shipped out to Brazil.

Brazil focused first on suppressing serious rebellions, including along much of the Atlantic coast: in Pernambuco in 1832–5, Pará in 1835–6, Bahia in 1837–8, Maranhão in 1839–40, and Rio Grande do Sol and Santa Catarina in 1835–48. Thereafter, in the War of the Triple Alliance of 1864–70, Brazil bore the bulk of the successful alliance effort against an expansionist Paraguay. Warships played a role in this war, but they operated on inland rivers, not the Atlantic.

The largest power in South America, Brazil did not attempt to expand northwards along the Atlantic coast. Portugal had controlled Cayenne from 1809, but French power there was restored in 1817, and a border with Brazil accepted that was finally fixed in 1900. Differences over Brazil's borders with Dutch Guiana (Surinam), British Guiana (Guyana) and Venezuela were all settled without conflict. Brazil became a major supplier of exports to Europe and North America, notably of coffee which benefited from the increasing wealth of the greater number of middle-class producers.

The Nullification Crisis

'Like well-boiled rice, they remain united, but each grain separate.' The British diplomat Henry Addington was ably observant in 1823 about the United States, but in 1832 South Carolina attempted to nullify a new tariff on the grounds that it was unconstitutional as well as unfair, and that individual states could protect themselves from such acts by interposing their authority, and thus nullifying the federal law. The state raised an enthusiastic army of more than 25,000 men, purchased arms, and threatened secession if the federal government sought to enforce the tariff.

The federal government, however, did not give way and Charleston's government was reinforced by General Winfield Scott. Moreover, unsupported by the other Southern states and also facing opposition to nullification from within, South Carolina had to back down, to abandon the threat of nullification and to accept a settlement of the tariff issue that did not meet its goals. The dispute indicated the fragility of political and constitutional conventions, the clash between Southern notions of the Union as a voluntary compact among independent states and Northern views of the indivisibility of the one American nation, and the possibility of conflict. In 1832–3, talking about disunion proved an alternative to conflict, but the situation was to be very different in 1861.

ARGENTINA

Having fought Brazil over Uruguay, Argentina also faced civil war. Moreover, it claimed the Falkland Islands but had to accept the reality of British rule there from 1833. This was another state on the Atlantic that was not a power on, or across, the ocean. Argentina expanded southwards over the Pampas and down into Patagonia and Tierra del Fuego, but again did not intervene in Africa. Allied to Brazil in the successful War of the Triple Alliance against Paraguay, Argentina competed with Chile in southwards expansion, but without war. Nevertheless, the expansion of Argentina across the Pampas and, even more, Patagonia represented a very major change of the rulership of part of the Atlantic coastline. The key campaign, the 'Conquest of the Desert' in the late 1870s and early 1880s, notably from 1878 to 1884, saw the Mapuche vanquished and their lands taken and settled. Sheep farming became especially successful. Western infectious diseases hit local people.

The Flying Dutchman

Richard Wagner's opera of 1843 bases the action off Norway, but earlier accounts of the legendary ghost ship doomed to sail forever were in the Atlantic and (less commonly) further east, notably off the Cape of Good Hope. A terrible sin is usually held to be the cause of the curse. In practice, the most likely explanation of a ghost ship is that sightings arose from superior mirages or Fata Morganas. In the Wagner opera, invoking Satan is the cause of the curse, and, as at the climax of so many nineteenth-century operas, there is a final redemption through suicide.

The American Civil War, 1861–5

Atlantic naval power played a key role, with the Union (North) using blockade to cut the Confederacy (South) off from trade, and therefore hitting its revenues and supplies. The rapidly expanded Union navy also threatened amphibious attack along the length of the Confederacy's shores, a process aided by the charts produced by the impressive United States Coast Survey. These attacks had mixed success. The Union captured New Orleans on 1 May 1862, a key episode in the economic warfare of the conflict, and forced entry into Mobile Bay on 5 August 1864 but on 6 April 1863, Rear-Admiral Samuel Francis Du Pont commanded nine Union ironclads in an attack on Charleston, only to be hampered by mines and exposed to fire from shore batteries. Benefiting from offshore islands, Charleston was protected by a network of defensive positions. The thinly armoured USS *Keokuk* was sunk, and three ironclads were damaged enough to be sent for repairs. Charleston only surrendered in February 1865 when threatened by General Sherman with a siege, thus repeating the British pattern of success and failure in 1776 and 1780. Wilmington, North Carolina, only fell in January 1865. There were no fleet actions in Atlantic waters during the war, but there were clashes between particular ships, as in 1864 when the Confederate *Alabama*, a British-built commerce-raider, was sunk by the Union *Kearsage* off Cherbourg. The Civil War hit American merchant shipping hard.

The Civil War gave Spain an opportunity to intervene in the Dominican Republic and France in Mexico, but these were abandoned in 1865 and 1867 respectively. The British and French had considered intervening in the American Civil War, notably in November 1861, when conflict between Britain and America appeared a prospect after a Union frigate stopped a British steamer in the Old Bahama Channel and seized two prominent

Confederate politicians en route to Europe, a clear breach of British maritime rights, and again in 1862 when both Britain and France were in play. This brings to the fore one of the major counterfactuals in Atlantic history. Britain was the leading Atlantic naval power, but the Union's ironclads increased the risk to Britain of intervention, and therefore lessened British political leverage. In order to be any real threat to the Union, the Royal Navy needed to invest in a brown-water (i.e. coastal) ironclad force to operate effectively in North American coastal waters. The British also faced the vulnerability of Canada. Having drawn back from conflict in 1861 and 1862, Britain and America managed subsequent differences with care, while France focused on Mexico and on the Polish crisis of 1863.

Mary Celeste

The *Mary Celeste* was an American two-masted sailing ship found deserted off the Azores in 1872 with her lifeboat missing but plentiful food on board. All aboard were never seen again. The salvage hearings could not explain what had happened. Explanations included murder, insurance fraud, fumes from the cargo, and flight in the face of being becalmed or due to a natural disaster such as a waterspout. All have been suggested, but none is satisfactory.

The ship itself reflected the multiple links of the Atlantic. Built in 1860–1 in Nova Scotia, and named *Amazon*, the first voyage was to take timber thence to London, but, in 1862–3, the ship worked mainly in the West Indies. Driven ashore in a storm at Cape Breton Island in 1867, in 1868 the ship was sold as a wreck to a New York mariner who restored her and gave her the name *Mary* (not *Marie*) *Celeste*. Rebuilt in 1872, her first visit was to take denatured alcohol from New York to Genoa. Natural disaster or foul play?

POWER IN ATLANTIC AFRICA

The situation on the African shore was far more drawn-out and complex than that on the Atlantic side. In 1826, European power was relatively modest. Britain was increasingly present in the South Atlantic, adding Ascension (1815), Tristan da Cunha (1815), Gough Island (1816) and the Falkland Islands (1833) to Saint Helena, and in West Africa added to its existing possessions Bathurst in Gambia (1816) and Fernando Póo from 1827 to 1843, although an attempt to defeat the Asante was crushed in 1821 with Colonel Sir Charles McCarthy's head turned into a ceremonial drinking cup. Moreover, the British were not able to develop their position on the Mosquito Coast of Nicaragua and eventually had to recognise Nicaraguan sovereignty in 1860.

The 1830s saw scant European expansion, but the situation changed from the early 1840s. Spain received Fernando Póo back from Britain in 1843, the year in which it also established Río Muni, the basis of the modern state of Equatorial Guinea. France established colonies in Gabon (1842) and Ivory Coast (1843), adding to its existing colony in Senegal, from which expansion occurred in the late 1850s.

This still left much of the African coast outside European hands, but only Morocco had any naval strength and that was inconsequential, although Moroccan pirates were still a factor in the 1870s.

Abd al-Rahman, the sultan from 1822 to 1859, had revived piracy as a way to help the government's dire financial situation, but this led to a hostile reaction, the British bombarding Tangier in 1828, with punitive bombardments following from other powers on other cities, including Larache, Azila and Tétouan in 1829, and Salé in 1851. His rule was also undermined by frequent revolts between 1824 and 1858, notably from tribal and élite opponents.

Accused of supporting opposition to France in Algeria, Morocco had already been invaded by the French in 1844 and its forces defeated at Isly, the first successful European invasion of Morocco for centuries. A French squadron bombarded Tangier, and bombarded and occupied Mogador (now Essaouira), then Morocco's leading seaport, inflicting much destruction. The Moroccans agreed, by the Treaty of Tangier of 1844, not to help Algerian resistance to France and, by the Treaty of Lalla Maghnia of 1845, to fixing a border with French-occupied Algeria that was further west than that prior to the French intervention there. At this stage, however, France focused on Algeria. Despite the efforts of the sultan's son, the future Muhammad IV (r. 1859–73), to Europeanise part of the army after defeat at Isly, this was not Morocco as an equivalent to Japan, which became strong through modernisation, crushing domestic opposition and embarking on foreign expansion.

The other African powers, including those in coastal areas such as Dahomey, were essentially inland and used Europeans to provide their transatlantic commercial links. Moreover, the British navy increased its presence in West African waters in an effort to counter the slave trade. In 1851, Lagos, a major slaving port that exported many slaves as a result of the bitter Yoruba civil wars, and that served as an entrepôt for Hausa slave traders, was attacked, harbour facilities destroyed, and a new ruler installed who agreed to abolish the slave trade. Lord John Russell, the prime minister, was to note: 'I hate slavery and the slave trade beyond measure.' A decade later, concern about continual slaving from Lagos, and about French interest, led to successful pressure for its cession to Britain.

Atlantic Diplomacy

'His slovenliness and untidiness are appalling. His table is covered literally a foot high with documents in their turn covered with dust. This is probably the dust-heap into which disappear many of our carefully prepared private letters and memoranda on pressing matters and possibly even our Notes, of which we never hear anything again.' Thus the British envoy, W. H. D. Haggard, in 1907 described José, Baron do Rio Branco, foreign minister of Brazil from 1902 to 1912, who had a high reputation. Another envoy's description of another foreign minister in 1921: 'It is difficult to describe the extraordinary sense of ineffectiveness which attaches to all dealing with the Minister.'

Trade was a key aspect of diplomatic relations with Latin America. In 1852, Sir Charles Hotham, who had defended trading interests in the Plate estuary in the 1840s as a naval officer, was sent back as envoy to negotiate a trade treaty with Argentina.

By then, European expansionism was increasingly affecting Atlantic Africa across its full range. Thus, in 1859–60, a Spanish campaign in Morocco which included the naval bombardment of Tangier, Azila and Tétouan, led to the capture of Tétouan and Ifni and the imposition, under the Treaty of Wad Ras of 1860, of a heavy indemnity to which half of all customs duties were allocated by treaty. This defeat ensured that Muhammad IV was unable to press forward with his policies for governmental modernisation, although he tried to appoint tribal leaders rather than letting them be elected. Despite being faced by widespread tribal opposition to attempts to increase the sultan's power, notably revenue raising, Hassan I (r. 1873–94) was able to try to consolidate control over the southern Berber tribes by, for example, founding the town of Tiznit in 1881 and touring the south in 1893.

The pace of Western imperial activity increased in the 1870s when the British defeated the Asante in 1873–4 in a campaign characterised by logistical support, firepower and adaptation to campaigning in the tropics.

The 1880s launched more expansion as did increased competition between the European powers, not least the determination of Germany to play a colonial role, which led to the establishment from 1883 of colonies in Togo, Cameroon and Namibia, with rebellion in the last in 1904–5 by the Nama and Hereros crushed with terrible brutality. France, Germany's major European rival, responded by driving forward its imperialism in West Africa, taking over Dahomey in 1884 and Ivory Coast in 1891, and also establishing a protectorate over most of Morocco in 1912, the latter in part to thwart German intervention.

The conquest of Morocco, eased by the 1904 Entente Cordiale with Britain, had really begun in 1907 with the bombardment of Casablanca. Violent opposition to the construction by the French of the port, as well as to other aspects of French influence, led to a heavy bombardment by French warships with a large number of casualties. Troops were landed and the heavily damaged city seized. A rebellion in 1911 against the sultan and growing French influence resulted in increased French intervention, as well as the Spanish occupation of Larache and the dispatch of a German warship to Agadir in an attempt to use the issue for German ends. In support of France, which had accepted the British position in Egypt and Sudan, Britain sent battleships to Moroccan waters and the Germans backed down, accepting compensation from France in Equatorial Congo. With the sultan deposed in 1912, French power was presented in terms of a Protectorate of Morocco, which was a different goal to that represented by the conquest of Algeria, and notably without the comparable European settlement. Important to the French plan was the consolidation of control over the areas of Morocco where the sultan had wielded only limited power, while the modernisation of Morocco was important to French intentions and their exposition.

Operating in part from the Canaries, Spain had established a protectorate in the Río de Oro in 1884, adding the Spanish Sahara to the north in 1912 when the north of Morocco became a Spanish protectorate.

Meanwhile, the Boer War of 1899–1902 between Britain and the inland Boer (Dutch Afrikaner) republics of Transvaal and the Orange Free State very much had an Atlantic dimension. British ministers were greatly influenced by the fear that if, given the gold and diamond discoveries, the Boers became the most powerful force in Southern Africa, it might not be long before they were working with Britain's imperial rivals, especially the Germans in South-west Africa, and threatening its strategic interests at the Cape. In West Africa, Britain had established the Oil Rivers Protectorate in 1885, and that and Lagos had become the basis of Nigeria. The British also had colonies in Gambia, Sierra Leone and Ghana, the Portuguese in Portuguese Guinea (Guinea Bissau) and Angola, and Belgium in what became Congo. By 1913, all of Atlantic Africa was under European colonial control with the exception of Liberia, which had been established in 1821 as a state for formerly enslaved Americans. In practice, once established, they treated the local Africans harshly.

THE ROYAL NAVY IN THE FRONT LINE AGAINST SLAVERY

The name HMS *Pickle*, a schooner with only five cannon, may not call forth patriots today, but it was a stirring sight on the night of 5–6 June 1829 when, after a deadly exchange of cannon fire at close range, she captured the *Voladora*, carrying enslaved people bound for American plantations, off Cuba. The *Voladora* was larger and had a crew twice the size, but the *Pickle* under Lieutenant John MacHardy, later on Admiral, closed, and after an action of eighty minutes the *Voladora*, the mainmast shot away, the sails repeatedly holed and rigging trailing over the stern, surrendered. The British had lost four men, their opponents at least fourteen. Two hundred and twenty-three African men and ninety-seven African women who had been bought in Africa were freed. Thirty-two had already died on the voyage. The British crew imprisoned the slavers in their own chains. The victory was celebrated in Britain, with memorable paintings depicting the plucky triumph of the smaller crew.

The *Pickle* was not alone. Five days after its victory the navy's smallest warship, the schooner HMS *Monkey*, under Lieutenant Joseph Sherer, captured the far larger Spanish brig *Midas* after an action of thirty-five minutes even though the *Monkey* had only one 12-pounder cannon and a crew of twenty-six, while the *Midas* had four 18-pounders and four 12-pounders, and a crew of over fifty. *Midas* had bought 562 enslaved people from Africa, but only 369 were still alive when she was captured. Earlier in 1829, the *Monkey* had already captured an American slaver and a Spanish one, the latter, again more heavily gunned, carrying 206 enslaved individuals.

Stopping first the slave trade and then slavery in British colonies was but a prelude to vigorous action against them elsewhere. In 1807, when Britain was in a difficult war with France, two warships were still sent to African waters in order to begin the prevention of the slave trade.

Action increased after the Napoleonic Wars ended in 1815, with victory at Waterloo. The next year, Admiral Lord Exmouth and a fleet of twenty-one British warships, with the support of a Dutch frigate squadron, demanded the end of holding Christians as slaves in Algiers. When no answer was returned, Exmouth opened fire and 40,000 roundshot and shells destroyed the Algerine ships and much of the city; 1,600 enslaved people, mostly from Spain and Italy, were freed; and the message was driven home by the appearance there of British squadrons in 1819 and 1824, and off Tunis in 1824. The overwhelming firepower of the Royal Navy's 32-pounders at almost point-blank range destroyed the Ottoman–Egyptian fleet in Navarino Bay, helping Greece win independence from the Ottoman Turks, thus ending their ability to acquire Greeks as slaves.

The most important active British anti-slavery naval force, however, in the first half of the nineteenth century was that based in West Africa, which freed the enslaved and took them to Freetown in Sierra Leone, a British colony founded for free black people. They could not be returned to their homes, as they would only be captured anew by fellow Africans and sold. Indeed, in 1862, Viscount Palmerston, the prime minister, who stated his desire to put 'the slave trade down', observed, 'Half the evil has been done by the time the slaves are captured in the American waters. The razzia [devastating raid] has been made in Africa, the village has been burnt, the old people and infants have been murdered, the young and the middle-aged have been torn from their homes and sent to sea.'

In 1834, an outgunned British ship, the brigantine HMS *Buzzard*, under Lieutenant Anthony William Milward, took on the well-armed and larger Spanish brig *Formidable* off West Africa after a chase of seven hours. In a 'smart action' of forty-five minutes, the *Buzzard* had several injured and, as Milward reported, 'our fore and maintop-mast stays were cut, running rigging and sails much damaged, flying jib-boom shot away, and bumpkin [a short boom] carried away in boarding', but six of the slaver's crew were killed. Seven hundred people were freed. In the late 1830s, British naval action, such as that by the *Buzzard*, helped greatly to reduce the flow of enslaved people from the Bight of Biafra.

At the same time, warships based in Cape Town, a British possession from 1806, also played an important role, as anti-slavery patrols were extended south of the equator in 1839, enabling Britain to enforce the outlawing of the slave trade to Brazil. The navy gave the muscle to British diplomacy as the latter sought to negotiate and then enforce restrictions on the slave trade. In 1839, the Act for the Suppression of the Slave Trade authorised British warships to seize slave ships registered in Portugal and sailing under the Portuguese flag, a unilateral measure in part intended to hit the use of the flag as a cover by Brazilian slave traders. The Royal Navy vigorously implemented the Act.

In addition, the Royal Navy was in action in the Caribbean, where the French, Dutch and Spanish colonies retained slavery. In 1840, the nineteen-year-old Midshipman Cooper Key, later an admiral, wrote from the frigate *Cleopatra* off Cuba after chasing a slave ship: 'How glorious! Seeing one's name in the papers for something of that sort! Should not you like it, dearest mama? I was sharpening my sword in the most butcher-like manner all the chase. It was delightful to see how eager our men were to get up with her.'

The 1845 Slave Trade Act authorised the navy to treat suspected slave ships as pirates, leading to the capture of nearly 400 ships within five years. By the end of the 1840s, there were thirty-five anti-slaving patrol ships off West Africa. In 1850, moreover, British warships entered Brazilian ports to seize and destroy suspected slavers, much to the anger of Brazil that, nevertheless, agreed to ban the import of enslaved people, which anyway had become too expensive due to British naval action. The slave trade to Brazil, the largest market in the southern hemisphere, was ended by the Royal Navy, for the Brazilian navy had done very little against the trade.

The Royal Navy was to lose 17,000 seamen to disease, mostly yellow fever, a horrific killer, battle or accident in this lengthy commitment off West Africa.

There are criticisms. It is argued that the navy could and should have sent more and better ships, which ignores the need for warships to guard against the risk of war with America, France or Russia. It is pointed out that some naval officers disliked the mission, their reasons including a belief that freeing the enslaved often exposed them to difficult circumstances, Lieutenant Gilbert Elliott of the *Sampson* being horrified by the conditions of freed Africans awaiting movement: 'thousands of poor wretches huddled together where no sea breeze can blow on them'.

The key element was that in difficult waters, and in the face of terrible disease, officers and men devoted their service to a hard task. They did it with determination and skill, and the role of the Royal Navy was central to ending the slave trade. Powers that were willing to sign up for agreements they had no intention of enforcing were obliged by Britain to act, but, even more, the lawlessness of the oceans was brought under control and the slave trade forced into the backwater of history. That was a great achievement of imperial Britain, and Britain today remains a key state in the suppression of this vile trade in human misery.

Steam Power

The forces deployed by the powers by 1913 were transported by coal-powered steamships in a way that would have seemed fantastical in 1800. Steam, however, was not introduced at once, not only because of the capital already invested in existing shipping as well as the cost of steam engines, but also due to the deficiencies of early steamships and the difficulties of providing sufficient infrastructure. Steam power made journey times predictable and quicker, but also made the availability of coal and the ability to carry sufficient coal key issues. Change, therefore, was not immediate. Early steamships suffered from slow speed, a high rate of coal consumption and the difficulties posed by side paddlewheels, which included the considerable space they took up and their vulnerability to accident. The prevention of rolling was especially important in order to keep their paddles in the water, and ship designers still believed in the steadying power of canvas in order to prevent ships from rolling too heavily. There were also serious problems in producing and maintaining reliable engines. Thus, the shift to steam took time, with the screw propeller (placed at the stern) in the 1840s important as a feasible alternative to the paddlewheel, while sailing ships remained important throughout the century.

Steam power made it possible to try to ascend rivers that flowed into the Atlantic, thus increasing its economic significance by easing transport. For some rivers such as the Mississippi, the Paraguay and the Paraná, this was possible but there were greater difficulties with some others. In 1816, an expedition sought to travel up the River Congo in order to discover if it was the outlet of the River Niger. Led by Commodore James Tuckey in command of the *Congo*, the first steamship on an African river, the expedition was blocked by difficult cataracts on the river, the boat did not operate correctly, and Tuckey and many of his men died of disease.

Great Western and *Great Britain*

A paddlewheel steamship designed by Isambard Kingdom Brunel and completed in 1838, the SS *Great Western* was the first steamship purpose-built for crossing the Atlantic, and it was the largest passenger ship in the world for a while. She was used to make forty-five Atlantic round trips from Britain to carry passengers to and from North America, before going out of service in 1846. In 1838–40, the *Great Western* averaged sixteen days westward to New York, and thirteen days and nine hours back to Britain, alternating between Avonmouth and Liverpool. She was acquired in 1847 for use on the transatlantic mail service, first to the West Indies, with fourteen voyages to 1853, and then nine to Rio via Lisbon, Madeira, Tenerife, Saint Vincent, Pernambuco and Bahia, between 1853 and 1855. She was scrapped in 1856.

From her maiden voyage in 1845 until 1854, SS *Great Britain* was the longest passenger ship in the world, and also the first iron steamer to cross the Atlantic. She was designed by Brunel for the North Atlantic run, and for an initial complement of 36 passengers and 130 crew. The ship ran aground on the Irish coast in 1846–7, was refitted and then, after only one further round trip to New York, moved to the Australia service. Fuelled by opportunities and entrepreneurship, this was a period of increasing competition on the Atlantic service. This was not only from the Cunard Line, which had preceded the *Great Britain*, but also from the Collins Line and the Inman Line, both of which entered service in 1850. The latter was the first service (in 1852) to carry steerage passengers, which opened up a larger passenger market.

The development of transoceanic steamship systems reflected the economic return from trade, especially from rapid and largely predictable crossings, but government subsidies also played a part in the shape of mail contracts. The resulting communication system directly helped the cause of commerce, while other goods and people were also carried by the mail ships, the 1839 mail contract between the British government and the Halifax merchant and whaler Samuel Cunard for services to Halifax, Boston and Québec requiring that the ships be able to act as troop ships. The maiden voyage, in 1840, of the *Britannia* (built on The Clyde), marked the beginning of steam postal services across the Atlantic, and, by the end of the decade, the service had increased to satisfy the British government's demand for a weekly mail. The average ocean crossing from Britain to Halifax fell from forty days in 1837 to twelve in 1852. In 1855, an iron ship, the *Persia*, was brought into the run, and in 1862 was joined by the *China*, the first big boat to cross the Atlantic using a screw-drive rather than a paddlewheel. Prior to the Civil War, the Americans were increasingly major players in Atlantic trade; notably the New York-based Black Ball Line shortened the time it took to cross the Atlantic and sailed on fixed schedules.

Moreover, improvements in engine design and technology increased power and cut coal consumption, and thus the frequent need for coaling, making steamships more profitable and thus attractive. Their greater cost-efficiency hit the use of sailing ships and thus, in the 1880s, affected the Canadian manufacture of them which was largely for British shippers, notably from Liverpool. This manufacture, which reflected the timber and skills available in Canada, was an aspect of the integrated nature of the Atlantic economy, which was more pronounced in the anglophone North Atlantic than further south.

In the 1860s, high-pressure boilers were combined with the compound engine and, in 1874, the triple-expansion marine engine was introduced. It was to be followed by the increased use, from around 1900, of the water-tube boiler which was able to work at higher pressure and was appropriate for turbine propulsion. As opposed to reciprocating (piston) engines, steam turbines are lighter weight, smaller and more energy-efficient. The modern steam turbine was invented in 1884 by Charles Parsons and made the production of plentiful electricity by a dynamo possible. Turbines were more expensive, but easier to maintain. *Turbinia*, in 1894, was the first steam turbine-powered ship and was the fastest ship in the world; the first turbine-powered merchant vessel followed in 1901. In 1905, the Admiralty decided that all future warships would be turbine-powered. That year saw *Victorian* and *Virginia*, the first turbine transatlantic liners, on the Liverpool–Montreal run for the Canadian Allan Line. *Victorian* could carry 1,690 passengers and 8,000 tonnes of cargo, its refrigerated space useful on the eastward run for taking Canadian food to Britain. Founded in 1819, the Allan Line became highly successful, but was bought by Canadian Pacific Steamships in 1917. In 1906–7, the *Mauretania* and *Lusitania* were launched with four Parsons steam turbines each.

'Rolling Down to Rio'
. . . weekly from Southampton
Great steamers, white and gold,
Go rolling down to Rio.

Rudyard Kipling, in his *Just So Stories* (1902), captured the romance and scale of transatlantic services, and the result-ing integration of a world based on the port cities.

IRON

The shift from wood to iron in ship construction was an import-ant aspect of maritime change. It was delayed by a series of problems, notably the effect of iron on magnetic compasses, the degree to which iron hulls fouled very much worse than wooden hulls that were copper-bottomed, and the difficulties of securing consistency and quality in the iron. The ability, however, to overcome these problems reflected the strength of the British economy in the acquisition and application of relevant knowl-edge. Britain had major competitive advantages for ships built of iron and powered by coal, and this helped ensure a rise in its shipbuilding, and an increase in the percentage of trade carried in British ships. Shipyards were major economic sites: there were 4,000 workers in Scottish shipbuilding in 1841, but the number had risen to 51,000 by 1911. Whereas 341,000 tonnes of shipping was launched on the Clyde in 1881, the figure in 1914 was 757,000. In 1910–14, Britain still built 62 per cent of the world's ships, although in 1892–4 the percentage had been 82.

British coalfields, especially that of south Wales, coal from which was particularly useful for steam-raising, serviced the needs of British and other steamships. The peak year for the number of collieries in south Wales was 1910, when there were 688, and in 1913 the coalfield produced 57 million tonnes, compared to 10.25 million in 1860, a growth reflecting greater demand but also the improvements in drainage and ventilation that made possible the working of deeper seams.

The coal trade helped to increase the British presence around the Atlantic as coaling stations were established (the ships could not carry enough fuel for their whole voyage). This was notably so at Las Palmas in the Canaries, the last fuelling port before sailing on to the New World. Alfred Lewis Jones, a colliery and shipping owner, established the Grand Canary Coaling Company in 1886, taking back bananas, tomatoes and potatoes. Jones also took tourists, and hotels were built accordingly, as was the Holy Trinity Church in Las Palmas, opened in 1893. The British introduced into the Canaries frozen meat, the first golf club in Spain and the telephone. Cricket, football, freemasonry and tennis were also part of the British Atlantic. Another coaling station was developed by the British from 1838 at Mindelo on the island of São Vicente in the Cape Verde Islands. This had the advantage of being roughly halfway from Europe both to Cape Town and to the Plate estuary, and, in 1919, its acquisition by Britain was briefly considered; but higher prices and fewer facilities there helped ensure that Las Palmas became more successful.

Iron ships were structurally stronger and could be larger, and they eventually made wooden screw steamers redundant. Cutting the cost of trade brought enhanced profitability, and fostered economic specialisation and therefore growth, with the opportunities and disruption that followed. Large and well-trained crews, not least skilled engineers, were important to more effective trade.

Talent for the Atlantic

From 1875, the Thomson Sounding Machine was used to sound the Atlantic. The wire-based, depth-sounding mechanism had been invented in 1872 by Sir William Thomson, from 1892 1st Lord Kelvin. He added a pressure gauge. Thomson had worked on the transatlantic telegraph project and improved the method used to calculate a ship's position, as well as the mariner's compass, which was affected by the use of iron in shipbuilding.

Ocean Liners

The Holland America Line, established in 1873 in Rotterdam, was a reminder that the Atlantic did not only affect countries on its shores, a point also seen with important German and Italian lines. This was the key Dutch carrier to the New World, and operated until 1989 when it was sold to Carnival. The *Nieuw Amsterdam*, which had its maiden voyage in 1938, provided a luxury service to New York, but was requisitioned as a troop carrier during the Second World War, resuming transatlantic service in 1947 before jet travel led to her becoming a Caribbean cruise ship.

Similarly, the Hamburg America Line was founded in 1847 in Hamburg. It was one of the major transatlantic carriers, merging in 1970 with its rival, the Bremen-based Norddeutscher Lloyd, founded in 1857. Hapag-Lloyd is the successor company.

TRADE

Larger iron, and later steel, ships required deeper anchorages, more sophisticated, purpose-built facilities for particular goods, and linkages with the rail system; and cities such as Halifax and Buenos Aires developed as major ports serving the Atlantic trading system. About half of all Canadian exports by value in 1891–1915 were wheat and flour for Britain, while timber was also important.

Atlantic trade was affected, however, by protectionism and population growth, as well as by technological change. The difficulty of competing in Canada and the United States, and of expanding sales in traditional colonial markets in Canada and the West Indies, ensured that much of the rise in British exports after the Napoleonic Wars was obtained from markets in Latin America, Africa and Asia.

Latin America was part of the British informal empire, areas that were economically dependent but not politically controlled; and the same was true of Portugal, Portuguese Africa and Portugal's Atlantic islands. In Latin America, the sources of British influence were varied, and not limited to trade and finance. Some of the expatriates and naval mercenaries who had played a prominent role in the Wars for Independence then settled down to establish prominent naval and/or mercantile families, intermingling with the locals and embedding a British connection in the life of these new countries. British political and economic ideas and practice were admired by reformers such as Bernardino Rivadavia, who in 1826–7 was the first president of Argentina, and this admiration helped ensure that Britain's commercial role was widely accepted. The *British Packet and Argentine News* was an established weekly by 1835, with a strong mercantile emphasis, regularly reporting on the movement of foreign ships and the current prices of such commodities as skins, wool and salt. English became the language of business, as more generally in the Atlantic, a development that owed much to expatriate communities and the role of British finance and shipping. Finance helped British entrepreneurs such as Thomas Brassey (1805–70), who played a major role in the development of Argentinian railways, particularly moving agricultural products to Buenos Aires, and thus in serving the Atlantic trading system. Some Argentinean nationalists, however, complained about the British influence.

British commercial and diplomatic links, and the cultural, intellectual and political image of Britain helped ensure that Freemasonry developed in Argentina as in Brazil. So also with the spread of friendly societies, such as the Manchester Unity of Oddfellows, the Freetown, Sierra Leone, branch of which contained more than fifty black members by the 1900s.

Wilson Sons

Established in Salvador, Brazil, in 1837 by two Scottish brothers, and initially focusing on coaling, Wilson Sons expanded to Rio de Janeiro and developed the services of towing and ship repair. It built the first drydock in Brazil, opened in 1869, as well as working for the Brazilian navy and moving into Brazilian railways.

The British embrace of free trade, notably with the repeal of the Corn Laws in 1846, was also important to the Atlantic economy. Free-trade agreements were negotiated, as with Morocco in 1856, and an Anglo-French trade treaty in 1860. Linked to technological changes in the shape of large steamships, refrigerated holds from the 1870s, long-distance railways and barbed wire, the end of protectionism saw the British market become important for Argentinian beef and Canadian wheat in the closing decades of the century and, in turn, this attracted investment in these countries.

Transatlantic food exports hit domestic production in the British Isles, helping cause agrarian depression.

Britain was also the largest overseas investor in the world as well as the centre of the world's financial system: commodity prices, shipping routes, insurance premiums and much else were all set in London, and it was not surprising that the Greenwich Meridian, finalised for Britain in 1851, became the internationally recognised prime meridian in 1884 when over two-thirds of all ships and tonnage used it as the reference meridian on their charts and maps. British regulation was also seen with the Plimsoll line, the maximum depth to which the vessel may be safely immersed when loaded with cargo, a line compulsory under the United Kingdom Merchant Shipping Act of 1876 and, internationally, under Load Line Conventions of 1930 and 1966.

Fishing

The British cod fishery on the Grand Banks off Newfoundland collapsed in the early nineteenth century, being replaced by fishing by those resident in Newfoundland. In the second half of the century, as Canadian fishing as a whole rose in value, with Britain a major market for fish and lobster exports from Newfoundland and Canada, the role of American and French fishermen in this area became more important. Nevertheless, buoyed by the use of fish to provide cheap food for industrial workers, the British fishing industry in the late nineteenth century was in a much better state than it would be a century later, while Greenland whaling was a source of profit, for example releasing much capital into the Shetland economy. In Lerwick, the Shetland Islands' main town, there is still much evidence of the wealth from the herring industry prior to the First World War. So also with the town of Siglufjörður in Iceland, where there is a Herring Era Museum.

A measure of differentiation came from steam fishing boats, which required investment, running costs and the ready availability of coal. The introduction of these boats from 1877 made it easier to exploit North Atlantic fishing grounds, and brought greater prosperity to the fishing ports where they were based. Most Atlantic fishing, in contrast, remained less capitalised, and very much for local markets, as, for example, off Morocco and Portugal.

QUEST FOR INFORMATION

The Atlantic was speeded up by steam travel and was also made more accessible through increased and more widely spread information. The charting of coastal waters was particularly important to trade. Thus, Francis Beaufort (1774–1857) surveyed the entrance to the Plate estuary in 1807, a valuable aid to the warships in preparing for what was to be an unsuccessful attack on Buenos Aires, but later important for helping ships sailing to a major destination for British trade. From 1829 to 1855, Beaufort was hydrographer to the navy, trying to fill in the coasts not so far covered by surveys. As a result, Edward Belcher surveyed the coast of West Africa in the early 1830s. Under Charles-François Beautemps-Beaupré, using triangulation, the Atlantic coastline of France was mapped between 1815 and 1838.

This was but part of a quest for information. Tide prediction tables became important, as did the recording of wind velocity and direction. Robert Fitzroy, the Chief of the Meteorological Department of the Board of Trade, established in 1861 a system of storm warnings, which became the basis of what he called the 'weather forecast'. The first telegraphic weather reporting was carried out in 1865. The sea area Finisterre was renamed Fitzroy in 2002.

Information about the availability and distribution of whales, seals and fish led to an expansion of maritime activity, although this hit the livelihood of local people, for example the Yamana of

Tierra del Fuego. The eventual laying of a submarine cable to the United States for telegram transmission reflected the development of partial information about the ocean bed. The first cable, finished in 1858, only operated for three weeks, and the second, begun in 1865, ended when the very heavy cable broke, but the third was successfully laid in 1866, the mighty *Great Eastern* doing the laying, as it had done for the second. A number of cables rapidly followed in 1873, 1874, 1880 and 1890, and underwater cables were also laid via the Cape Verde Islands and Ascension to South America and Cape Town, and also to Bathurst and Freetown. In 1956, the first transatlantic telephone cable system was opened, in place of an earlier reliance on radio transmission; the first transatlantic phone call being made in 1876. In contrast, undersea links between Africa and South America were poor, the South Atlantic Cable System between Brazil and Angola, opening in 2018, however, ensuring that it was no longer necessary to go via the USA and Europe.

Migration

Steamships cut the cost of migration to passengers both by reducing the time of transit – to ten days from Britain to New York in the 1870s – and because their size and cost required the need for a greater number of passengers. A dynamic process, migration provided multiple links within the Atlantic world. Imperial links were important, including from Britain to Canada and, to a far lesser extent, the Cape Colony, but far less so than non-imperial links, as of the movement of Italians and Germans to Argentina, Brazil and the United States, and the over 8 million emigrants from the British Isles to the United States between 1815 and 1901. A large number was the result of emigration from Ireland in the aftermath of the potato blight that began in 1845. Indeed, migration in the Atlantic world was to be one of the defining factors of the Irish experience in the nineteenth century. The Irish created an Atlantic world that was to include significant space for anti-British activism including conspiracies in Britain and Canada, and members of the American Irish community were to be long-standing supporters of Irish nationalism, including terrorist organisations, although there were also deep ties across the American–Canadian border, ties that remain strong today. Boston was, and remains, a key place in this world. In contrast, there were very few European migrants to Atlantic Africa: Portuguese emigrants far preferred the economic opportunities and society of Brazil to Angola.

Migration, a Fictional Account

Dickens's novel *Martin Chuzzlewit* (1844), described a ship en route from Liverpool to America: 'A dark, low, stifling cabin, surrounded by berths all filled to overflowing with men, women, and children, in various stages of sickness and misery'.

In some cases, the intention of migrants from the outset was to return having made money, and this became easier as steamships cut journey times and costs. Most migrants, however, did not return, which contributed to the emotional wrench of emigration and to the character of Atlantic societies as separated families. Linkage, nevertheless, owed much to the degree to which migration took place within, or with regard to, friendship, family, locality or occupational networks.

The Atlantic world also provided an opportunity for individuals and groups to pursue hopes and implement ideas. Michael Jones, a committed nationalist, undertook an ill-fated attempt to establish a Welsh community in Patagonia in 1865. This proved more difficult than expected and did not fulfil the hopes of those involved, but a Welsh-speaking community has continued to the present. The Atlantic also offered the apparent prospect of a virtuous regeneration, which was why the British Salvation Army sponsored and organised the emigration to Canada of 200,000 people between 1890 and 1930, or, at least, an alternative to the poverty and despair of life in southern Italy and other sources of migrants.

The White Star Line

Established in 1845, and originally focusing on voyages to Australia, the company went bankrupt but was relaunched in 1868 in order to focus on the Liverpool–New York service. In 1873, the *Atlantic* ran aground trying to make Halifax, and 535 people were killed. The demand for Atlantic passage ensured that the White Star Line could replace liners and compete with Cunard. Harland & Wolff built the ships, which developed in the direction of larger size and thus more passengers. From 1907, White Star began a weekly service to New York from Southampton, which was closer to London than Liverpool. On its maiden voyage, the *Titanic* was lost in 1912, as were several White Star ships during the First World War. White Star was bought by the Royal Mail Steam Packet Company and, in 1934, the establishment of the Cunard-White Star Line reflected the travails of the Great Depression.

New York: Atlantic City

Of the roughly 1 million people squeezed into the burgeoning metropolis in 1875, some 40 per cent had been born abroad. By the end of the century, the population would explode to 3.5 million, in part due to new arrivals from Italy and Eastern Europe, adding to the prior immigrant surges of Germans and Irish. The city had expanded all the way north up Manhattan Island in a grid of city blocks, interrupted only by Central Park, which was laid out in 1857–8. The Hudson and the East River were both spanned by the energy of the expanding metropolis, as well as by the Hoboken steam ferries and the Brooklyn Bridge (opened 1883), so that Hoboken, Jersey City and Brooklyn all grew greatly. Installed in 1870, the city's first passenger lift was to lead to the birth of the skyscraper.

The Atlantic was crucial to New York, which was very much a port-city to which immigrants arrived by sea. It was also the primary port of entry to the USA for goods, and the domed Customs House on Wall Street was a major feature. In his poem 'The City' about New York, Richard Watson Gilder (1844–1909) referred to its having 'room to spare, on thy splendid bays / For the ships of all the earth!'

AN ATLANTIC SHIFT

War in the Atlantic appeared a prospect on several occasions in mid-century, as Britain and America disagreed over the American–Canadian border, and notably so in 1838 and 1844. Forced to consider the defence of Canada, the British relied heavily on the ability of the Royal Navy to attack America's Atlantic cities as a deterrent. The navy also played a role in moving troops, for example to Canada from the British Isles, Gibraltar and the West Indies, and from Halifax to Saint John's, New Brunswick, and Québec.

British military involvement again seemed a prospect during the American Civil War (1861–5). Relations were tense, as the British government appeared to the Union to be unduly pro-Confederate, while the Union blockade of the Confederacy badly hit British trade links, and notably of cotton to the Lancashire mills. There were specific crises over the Union seizure of Confederate diplomats from a British Royal Mail steamer in November 1861 and over the possibility of Anglo-French mediation in late 1862. Preparations for conflict included the strengthening of the Royal Navy in North American waters, the dispatch of reinforcements to both Bermuda and Canada, and defensive preparations. Thus, Fort Hamilton was designed to protect Hamilton Harbour, Bermuda, from an American invasion, and had a moat, underground passageways and powerful guns.

Battle, however, was avoided, and the rapid demobilisation of the Union fleet after the war improved the British position. There was to be no conflict between the two powers over Canada or American expansion. Differences were settled by the Treaty of Washington of 1871. Furious with what he saw as American aggression during the Venezuela crisis in 1895, Robert, 3rd Marquess of Salisbury, the prime minister, argued that Britain should have supported the Confederacy so as to make American power more manageable.

Meanwhile, Britain had not sought to become a major colonial power in South America. The British had thwarted both Argentina and the United States in establishing control of the Falkland Islands in 1833, the government being concerned about the potential threat that the islands in other hands might pose to British seaborne and political interests in South America and the southern oceans. Viscount Palmerston, the Foreign Secretary, was influenced by the views of William Gore Ouseley, envoy in Rio, who argued that, if the Falklands were developed as a centre for trade, ship repair and shipbuilding, they would assist British maritime activity. Britain had been concerned about American views after the Monroe Doctrine, stating that any interference in the Americas could be deemed a hostile act against the United States, was declared in 1823, but America proved reluctant to cooperate with Argentina against Britain.

British Guiana, the consolidation in 1831 of the separate colonies of Berbice, Demerara and Essequibo, became an important plantation colony, especially for the production of sugar. It was expanded into the interior, but this expansion was challenged by Venezuela, which claimed all lands west of the Essequibo River, and, although international arbitration in 1898–9 largely found for Britain, the colony was not the basis for future expansion. So even more with British Honduras, while the British surrendered their position on the Mosquito Coast of Nicaragua.

In the Caribbean, Spanish weakness was exploited, not by Britain, but by the United States, which gained Cuba and Puerto Rico in 1898. The key naval battle, off Santiago de Cuba on 4 July, was a total victory for the Americans. There was no equivalent in the New World to the conflict with settlers of European descent seen with the Anglo-Afrikaner Boer Wars of 1881 and 1899–1902 in Southern Africa. The latter left Britain dominant there, albeit after initial failures and much expenditure.

An Atlantic Prince

In 1893, James Harden-Hickey (1854–98), a Franco-American adventurer, monarchist, novelist and accomplished duellist who had travelled to India and become interested in Buddhism, decided that the uninhabited island of Trinidad (otherwise known as Trindade), about 1,100 kilometres (680 miles) from the coast of Brazil, which he had passed while en route to Tibet, could be the basis for his position. In 1893, he claimed the island, proclaiming himself James I, Prince of

---

Trinidad, opening a New York consular office, selling government bonds, founding the Order of Trinidad, and purchasing a boat to transport colonists. In 1895, Britain seized the island as a telegraph cable-relay station. James I sought American backing to regain it, but was ridiculed. James, who had a homemade crown, then envisaged invading Britain from Ireland, but could not raise the funds, while the idea of becoming king of Hawai'i was also fruitless. He committed suicide.

BRAZIL, A MAJOR NAVAL POWER

One of the leading second-tier navies in the world, Brazil had an impressive fleet, in part due to competition with Argentina. Two powerful ironclads, the *Riachuelo* and the *Aquidabá*, were bought from Britain in the 1880s, being replaced in the 1900s by two dreadnoughts, also British-built, the *Minas Geraes* and the *São Paulo*. They remained in service until after the Second World War, and were an aspect of British influence. Brazil's navy was at times the fifth or sixth largest in the world, but there was nothing to match Japan's entry into the naval power stakes. A series of naval revolts, notably in 1893–4, helped to lead to a focus instead on the army, and the navy became relatively obsolescent in the late 1890s and again in the Second World War.

A CHANGING ATLANTIC

The end of the Atlantic slave trade was followed by the end of Atlantic slavery, with those powers that had been initially reluctant abolishing slavery from the 1860s: Portugal in 1861, the Dutch in 1863, the United States in 1865, Spain in 1886 and Brazil in 1888. British action against the slave trade helped push up the price of enslaved people from the 1850s, ensuring that slave owning became too expensive. Systems of servitude, however, continued, with indentured labour for example in British Guiana, Surinam, Cuba, Trinidad and São Tomé, and the very brutal collection of rubber in the Congo Free State on behalf of King Leopold II of the Belgians.

Western exploitation of Africa took several forms. In 1871, when the Dutch sold their forts on the Gold Coast to Britain, the views of the King of Asante, Kofi Kakari, who saw them as trading bases under Asante sovereignty, were neglected, helping lead to war with Britain in 1873.

Alongside imperial rule, Western interests, in place of enslaved African labour to grow crops or mine in the New World, became more focused on obtaining products for export, such as sugar and coffee from Angola, rubber from the Congo, and cocoa and palm oil from West Africa. Moreover, in contrast to the eighteenth century, Western goods, especially textiles and metals, became available in larger and cheaper quantities, thanks to the economies of scale brought by the use of steamships, which hit African industries.

Economic pressures and resulting social changes were felt around the Atlantic thanks to its integration through large-scale trade. Thus, in Gran Canaria, banana production for European markets developed, with the fishing harbour at Puerto de las Nieves used for shipping the fruit to Las Palmas and thence to Europe. The British also introduced banana plantations to Tenerife in the late nineteenth century. In London, the banana boats went to what was named in 1936 Canary Wharf. Exports of salt from the saltpans on the Cape Verde island of Sal developed from the mid-nineteenth century. The living standards of workers around the Atlantic were often under great pressure, for example on Cape Verde where drought, famine and low wages in the coal-bunkering trade combined to cause destitution and industrial and social strife, as in 1910 and 1920.

Very differently to West Africa, in the Highlands and Islands of Scotland, where potato famine in the late 1840s had led to emigration, there were 'clearances' of cultivation and settlement from the land by landowners in order to make way for sheep farming and deer stalking. By 1884, 1.98 million acres, over 10 per cent of Scottish land, was reserved for deer and thus the hunting interests of a small minority. In turn, the 'Battle of the Braes' against clearances in Skye grew more intense and was a focus on an Irish-type resistance to clearing: the Land League, modelled on the Irish Land League, had 15,000 members by 1884. The crisis led to the Crofters Holdings Act of 1886, which established crofting rights and ended the major phase of the clearances. The colonial populations had far fewer options.

The captured Africanisation of the New World stemming from the slave trade had ceased in terms of new numbers crossing the Atlantic. Instead, in Brazil, there was a shift toward new labour from Europe as part of a new process of capitalist development linked to different labour demands and a new racial-political image as a white democracy. More generally, this shift affected the character of the South Atlantic, as with the marked increase in European numbers in Argentina and South Africa. In contrast, formerly enslaved people, in Brazil and elsewhere, were often very much second-class citizens, usually with poor jobs and low living standards. At the same time, some free black Brazilians sought opportunities back in Africa, helping to create a new dimension to creole communities, for example in Porto Novo, Benin, which had been an important slave port.

Further north, there was only a limited European flow, in the era of large-scale steamship migration, to the Caribbean, Central America, Mexico or the states of the former Confederacy, none of which areas had the opportunities offered by the expanding and growing industrial United States, which, by 1898, was already emerging as an Atlantic great power very different to Britain but of increasing significance. Indeed, in his *The Influence of Sea Power upon History, 1660–1783* (1890), Captain Alfred Thayer Mahan, president of the (American) Naval War College at Newport, Rhode Island, pressed the case for an American oceanic destiny with naval strength as a strategic tool, an argument backed by powerful east coast industrial and commercial interests.

CONCLUSION

Yet, alongside the unprecedented scale and significance of oceanic trade, and the importance thereby attaching to sea power, came the extent to which, irrespective of their oceanic profiles and strength, the industrialisation and political coherence of large land powers – the United States, Germany and Russia – both appeared to challenge the value of sea power and gave it a new direction and energy. They did this by linking this naval strength to continental ambitions and basing their strengths on continental (land) resources. Indeed, in his *Britain and the British Seas* (1902), Halford Mackinder, reader in geography at the University of Oxford, argued that the development of rail technology and systems altered the paradigm of economic potential away from maritime power, while in 1904, speaking at the Royal Geographical Society, he claimed that an international system based on sea power, which he termed the Columbian epoch, was coming to an end as a result of the reassertion of land power made possible by the railway: 'a generation ago steam and the Suez Canal appeared to have increased the mobility of sea-power relative to land-power ... trans-continental railways are now transmuting the conditions of land power'. The twentieth century, however, was to suggest that Mackinder was less the prophet of geopolitics than he was prone to suggest. The significance of oceanic power was far from over.

The *Titanic*

The graveyard in Halifax is sombre by any standard, even in the sun. The sinking, on 15 April 1912, of the largest ocean liner then in service, four days into her first Atlantic crossing from Southampton to New York, led to over 1,400 deaths and caused not only an international drama but also a lasting cause of contention and speculation. The often-retold account of the sinking has been used to make a multitude of points, including class and ethnic ones. In practice, the sinking was in part a result of a failure to heed six messages about drifting ice, but also poor construction techniques.

Devil's Island

The island was a French penal colony in the Salvation Islands of French Guiana (Cayenne) from 1852 until 1953 with a high death rate due to tropical diseases. Political prisoners were among those sent, including Alfred Dreyfus for five years. Several prisoners escaped successfully. Prisoners referred to the penal colony as *la guillotine sèche* (dry guillotine), the title also of the memoir of René Belbenoît who escaped to the United States.

8

The First World War and After, 1914–38

The drama off the Falkland Islands on 8 December 1914 was the most impressive British naval action of the world war. The German East Asiatic Squadron under Vice-Admiral Maximilian Graf von Spee, the leading German naval force outside Europe, had defeated a weaker British force off Coronel in Chile on 1 November and then sailed into the Atlantic in order to destroy the wireless station at Port Stanley and seize coal. Instead, it found that the Admiralty had sent two powerful battlecruisers, the *Invincible* and the *Inflexible*. Their speed had got them to Port Stanley first, and, in the resulting battle, all bar one of the German ships were sunk, although only after a prolonged chase that practically exhausted the magazines of the battlecruisers. The strong sense of commitment by the sailors was recorded by Henry Welch of HMS *Kent* reporting on the sinking of SMS *Nürnberg*: 'We have avenged the *Monmouth* [lost at Coronel]. I really believe it was in the *Nürnberg*'s power to have saved many in the *Monmouth*'s crew. Instead, she simply shelled her until the last part was visible above water. Noble work of which the German nation should feel proud. Thank God I am British.'

Alongside British control of the Channel and the northern approaches to the North Sea, the battle of the Falkland Islands ensured that no German squadron was able to attack Atlantic shipping routes and that situation was fundamental to Britain's success in the war, for Britain was a country that could not feed itself, an imperial economy that relied on trade, and a military system that required troop movements within the empire. No significant warships were based in Germany's Atlantic colonies, and the Belgian ports conquered in 1914 by the Germans did not end the confinement of the latter's surface shipping by Britain.

The crucial nature of Atlantic shipping led Germany to turn to unrestricted submarine warfare, which began on 18 February 1915. This entailed attacking all shipping, Allied and neutral, and without warning, within the designated zone. The *Lusitania*, the largest liner on the transatlantic run, which had made its maiden voyage in 1907, was sunk off Ireland by *U-20* on 7 May; 128 Americans were among the 1,192 killed, and there was savage criticism in America. Indeed, unrestricted warfare was cancelled on 18 September in order to avoid provoking American intervention. Moreover, although the Germans sunk 748,000 tonnes of British shipping in 1915, Britain launched 1.3 million tonnes.

The resumption of such warfare in 1917, a measure of the German turn toward total war, brought America into the war, and was followed later that year by Brazil, which in 1918 provided warships, based at Dakar, to patrol against submarines in the Atlantic Narrows between north-east Brazil and West Africa. America's entry into the war itself increased the very importance of submarines to German capability as it further shaped the balance in surface warships against Germany. America had the third largest navy in the world after Britain and Germany, and the Naval Act of 1916 increased the American shipbuilding programme.

The initial rate of Allied shipping losses was sufficiently high to threaten defeat. In February to April 1917, 1,945,240 tonnes of British shipping was sunk, with only nine German submarines lost. The Germans calculated that if they could sink 600,000 tonnes of British shipping per month for six months, it would drive Britain out of the war, a calculation also based on the assumption that 40 per cent of neutral trade would not enter the war zone due to the threat and, especially, the high maritime insurance rates.

In the event, as in the next world war, Britain defeated the attack. The introduction, from 10 May 1917, of a system of escorted convoys cut shipping losses dramatically and helped lead to an increase in the sinking of submarines. Convoying was unpopular for a variety of reasons, not least delay, harbour congestion, a desire for naval boldness rather than defensive tasks, and the risks of providing a larger target; but it was introduced as likely to be the most effective protection, which it definitely was. Indeed, convoys facilitated the transport in 1917–18 of over 2 million American troops to Europe aboard thousands of ships, and only sixty-eight soldiers were drowned as a result of U-boat attacks. Another 2 million troops were ready to sail to France at the point when the war ended.

The stationing of American escort vessels in the eastern Atlantic at Queenstown, Ireland, and Gibraltar, was significant in increasing and sustaining the anti-submarine force and helping convoying. The Americans proved proficient in anti-submarine warfare. Convoys reduced the targets for submarines and ensured that, if they found the convoys, the submarines could be attacked by escorts with appropriate goals and weapons. The tonnage of merchant shipping lost fell below half a million in August 1917. The Allies sought also to close the Atlantic, adding in 1918 a minefield across the North Sea between the Orkneys and Norway to that laid in 1916 across the Strait of Dover. Convoy escorts helped keep submarines submerged, which reduced their effectiveness, as they had an inherent disadvantage in that it was not necessary to sink the submarine but only to have shipping come safely home. The battle of the Atlantic extended to the Home Front, not only in shipbuilding but also with the drive to increase grain production and ration food and coal, moving Britain toward a total war mobilisation of the resources of society and the capabilities of government.

The Halifax Explosion

The collision in Halifax, Nova Scotia, on 6 December 1917 of a French cargo ship laden with high explosives with a Norwegian ship led to the detonation of the explosives causing what was then the largest human-made explosion. Much of the city was damaged, with 1,630 houses destroyed, 12,000 damaged, and the harbour, a key node on the trans-atlantic movement of munitions, badly hit; 1,782 deaths were confirmed, while 9,000 people were injured. Because Bostonians helped out in the aftermath of the explosion, Nova Scotia sends a Christmas tree for Boston Common every year.

The war also saw the British and French Atlantic imperial systems work, with troops and resources provided accordingly, notably by Canada and South Africa. Lieutenant-General Sir William Birdwood noted in Gallipoli in 1915 that the Martinique and Guadeloupe troops 'are treated in precisely the same way as if they were Frenchmen which from our Indian Army point of view strikes one as curious'.

Armed resistance within the Atlantic empires was largely restricted to a small minority of Irish nationalists and a fraction of the Afrikaner population of South Africa. In September 1914, the French cruiser *Cassard* and the British armed merchant cruiser *Victorian* (a converted liner) bombarded rebellious sites on the Moroccan coast.

Informal empire also worked, with resources provided by allies such as Portugal, which entered the war in 1916 after confiscating, at

Britain's request, German ships docked in Portuguese ports, as well as by neutrals such as Argentina.

The war led to debt-fuelled purchasing by combatants that drove demand for production for Britain and France, and this helped the economy of many Atlantic states, including the United States and Spain, the latter for example shipping timber to Britain. Thanks to demand, investment in production and communications was seen, such as the linkage of the railway system of South Africa with South-west Africa, which had been acquired as part of the partition of the German empire. In the peace settlement of 1919, France also gained much of Togo and most of Cameroon, and Britain part of Togo and a sliver of Cameroon.

After the War, 1919–38

During the war, there was a shift of emphasis in power within the British empire, with the Dominions increasingly influential, which, for the Atlantic, meant Canada and South Africa. British power in Ireland had been weakened and, after the war, a rebellion led to the eventual establishment over most of the island of Ireland of the Irish Free State (Eire), a new Atlantic country but one without a navy. The Anglo-Irish treaty gave Ireland responsibility for policing its fishing, and a former British steam yacht was bought and commissioned in 1923 as the *Muirchú*, and subsequently given two guns as opposed to one in 1936. Because of anxiety about a resumption of submarine warfare, the United Kingdom remained in control of three deep-water treaty ports – Cork, Berehaven and Lough Swilly, until they were handed over in 1938 in order to ease relations with Ireland at the end of the 'Economic War' begun in 1932, a handover criticised by Winston Churchill who correctly presented the ports as essential to the security of the Atlantic trade routes. Meanwhile, French intervention in 1925–6 helped Spain suppress initially successful resistance in the Spanish zone of Morocco.

The Atlantic was an uneasy condominium in the 1920s. The Washington Naval Treaty of 1922 established equality in capital ship tonnage, and in part reflected the degree to which Britain could not match an American naval build up. There was also a *de facto* division of spheres of activity, with the Americans having an interventionist role in the Caribbean, including control over the Panama Canal opened in 1914. In contrast, the British were more prominent in the South Atlantic. There was tension between the American and British navies and governments, although Japan, and later Germany as well, were the powers of most concern. From 1936, helped on by an increase in the naval estimates, the Royal Navy increased its strength.

Running down its navy greatly and relying on Britain and America for its security, Canada had only six destroyers and four minesweepers in 1938. In the imperial conferences of 1923 and 1926, Canada emphasised its determination only to heed the British lead if in Canada's interests. In 1922, in the Chanak crisis with Turkey, Canada refused to pledge help to Britain and, in 1937–8, was in favour of the appeasement of Japan and Germany. Meanwhile, Britain remained the major shipper in Atlantic trade and travel, with regular liner services to North and Latin America, and South Africa.

Queen Mary and Normandie

Sailing the North Atlantic from 1936 to 1967 for Cunard, the *Queen Mary*, built on the Clyde, was designed, with the *Queen Elizabeth*, to provide a weekly fast service on the Southampton–New York run and to benefit from the demand for luxury transatlantic crossings. The *Mary* held the Blue Riband in 1936–7 and 1938–52. At 80,774 tonnes and over 300 metres (1,000 feet) long, the ship had twelve decks and four Parsons steam turbines, and did 28.5 knots

---

when in service, although it had average speeds of 30.99 west-bound and 31.69 eastbound when winning the Blue Riband from the *Normandie* in 1937. It could carry 2,139 passengers and had a crew of 1,101. There were two indoor swimming pools. The ship was used as a troopship in the Second World War.

Built in Saint-Nazaire, the *Normandie* had its maiden voyage in 1935 and was then the largest and fastest passenger ship afloat, with a new streamlined design and an art deco extravagance. Expropriated by the Americans in the Second World War and renamed USS *Lafayette*, the ship was converted into a troop transporter. In 1942, it caught fire in New York harbour as a result of sparks from a welder (not German sabotage as was claimed), and became a hulk that was sold as scrap in 1946.

Blue Riband

The Blue Riband is the accolade for the passenger liner crossing the Atlantic in regular service with the record highest speed. Traditionally, it is based on average speed, not passage time, due to ships following different routes, with eastbound and westbound speed records assessed separately. Twenty-five of the thirty-five liners to hold the Blue Riband were British. The record set by the *United States* in 1952 is unbroken, the second longest period for the record being Cunard's *Mauretania*, which was the world's largest ship from her launch in 1906. Named after the Roman province of Mauretania, not the current state of Mauritania, the ship held the Eastbound Blue Riband from 1907 and the Westbound from 1909, until 1929. She went out of service in 1934. The *United States* retired in 1969.

At the same time, oil-powered ships and air routes offered a new Atlantic. Oil-powered vessels had a greater range than coal-fired steamers, and coaling stations became redundant. There were two rival systems for air routes, airships and aircraft, both of which first crossed the Atlantic in 1919: an aircraft flown by John Alcock and Arthur Brown, and then the R-34 airship. The first attempt to fly the Atlantic by airship had ended in 1910 after the engine failed. The first non-stop transatlantic commercial flight, by the airship *Graf Zeppelin* from Friedrichshafen to Lakehurst, New Jersey, took 112 hours in 1928, the return, benefiting from westerly winds, taking 72. Two years later, the British R-100 flew 5,300 kilometres (3,300 miles) from Bedfordshire to Montreal, taking 78 hours. The airships were faster than liners and luxurious, but could not carry many passengers. Several German airships flew across the North and South Atlantic until 1937, when the hydrogen-filled *Hindenburg*, which had entered service the previous year, caught fire at Lakehurst while trying to dock: of the ninety-seven people on board, thirty-five died and that disaster ended the service. Airships had earlier fallen victim to violent storms.

Aircraft services also developed, with Imperial Airways, a company founded with government support in 1924, linking the empire to Britain. Weekly flights from London to Cape Town began in 1932, and took nine days in 1936. The flights ran via Egypt, Khartoum and Nairobi, and not via Gibraltar and West Africa. Similarly, again defined by the empire, French airlines flew to Morocco and Dakar. In 1939, commercial air services between London and New York began, only to be interrupted by the war, resuming thereafter.

Very differently, the Intracoastal Waterway authorised by Congress in 1919 provided a protected maritime route along the Atlantic coast of the United States.

Flying Boats

In 1913, the *Daily Mail*'s £10,000 prize for the first non-stop aerial crossing of the Atlantic led to interest in flying boats, which was then encouraged by service in the First World War. Some of the largest flying boats of the period, built in New Jersey from 1917, provided air services from America to the Bahamas and Cuba. In 1919, an American Curtiss NC-4 became the first aircraft to fly the Atlantic, crossing not non-stop but via the Azores, although only one of the four planes that set off succeeded.

From the mid-1920s, commercial services developed, notably from London to Cape Town, and from Stuttgart, Germany, to Natal, Brazil, the latter, from 1934, with stops including Bathurst in Gambia and the Brazilian Fernando de Noronha archipelago. Initially, there was a refuelling stop in mid-ocean, with the flying boat landing on the Atlantic near a refuelling ship, being then winched onto the ship, refuelled and sent forth by catapult. The Dornier Do J Wal (Whale), which flew from 1922, provided the latter service, while one flew from Sylt in Germany via Iceland and Greenland to New York in 1930 in forty-seven flight hours. Having earlier lost many aircraft at sea, Air France began an all-air service from France to Brazil in 1936, via Dakar: initially, from 1925, the section on from Dakar had been by ship.

Flying Down to Rio

The first Fred Astaire–Ginger Rogers pairing, this 1933 musical film included an aircraft-wing dance. The flight down is from Miami to Rio via an unspecified deserted island.

Alongside developing links, the Atlantic world was greatly affected in the aftermath of the First World War by protectionism, both restrictions on immigration, notably the American ones in 1924, which also hit liner traffic, and on imports, particularly as a result of the Depression that began in 1929. This was not the free-trade, liberal Atlantic that Victorian Britain had sought with much success to develop. Instability after the war included major labour disputes in 1919, not least in many Atlantic ports, such as Glasgow, where tanks were deployed, and Buenos Aires, where troops quelled a general strike. Economic problems also contributed to political instability. The unsuccessful revolts of the 1920s, as in Brazil in 1922 and 1924 and Venezuela in 1928, were accompanied by successful coups, including in Portugal in 1926, Argentina, Brazil and the Dominican Republic in 1930, Uruguay in 1933 and, eventually, Spain in 1936–9. As a result, authoritarian regimes were established.

In the late 1930s, as a consequence of protectionism elsewhere, the British exported more to South Africa than to the far larger but more self-sufficient and protectionist United States; while American businesses made major inroads in Latin America and Canada, hitting British exports to both. There was also the cultural and social model of America around the Atlantic world. In July 1939, Philip Kerr, 11th Marquess of Lothian, en route to take up the British embassy in Washington, spoke of 'the extent to which we in Britain have become Americanised, in the best sense of that word, in the last twenty-five years – not merely in the

mechanisation of our private lives but in our social and democratic life.'

Other powers were entering the Atlantic sphere, in part by
using aircraft. In 1931, an Italian squadron of eleven double-
hulled flying boats reached Brazil after a journey of 10,400 kilometres (6,500 miles), the first for a squadron of such a size. The
politics as well as drama of flight across the Atlantic was apparent, as the Italian-made aircraft were sent by Benito Mussolini,
Italy's fascist dictator, as a gesture of support to Getúlio Vargas,
the new president of Brazil, and were led by Italo Balbo, the
commander of the Italian air force and a prominent fascist,
who, in 1933, also led a flight of twenty-four of these flying boats
to the United States.

By the end of the decade, Germany, in turn, was actively seeking to expand its influence in Latin America, notably Argentina,
in part by using existing émigré communities and economic links
and in part by developing air services.

The fascist Atlantic was an aspect of unwelcome developments, one enhanced by the degree to which the authoritarianism
in Portugal was joined by Brazil, and then by a more explicit
fascist Spain where the Nationalists who launched the takeover
attempt in 1936 were in part based in Spanish Morocco.

There was also a liberal Atlantic, in which many, notably in
Argentina and Brazil, looked to France, which had an anticlerical
Catholicism they sought to emulate. Cultural links included those
focused on Le Corbusier's visit to South America in 1929, which
led him to draw up new city plans including for Montevideo. The
liberal Atlantic led to support for the Republican cause during
the Spanish Civil War of 1936–9, especially from Mexico. The
communist Atlantic was far weaker.

Pan-Africanism became important with the African diaspora a
basis for a range of ideas including the Back-to-Africa movement
developed by the Jamaican born and (for long) New York-based
Marcus Garvey, who wanted an end to European colonial rule. In

1919, he founded the Black Star Line designed to facilitate diaspora links and help immigration to Africa. Its first ship had an all-black crew and a black captain, and sailed between New York and the West Indies. Mismanagement and American governmental opposition led in 1922 to bankruptcy and to Garvey being jailed for fraud. The American Pan-Africanist, W. E. B. Du Bois, a founder in 1909 of the National Association for the Advancement of Colored People, proved a more substantial figure, opposing both racism and colonial rule. His last years were spent in Ghana, where he was given a state funeral in 1963.

The British Atlantic remained significant, not least, outside the empire, in Argentina where the married Captain Hastings acquires a ranch in Agatha Christie's Poirot novels. The standard British view of empire very much centred on an oceanic destiny with, partly due to the location of the British Isles, the Atlantic the most prominent in the maps, followed by the Indian. Meanwhile, the steamers continued their ocean-weary travels, creaking under the burdens of high seas. In *The House on Tollard Ridge* (1929), John Rhode described a Clyde-built 1,500-tonne British ship off Spain carrying coal to North Africa: 'this ceaseless rolling . . . the unending swell which swung resistlessly eastward . . . in the engine-room, the heat was intense. No air seemed to come down the big ventilators, and a thin, oily steam formed a mist . . . The shining connecting-rods whirled ceaselessly . . . Towering above them were the wood-encased cylinders . . . If it was hot in the engine-room, the passage-way between the boilers vomited the very breath of hell.'

Josephine Bell began *The Port of London Murders* (1938): 'In the early afternoon of a bleak first of November, the *San Angelo*, with a mixed cargo from the East, and after a voyage remarkable in its latter part for almost continuous storm and gale, steamed thankfully into the wide mouth of Thames river. She was British-owned, and most of her crew of eleven, including her captain, were also British.'

The Dominion of Newfoundland

Newfoundland, a self-governing colony from 1855, was a British Dominion in 1907–34 but in 1934, in response to the Depression, the risk of a default on its public debt and public disquiet, gave up self-government to become a dependent territory of the United Kingdom, although it de jure remained an independent Dominion. The Commission of Government took over, with three commissioners from Newfoundland and three from the United Kingdom, and the governor as chairman. This continued until two referenda were held in 1948 over the future status of Newfoundland. In the second, held after the option of a continued Commission had been rejected, 52 per cent voted for confederation with Canada and 48 per cent for Dominion status; and Newfoundland joined Canada in 1949, reducing the number of Atlantic states. Labrador had been transferred by Britain from Lower Canada to Newfoundland in 1809, which led to a long-standing border dispute with Québec.

9

The Second World
War, 1939–45

The American troops landing in the heavy surf at Casablanca, Port Lyautey and Safi in Morocco on 8 November 1942 as part of Operation Torch had a difficult time that was not eased by Vichy French opposition, especially around Casablanca. Surprise on the beaches was complete, which was just as well as the Americans had sailed directly from Norfolk, Virginia. Moreover, thanks to successful Allied disinformation, Axis submarines in the Atlantic were positioned further south to prevent a reported attack on Dakar while the Americans were strongly convoyed. A lack of understanding of beach conditions, inadequate training and equipment, and a poor tempo of landing and exploitation were all a problem for the Americans, but thanks to careful cultivation of the French military leaders in North Africa, a general ceasefire was ordered on 10 November. Moreover, a misleading view of the Casablanca landing was soon after spread when the film *Casablanca* was released on 26 November, being hurried into release to take advantage of the publicity around the landings and then, in January 1943, the Casablanca Conference of Winston Churchill and Franklin D. Roosevelt.

This was not the only fighting on the coasts of the Atlantic during the war, but it was the most significant. None of the French Atlantic colonies put up resistance to the Allies comparable to that earlier against British attacks on Syria and Lebanon in 1941 and Madagascar in 1942; but there was still fighting. A badly planned and poorly commanded British–Free French expedition to capture Dakar in Senegal, which was seen, with reason, as a potential German submarine base, was a total failure in September 1940, and the Vichy authorities in Senegal did not change sides until after the Operation Torch landings. Free French forces had more success in capturing Libreville, the capital of Gabon, in the face of strong resistance in November 1940. The islands of Saint Pierre and Miquelon were peacefully occupied by the Free French in December 1941, while French Guiana and the French West Indies changed sides without fighting in 1943, although Martinique and Guadeloupe had earlier been blockaded, first by the British and then the Americans.

The French empire was not the only one at issue in the Atlantic. With neutral Denmark rapidly conquered by the Germans in April 1940, the Danish world came into the spotlight. Iceland, a sovereign kingdom in personal union with Denmark, declared neutrality, but the British occupied Iceland that May to pre-empt German moves. In turn, the Americans took over the occupation in July 1941 as part of a growing commitment to Atlantic security. Iceland remained neutral and, in June 1944, ended its union with the Danish Crown and declared itself a republic. The Allied occupation of Iceland meant that warships and aircraft could be based there, which was an aspect of the very different geography of the Atlantic to that during the previous world war. The Atlantic was accordingly remapped to show the potential range of anti-submarine escorts.

Greenland, a Danish colony, meanwhile rejected orders from Copenhagen, and sought American protection, in part in order to avoid British and/or Canadian occupation and possible Free Norwegian intervention, and it joined the Free Denmark movement in 1940. The Germans established meteorological stations on its largely uninhabited east coast, as well as in Labrador, and the Allies sought with considerable success to hunt them down, while also establishing their own stations.

The British, meanwhile, considered military action against Spain if German submarines were allowed to use the Canaries or if Franco, its fascist dictator, joined the Axis powers and attacked Gibraltar. They also envisaged occupying the Azores and the Cape Verde Islands to pre-empt German or Spanish moves to seize control from Portugal. Franco, who occupied the international zone of Tangier in June 1940, indeed envisaged a new Spanish empire, including Gibraltar, French Morocco and part of French West Africa, to add to Spain's existing territories; but, unwilling to abandon Vichy France, Hitler rejected this plan in late 1940. Franco did not push his sympathies to the point of war and sent men to fight the Soviets, but not the British to whose naval power Spain was exposed.

As, unlike in 1914, there were no German colonies in Atlantic Africa, the war on land around the Atlantic was less of an issue than that at sea. There it was made far more difficult for the Allies because the Germans conquered Norway and France in 1940 and therefore had bases for their navy that they had lacked in the First World War. As a result, German surface raiders were more of a factor than in the previous conflict.

As in that war, the first major clash occurred in the South Atlantic. The German pocket battleship *Admiral Graf Spee*, which had left Germany before the war in order to raid commerce, encountered three lighter British warships in the River Plate on 13 December 1939 and, with her fuel system crippled in the resulting action, was driven to take refuge in neutral Montevideo, Uruguay. Told that only seventy-two hours of refuge could be provided, the ship was scuttled on 17 December rather than facing a renewed battle. The arrival of reinforcements was exaggerated by British misinformation and the *Graf Spee* was short of ammunition.

In September 1940, as an important gesture to Britain, the United States provided fifty surplus destroyers (seven of them to the Canadian navy) in return for ninety-nine-year leases on bases in Antigua, the Bahamas, Bermuda (not actually part of the exchange but nevertheless provided), British Guiana, Jamaica,

Newfoundland, Saint Lucia and Trinidad. The following March, under the Lend-Lease Act, President Roosevelt was granted $7 billion for military materiel that he could sell, lend or trade to any state vital to American security, which opened the way for the shipping of supplies to Britain.

The *Bismarck*, the leading surface ship in the German navy, with eight 15-inch guns, was a more formidable threat than the *Graf Spee* as it was strong enough to defeat convoy escorts. On 24 May 1941, en route into the Atlantic from Norwegian waters in order to attack Allied merchant shipping in Operation *Rheinübung*, the *Bismarck*, in the battle of the Denmark Strait, sank the elderly battlecruiser *Hood* with over 1,400 of her crew, and damaged the battleship *Prince of Wales*, inflicting serious damage to her forward fuel tanks. The latter had hit the *Bismarck*, which abandoned its cruise and turned toward Saint-Nazaire in France and repairs. A massive British deployment, including two battleships, two carriers, two battlecruisers and thirteen cruisers, led to the sinking of the *Bismarck* on 27 May.

Roosevelt had followed the hunt with great interest as the Americans were concerned about the *Bismarck*'s capability. Indeed, they had already deployed land-based 16-inch guns capable of outfiring the *Bismarck* in the event of the latter trying to attack the naval base at Norfolk, Virginia. Moreover, the B-17, the Flying Fortress, the first effective all-metal, four-engine monoplane bomber, had been presented as extending America's coastal perimeter by being able to attack an incoming fleet well out into the Atlantic, in other words as a form of mobile coastal fortress.

From 1943, the German naval effort was focused not on surface warships but on the U-boats (submarines) in the battle of the Atlantic, which had been a serious challenge to Britain from late 1940. Despite heavy casualties, and the major strain of the continuous risk of attack, the strength and resilience of the Royal Navy were an important defence against the submarines, as was the size of the merchant marine and the emphasis on convoys.

America's entry into the war in December 1941 provided more targets for the submarines, but also far more resources for the Allies, both maritime and naval. As in the First World War, the introduction of effective convoying was important. The roughness of the weather in the vast Atlantic, the small size of the ships and submarines, and the problems of visibility, combined to make anti-submarine warfare difficult, but the British were helped by intelligence from intercepting German naval codes. Changing goals were also significant. Thus, U-boat warfare in the Atlantic in late 1941 was reduced as submarines were moved to Norwegian and Mediterranean waters in order to attack Allied convoys to the Soviet Union and to deny the Mediterranean to Allied shipping. Nevertheless, the peak of tonnage sunk by the Germans was reached in November 1942.

The Cruel Sea and *Das Boot*

The Cruel Sea is a 1951 novel by Nicholas Monsarrat, who had served in escort ships in the war of the Atlantic, becoming a lieutenant-commander. Alongside the Germans, the stormy sea and the cold weather are harsh enemies, the majority of the crew of the fictional corvette *Compass Rose* dying in the cold sea off Iceland when it is torpedoed in 1943. The German equivalent, *Das Boot* (The Boat, 1973), was by Lothar-Günther Buchheim, who, as a naval war correspondent, had joined *U-96* on a 1941 patrol in the battle of the Atlantic. His novel was a fictionalised autobiographical account with an anti-war tone.

The political geography of the Atlantic moved against the Germans, whose naval staff had fruitlessly hoped to acquire bases in the Azores and the Canaries in order to threaten British convoy routes, increase German influence in South America, and challenge American power. Instead, America's entry into the war was followed by that of much of Latin America, notably Brazil on 22 August 1942, although not Venezuela until February 1945 and Argentina until 27 March 1945. Argentina, indeed, in 1941 considered a plan to invade the Falkland Islands, but it was not viable, while there were also rumours of (non-viable) German interest in Patagonia. America, Britain and Brazil put pressure on Argentina where the army was Germanophile, as was the government that gained power through a coup in 1943 and that was increasingly dominated by Juan Domingo Perón. Venezuela provided crucial supplies of oil to America and Britain, while the Allies also allied with Cuba, the Dominican Republic and Haiti, helping them by purchasing their goods, notably Cuba's sugar.

American airbases were constructed in Cuba, the Dominican Republic, Brazil, Haiti and Panama in order to patrol against submarines, and the Brazilian air force and navy, both provided with American equipment, also operated against the U-boats, destroying at least six of them. More British resources were devoted to very long-range aircraft from November 1942 and, in October 1943, the deadly mid-Atlantic 'Air Gap' to the west of the Azores, where air cover against submarines was not provided, was closed: neutral Portugal, which had already built naval trawlers for the British navy in 1941–3, permitted the establishment of airbases on Terceira and Santa Maria.

Successful against the U-boats in key convoy battles in early 1943, by 1944 the Allies had clear mastery in Atlantic waters. In the early stages of the war, Hitler hoped to starve Britain of food and raw materials by hunting down her merchant shipping with his U-boat packs. Just how those hopes had been dashed was revealed early in 1944, when Britain's First Lord of the Admiralty, A. V. Alexander, stated in the House of Commons that there had been periods when more U-boats had been sunk than merchant ships. He added: 'The reduction is further exemplified by the falling proportion of ships lost in main North Atlantic and United

Kingdom coastal convoys. In 1941, one ship was lost out of every 181 which sailed; in 1942, one out of every 233; in 1943, one out of every 344. The losses in these convoys during the second half of last year were less than one in 1,000.' This remarkable record had been achieved by the unceasing watchfulness of RAF Coastal Command, which sank more U-boats in 1943 than in all the other years of the war put together; by the growing number of escort vessels safeguarding convoys; and by the pounding of U-boat bases and factories by the Allied air forces.

In turn, only three Allied merchantmen convoyed across the Atlantic in January–March 1944 were sunk, a situation won at sea that was enhanced when, in response to the Allied breakout from Normandy, the Germans evacuated their submarines from western French bases and moved them to Norway. The fitting of snorkel devices meant that U-boats could charge their batteries while submerged, plus start and run their diesel engines underwater, but the snorkel did not permit running the diesels at sufficient depth to avoid detection from the air.

A Flawed Governor

Edward, Duke of Windsor, formerly King Edward VIII (r. 1936), an unpredictable individual with fascist sympathies, was parked as governor of the Bahamas in 1940–5 in order to keep him under surveillance and away from undesirable elements. The Duke disliked the job and displayed his characteristic racism, but helped to tackle poverty and labour unrest. The Bahamas themselves served as a major anti-submarine base.

The submarine war was waged at a smaller scale in the distant South Atlantic. The closure of the Mediterranean to most Allied shipping in 1941–3 helped lead to an emphasis on convoys round the Cape of Good Hope. Four hundred convoys used South

African ports during the war, and the South African economy grew greatly to meet war demand. Although ships there were sunk by submarines, they were relatively few, in part because individual U-boats, and not U-boat groups, operated in these distant waters.

This was another instance of the extent to which, despite German hopes to the contrary, the U-boats had only an operational capability for the strategic threat they posed, whereas the Allies were able to make a strategic response. Mass was a key element, the Americans building over 300 escort destroyers, while, by the end of the war, Canada had the world's third largest navy. Increasing in 1944, construction, in turn, maintained the overall numbers of U-boats, obliging the Allies to continue to devote considerable naval resources to escort duty and anti-submarine warfare, but, given Allied, especially American ship-building capacity, including in Atlantic shipyards such as Newport News, Charleston and Savannah, this did not prevent other uses of Allied naval power, while merchant marine losses were more than covered. The Americans rapidly used effective factory methods to roll out vast numbers of ships, breaking all records for speed of building. Bombing, moreover, delayed the construction of a new, faster class of German submarine. The crucial battle of the Atlantic was waged in the North Atlantic and was, albeit at a heavy cost in sailors and ships, a complete Allied victory.

The Atlantic was also crucial to the movement of aircraft from North America to Britain in order to support operations against Germany. A number of routes were used, including via Newfoundland, Labrador, Greenland, Bermuda and the Azores. The South Atlantic route took American aircraft to Africa in order to help British forces operating there, with the key bases at Belém and Natal in Brazil, Ascension Island, Monrovia in Liberia and Takoradi on the Gold Coast (Ghana). The system put in place was completely different to that in the First World War, and part of a new activation of the Atlantic as a strategic space.

Fishing in the Second World War

Ocean fishing continued, notably off Iceland, but with many restrictions, although these varied by combatant. The requisitioning of numerous fishing vessels (including about 1,016 English and Welsh ones) and particularly the larger and more modern ones, for example to act as minesweepers and auxiliary patrol boats, ensured that there was far less ocean fishing, as did the sinking of many boats, the conscription of many fishermen and the limitation of fishing movement. As a result, fish stocks rose. About 260 British trawlers were lost in action during the war to mines, submarines and aircraft, and particularly in 1940–1. German trawlers used as weather ships were systematically pursued by the British. American fishing vessels were made much more cautious by the U-boat campaign in American waters from 1941.

Filming the Battle of the Atlantic

Although Britain's leading naval film of the war, *In Which We Serve* (1942), was set off Norway, Dunkirk and Crete, the battle of the Atlantic has been covered in a number of films including *Atlantic Convoy* (1942), about American naval vessels off Iceland, *Corvette K-225* (1943), an American film about a Canadian warship with German savagery to the fore, *San Demetrio London* (1943), a British docudrama about the salvage of a tanker set on fire by German shells, *The Cruel Sea* (1953), *The Enemy Below* (1957), *Das Boot* (1981), a West German adaptation of the 1973 novel, in which boredom, gales and British action are all challenges, *Enigma* (2001) and *Greyhound* (2020). In *The Enemy Below*, an American escort destroyer and a U-boat sink each other, and there is a mutual respect absent in the original, a 1956 novel by Denys Rayner, a British naval officer involved in the battle of the Atlantic who wrote about a British warship. In *Greyhound*, a convoy in the mid-Atlantic Gap in early 1942 is attacked by a wolfpack, Tom Hanks proving a resilient commander who rises to the challenge of his wartime command. The conflict is shown as a battle of brain power as well as of will and courage.

10

The Atlantic in the Cold War, 1945–90

COLD WAR CONFRONTATIONS

Dropping warning depth charges to force three Soviet submarines to the surface was one of the most dramatic episodes of the 1962 Cuban Missile Crisis. The naval dimension of the Cold War very much focused on the Atlantic and, as in the Second World War, particularly the North Atlantic, and became more serious from the 1960s as the Soviet Union built up its navy, indeed, in 1971, supplanting Britain as the world's number-two naval power. Over three-quarters of Soviet naval expenditure was on the submarine force, with the Northern Fleet based at Murmansk and nearby Severomorsk able to use waters that the Gulf Stream kept from freezing, and clearly aiming to operate in the North Atlantic against oceanic maritime links. In response, the British and Americans established underwater listening posts and developed anti-submarine capabilities. With the development of the American base at Thule, Greenland became of far greater strategic significance. Under a 1951 agreement with Denmark, a major airbase was completed in 1953 and became a centre for aerial reconnaissance and deterrence of the Soviet Union.

The South Atlantic, in contrast, saw far less naval activity and geopolitical competition, which is a reminder of the extent to which the scale of the ocean helped ensure a range of strategic environments. At the same time, the closures of the Suez Canal in 1956 and 1967–75, combined with the larger scale of oil tankers, put a far greater emphasis on trade round the Cape of Good Hope, and therefore the strategic importance of both the South Atlantic and South Africa. Britain had lost control of the Simon's Town naval base, on the eastern side of the Cape Peninsula, which was the major naval base in South Africa, having been extended in 1900–10. The naval base was handed over to South Africa in 1955, under an arrangement by which Britain was promised use of the base and South Africa agreed to buy British warships. An understanding on the defence of sea routes around South Africa, including in the South Atlantic, was part of this agreement. Essentially because of opposition to apartheid, the British government terminated the agreement, however, in 1975, and the Royal Navy was not able to use South African ports during the Falklands War in 1982. Already in 1967, the post of Commander-in-Chief South Atlantic had been ended by the Royal Navy, with responsibilities absorbed into the Western Fleet.

Meanwhile, the Soviets were able to establish a presence in Angola once the Portuguese had left in 1975. Surveillance aircraft flew out of Luanda, and warships called there and at Lobito and Moçâmedes. The Angolan navy was developed with Soviet warships in the 1980s, especially six Osa II fast missile craft intended to launch anti-ship missiles. However, the Soviet navy did not put an emphasis on the region comparable to that on the North Atlantic.

In the central Atlantic, in 1969, the Soviet Union had provided four motor torpedo boats to the guerrilla movement in Portuguese Guinea, but these, plus three missile boats of the Guinea navy, were sunk by a Portuguese naval raid on the Guinea capital, Conakry, in 1970, a raid carried out by four patrol boats and two landing ships. Subsequently, the Soviet Union delivered four motor torpedo boats to Guinea in 1971–2, and three patrol boats to the guerrillas in Portuguese-Guinea, but the crew of these last three mutinied in 1973, only then to be seized by a Soviet destroyer and the Guinea navy. However, Guinea moved away from the Soviet bloc and did not become a significant base. In contrast, in Cuba, where Fidel Castro had seized power in 1959 and subsequently became a close ally of the Soviets, they began major visits by surface naval units in 1969 and from 1962 had based spy vessels near Havana.

Six Typhoon-class ballistic missile submarines entered Soviet service from 1980, as did their most impressive surface warships. The Typhoon-class competed against the American *Ohio*-class, as the submarine evolved into an ocean-going underwater capital ship as large as First World War *Dreadnought*-class battleships, and with a destructive capacity never seen before (or since) in any other type of warship. The USS *Ohio* and its sister submarines were 170.7 metres (560 feet) long with an 18,700-tonne submerged displacement. The Soviet Typhoon-class was 171.5 metres (563 feet) long with a 25,000-tonne submerged displacement. In each case, the submerged displacement was somewhat greater than the surface displacement. By comparison, the British battleship *Dreadnought* of 1906 was 161 metres (528 feet) long and displaced 18,420 tonnes. Super-dreadnoughts from 1911 on were 18 to 24 metres (60 to 100 feet) and 8,000 to 10,000 tonnes larger. These submarines were in a completely different league to the German U-boats of the Second World War. There were also important developments in ballistic missile technology.

Although the Soviets deployed ballistic missile submarines near the American coast in 1985, the Typhoons, since they carried newer, long-range missiles, could remain under the sanctuary of the Arctic ice cap, surface just at the edge of it, fire their missiles and then retreat under the ice cap, or could stay in their home base and move out. The Typhoons looked monstrous because they were triple-hulled, possibly because the Soviets did not trust the quality of their welding of the second hull. The titanium used for the pressure hull required more sophisticated welding than regular welding: the welding temperature is much higher and must be done in a vacuum. The Soviets were aware of, or at least feared, the shortcomings in their ability to construct minutely calibrated, pure micro-environments for difficult product fabrication, whether it be computer chips or titanium parts.

More generally, as was increasingly ascertained from the 1990s, Soviet-era surface warships and submarines were poor, certainly compared to American and British models, and especially in terms of workmanship and maintenance. Nevertheless, although their safety record was poor, the Typhoons were formidable. In response, the Americans, to protect the Atlantic axis, focused on a forward strategy of deployment of warships in the north-east Atlantic and forcing battle on the Soviets.

THE FALKLANDS WAR, 1982

Short of resources, ambition and confidence, Britain very much drew in its military roles in the late 1960s and 1970s in order to focus on the British Isles, Western Europe and the North Atlantic. Much of the British navy was allocated to a permanent Allied Atlantic naval contingency force that was activated as Standing Naval Force Atlantic in 1968. That Britain was to fight a last imperial war in 1982 with a major naval component was totally unexpected. The Falklands had been under British control from 1833, but were claimed, as the Malvinas, by the Argentinians. Their dictatorial ruling military junta was convinced that, because the British government was uncertain of the desirability of holding on to the colony, it would accept its seizure by the Argentinians. The decision, in 1981, to withdraw the Antarctic patrol ship *Endurance* was seen as a sign of British lack of interest in the South Atlantic, and, on 2 April 1982, the virtually undefended islands were successfully invaded in a surprise attack.

Assured that the Royal Navy could fulfil the task, and determined to act firmly in what was seen as a make-or-break moment for the government, the British prime minister, Margaret Thatcher, decided to respond with Operation Corporate: an expeditionary force, dispatched from 4 April, that included most of the Royal Navy. Fifty-one warships were to take part in the operation. As another sign of British maritime strength, a further fifty-four ships were 'taken up from trade', chartered or requisitioned, including the cruise ships *Queen Elizabeth II* and *Canberra*, which were used to transport troops, fourteen tankers and the container ship *Atlantic Conveyor*, which was sunk by an Exocet missile, taking a large amount of stores to the bottom, including helicopters which would have aided the mobility of the landing force. Sixteen of the ships were fitted with helicopter flight decks and all had rapidly to be installed with military communications equipment and gear for replenishment at sea. The naval supply line moved over 400,000 tonnes of fuel, 100,000 tonnes of equipment and supplies, and 9,000 troops within range of the Falklands, 12,000 kilometres (7,500 miles) from Britain, in six weeks. Meanwhile, alongside highly helpful American military assistance, including regular satellite intelligence, American mediation attempts that would have left the Argentinians in control of the islands were rejected.

Thanks to the shift from large fleet carriers, not least the cancellation of the CVA-01 aircraft carrier project in 1966, the expeditionary force, which was operating beyond the range of its land-based air cover in the NATO area, lacked a large aircraft carrier, and therefore airborne early warning of attacks. This was a serious problem. However, Britain had two smaller carriers, *Hermes* and *Invincible*, intended for anti-submarine warfare. Each carried V/STOL (Vertical/Short Take Off and Landing) Sea Harriers designed as fighters. Furthermore, the Argentinian aircraft carrier, *Veinticinco de Mayo*, built for the Royal Navy in the Second World War as *Venerable*, and sold to the Dutch in 1948 before being taken out of service by them in 1968 and sold to Argentina, had not been refitted to operate the impressive Super Étendard bombers Argentina had bought from France. As a result, it was unable to play a role in the war.

On 25–6 April 1982, the British recaptured the subsidiary territory of South Georgia and, on 2 May, large-scale hostilities began when *Conqueror*, a nuclear-powered submarine, sank the Argentine cruiser *General Belgrano* with 321 fatalities. This step was crucial to the struggle for command of the sea, as it led the Argentinian navy to desist from threatening attack and to return to port. At the time of writing, the *Belgrano* was the largest ship so far sunk by naval action since the Second World War, and the first ship to be sunk by a nuclear-powered submarine.

Air-launched Exocet missiles and bombs led to the loss of a number of British ships, showing that modern anti-aircraft missile systems were not necessarily a match for manned aircraft and revealing a lack of adequate preparedness on the part of the British navy. The Royal Navy lacked, as did most units of the American navy, an effective close-weapon system against aircraft and missiles. An Exocet was responsible for the loss of the destroyer *Sheffield* and bombs for that of the destroyer *Coventry*, both of which affected British public opinion. However, many of the bombs did not prove reliable – hitting ships but not exploding – while, despite initial reports that the *Hermes* not the *Sheffield* had been hit, the Argentinians did not sink the two carriers, which provided vital air support (but not superiority) for both sea and land operations. Designed for anti-submarine warfare in the North Atlantic, the carriers' Harriers and their Sea King helicopters demonstrated their versatility, while the ships served as amphibious assault command ships. Ultimately, the fleet and its air power won the struggle to isolate the Falklands, a struggle helped by the cautious Argentinean response to British naval persistence and fighting determination.

The Argentinians on the Falklands outnumbered the British force, and also had both aircraft and helicopters, while the British were short of ammunition because they had underestimated requirements. Nevertheless, landing on 21 May, British troops advanced on the capital, Port Stanley, fighting some bitter engagements on the nearby hills, and forcing the isolated, demoralised and beaten Argentinians to surrender on 14 June. American logistical and intelligence support aided the British but, in the end, it was a matter of an effective strategy of indirect approach, bravely executed attacks, the careful integration of infantry with artillery support, the ability to continue without air control, and the resolve of the British officers, soldiers, marines and sailors.

TRADE AND SHIPPING

Meanwhile, there was a growing split in the Atlantic, between goods, which continued to go by sea, and people, who increasingly travelled by air. Technology was important in both respects. The use of containers made freight movement by sea more cost-effective (as well as reducing pilfering), while also requiring major investments in port facilities. The repurposing of shipping was linked to major changes in trade routes and shipping stock. Atlantic shipbuilding declined, notably in Britain, as that of East Asia rose, and the Atlantic's share of world shipping tonnage also fell.

Britain led the world in shipbuilding until 1955 when it was supplanted by Japan. In the late 1940s and early to mid-1950s, while American war-surplus ships helped many countries renew their merchant fleets, British shipyards benefited from rising world demand but, by the 1960s, they were losing orders to the lower charges of foreign yards. In addition, the latter were able to promise earlier and more reliable delivery dates, a result of the lack in Britain of modern yards able to offer flow-line production and, therefore, higher productivity. This absence reflected problematic labour relations and a lack of investment, born of short-term attitudes and limited planning for the longer term.

As the market became more competitive from the 1960s, the decline of British competitiveness in this sphere hit hard. Business was lost and shipyards were closed, so that, whereas the UK had delivered 12.4 per cent of the ships that entered service in the world in 1962, by 1971 the percentage was down to 5.1; although, in terms of tonnage, this represented a larger figure. The Suez crisis of 1956 exposed a particular problem in British shipbuilding capacity, as it led to a shift towards supertankers, designed to take oil from the Middle East round Africa rather than to go through the Suez Canal, a shift encouraged by the conflicts between Egypt and Israel in 1967–73, but a challenge that British yards, with their limited facilities on narrow rivers such as the Clyde and the Tyne, could not meet. Merchant ship-building was in terminal crisis by the 1970s. As with the car industry, the Labour government of 1964–70 went for larger groupings, rather than the reform of working practices. In 1977, Labour nationalised the industry. Trading losses and a lack of support from the succeeding Conservative government and the European Union compounded the problem and, by 1992, the percentage of world output was 1.2, while most British shipyards had closed. This was due not only to the growth in the shipping of other countries, but also to serious problems in the British indus-try, especially labour disputes, anachronistic working practices, poor management and under investment; labour problems hit profits ensuring limited investment, which, in turn, affected British shipbuilding. In 1997, the percentage fell to 0.7.

Britain's merchant marine also declined, with, again, a major implication for the nation's once close relationship with the sea. In 1900, the UK owned about half of the merchant shipping afloat and, in 1914, 39.3 per cent. Thereafter, there was a serious decline, to 29.9 per cent in 1930, 26.1 per cent in 1939 and, after the wartime destruction of other merchant navies, a rise to 32.4 per cent in 1948. By 1960, the share was down to 16.3 per cent. Although Britain's merchant fleet was not to reach its post-war peak until 1975, in 1967 she lost her position as the world's lead-ing shipper to Liberia, which operated as a flag of convenience for the United States, helping to provide American-owned shipping with lower taxation and cheaper crews.

By 1983, Britain had only the eighth largest merchant fleet in the world, and increasingly traded with Europe. Atlantic shipping routes were affected. By the late 1980s, Latin America, once a major field of trade and investment, supplied only 1.5 per cent of

British imports, took only 1.4 per cent of its exports, and invest-ments in the region totalled only 6 per cent of British foreign investment. In Britain, the shadowing of the Atlantic was in part an aspect of the decline of the country, one seen most clearly in Liverpool's once-mighty docks. However, a different picture was seen in some other Atlantic centres.

Atlantic Ferries

In 1971, a Southampton to Lisbon–Casablanca–Tangier cruise ferry service opened, the *Eagle*, providing a cross between a cruise and a car ferry. After five seasons, in some of which storms in the Bay of Biscay had been a hazard, recession put paid to the service and the ship became a Marseille-based cruise liner. In 2019, in contrast, there were four sailings weekly of ferries from France to Morocco, with Sete to Nador and Sete to Tangier the two routes. There was no comparable service, however, further along the coast, notably to Dakar.

FISHING

Waters distant from major areas of settlement became more heav-ily fished from the 1980s as more countries entered long-distance deep-sea fishing and as the technology improved with, for example, sonar devices to detect shoals. Thanks to improved detec-tion and exploitation techniques, the needle in the haystack approach was now defunct. Fish instead were hunted systemati-cally, although that was apparently made more acceptable by refer-ring to the harvesting of the seas. In practice, the ability of fish stocks to reproduce was challenged, which greatly threatened the biodiversity of the Atlantic, not least because fishing fleets refused to use nets that permitted smaller (young) fish to swim on in order to restock the fishery. Fishing, moreover, was a cause of disputes, notably the Cod Wars of 1958–61, 1972–3 and 1975–6 between Britain and Iceland over fishing rights in territorial waters claimed by Iceland. These were won by Iceland, badly hitting the already declining British fishing industry, and leading Britain to follow Iceland in abandoning an 'open seas' fisheries policy.

These were not the only clashes. Thus, in 1980, the detention of a Spanish fishing boat by a Moroccan patrol boat close to the coast of the Western Sahara led to the intervention of a Spanish destroyer, which was then strafed by a Moroccan aircraft. In 2021, there was Anglo-French confrontation off Jersey.

Decolonisation

The rapid collapse of European empires was significant in the Atlantic with Britain, France, the Netherlands, Portugal and Spain all granting independence to parts of the Atlantic coastline. Compared to the situation in South Asia and the Middle East, this was a slow process, not beginning until Morocco (from France), Ghana (Britain) and Guinea (France) gained independence in 1956, 1957 and 1958 respectively. There was a rush in 1960, with Mauritania, Senegal, Ivory Coast, Togo, Dahomey, Cameroon, Gabon and Equatorial Congo (Congo-Brazzaville) all gaining independence from France, Nigeria from Britain, and Congo (Zaire) from Belgium. Sierra Leone from Britain followed in 1961, and Spanish Guinea, as Equatorial Guinea, from Spain in 1968, while Guyana gained independence from Britain in 1966, Surinam from the Netherlands following in 1975. There was a rush of independence in the Caribbean, with Jamaica and Trinidad and Tobago beginning in 1962, Barbados following in 1966, and the Bahamas, Grenada, Dominica, Saint Lucia, Saint Vincent, Belize, Antigua and Barbuda, and Saint Kitts and Nevis by 1974.

The empires that were left were those of Portugal, Spain, South Africa and Denmark, but the first two collapsed in the

1970s, bringing independence in 1975 for Portuguese Guinea (Guinea-Bissau), Angola and Cape Verde (as well as Mozambique in South-eastern Africa). Also, in 1975–6, much of the Spanish Sahara was occupied by Morocco, beginning a war with the local independence movement, Polisario Front, that lasted until 1991 when a ceasefire took effect that left most of the territory, now the Western Sahara, including the coast, under Moroccan control. Many Sahrawis were displaced into refugee camps. South Africa accepted independence for South-west Africa (Namibia) in 1990, bringing a long independence struggle to a close.

The Green March

Allegedly 350,000 Moroccans crossed into the Spanish Sahara in November 1975 in order to substantiate the Moroccan claim to the territory. Green is a symbol of Islam. There was no Spanish resistance and the march increased successful Moroccan pressure on Spain over the fate of the territory.

Flying the Atlantic

Introduced in 1958, jet aircraft, in the shape of the Boeing 707 and the DC-8, took seven hours to cross the Atlantic, but this was to be cut further when the supersonic Concorde entered service, first with routes from Paris to Rio, Caracas and Washington, and London to Washington in 1976, and then with services from both to New York from 1977 after noise complaints had been overruled. There were extensions to serve Mexico City in 1978–82 and Dallas–Fort Worth in 1978–80.

Jet aircraft also led to a major expansion in tourism around the shores of the Atlantic, notably to the West

---

Indies, the Canaries, Madeira, Yucatán and the Algarve. A new airport at Tenerife, Tenerife South Airport, was inaugurated in 1978. Within the first year, it had handled a million passengers. In 2019, it handled 11.2 million passengers.

Civil wars followed the end of colonial rule, notably in Angola (1975–2002) and Nigeria, the latter, the Biafran War of 1967–70, causing the starvation and killing of perhaps up to two million Igbo people in their unsuccessful attempt to win independence. That was a conflict in which control of the ocean played a role as the federal forces, who also enjoyed air superiority, were able to seize the Biafran coast, thus enforcing a blockade. In contrast, in the conflicts in Angola, Namibia and the Spanish Sahara this control was of far less consequence.

Great power competition played a role both in civil wars and in politics. Thus, the federal forces in the Biafran War were backed by the British and Soviets, and their opponents by the French who, in a continuation of earlier imperial rivalry, sought to undermine the position of Britain in its former colonies. In Brazil, the army seized power in 1964 with American encouragement, but not the troops sent into the Dominican Republic the following year in order to stop the greatly overstated threat of a Communist takeover, nor into Grenada in 1983 and Panama in 1989. The most significant commitment was that of Cuban forces, up to 50,000 troops, in Angola, from 1975 to 1991. This helped block the South African-backed UNITA movement, but also protracted the destructive civil war as well as proving a major burden for Cuba, which very much saw the commitment in terms of a revolutionary globalism. This transatlantic character to the conflict ensured that the Cold War in the Atlantic had an important South Atlantic dimension. More positively, many Cuban doctors and teachers were sent to Africa. The end of the Cold War saw the pro-Soviet regimes survive in Angola and, albeit with greater economic difficulties, Cuba, but not in Nicaragua.

Biafran War: The Naval Dimension

An emphasis on the slave trade can lead to an underplaying of other episodes in Atlantic African history and notably the Biafran War of 1967–70, a civil war in Nigeria arising from Igbo separatism. Up to 2 million Biafran civilians died of famine in part due to a naval blockade imposed in order to cut off Biafra in particular from arms supplies. Both France and Portugal backed Biafra, while Nigeria was supported by Britain and the Soviet Union. Control of the sea was important to the federal forces, enabling them to seize the significant oil facilities in the extensive Niger delta as well as the major cities of Calabar and Port Harcourt, which were captured in October 1967 and May 1968 in what were major blows to the separatists. Calabar was captured in an amphibious operation launched from the port of Bonny, which had been captured earlier in October. As in earlier fighting in Atlantic Africa, inshore waters were very important to amphibious operations.

KNOWLEDGE

Knowledge of the ocean bed was transformed during the Cold War, with need and opportunity working in harmony. The increased scope of knowledge came in a number of ways: from aircraft, satellites, submersibles, surface ships using sonar, and from boring into the ocean floor. Water temperatures measured in the same way provided warning of forthcoming storms, as did radar. The floor's effect on the water surface, and its contours, could be picked up on radar images taken from aircraft and satellites, while ship- and airborne towed magnetometers and deep-ocean borehole core sequences provided widespread data about magnetic anomalies. Submersibles able to resist extreme pressure took explorers to the depths of the ocean.

From the 1970s, metals on the ocean floors were mapped, while unmanned submersibles with remote-controlled equipment furthered underwater exploration. Thermal hotspots on ocean floors were charted and an understanding of their causes and impact developed. The role of the thermal layer on the effectiveness of sonic systems encouraged charting, and imagery from the Seasat satellite helped provide a full map of the ocean floor.

The Cold War helped drive this process, with secret underwater mapping and hydrography important to the establishment of patrol areas for submarines and to communications with them, as well as for the location and maintenance of far-flung systems of underwater listening devices. The United States was particularly active while the Soviet Union established a Marine Cartographic Institute in 1946 and it focused on foreign waters in the NATO area. By 1955, the northern hemisphere had been covered by Soviet navigational charts.

The Forgotten Atlantic: Brazilian Islands

Brazil has numerous islands in the Atlantic, many far out into it, such as the Saint Peter and Saint Paul Archipelago, which is 940 kilometres (590 miles) from mainland South America, and the only Brazilian islands in the northern hemisphere. Most of Brazil's Atlantic islands are uninhabited bar scientific stations, with one in this archipelago since 1998.

In contrast, the island of Fernando de Noronha in the archipelago of that name, 354 kilometres (220 miles) offshore, has about 3,000 inhabitants, with tourism and

---

charter fishing important. Discovered by the Portuguese, probably in 1503, the island was a prison from the late eighteenth century until 1957. The Americans built an airport there in 1942 as part of their warfare against German submarines.

Further south, Trindade and Martin Vaz is an archipelago about 1,100 kilometres (680 miles) offshore with a population of thirty-two naval personnel. Volcanic in origin, it was discovered by the Portuguese in 1502, but claimed or occupied by Britain in 1700, 1781–2 and 1895–6, and was where James Harden-Hickey appointed himself prince in 1893. In 1914, the Germans tried to establish a secret coaling base there, but, on 14 September 1914 in the battle of Trindade, the HMS *Carmania*, a converted liner, defeated and sank the *Cap Trafalgar*, a former German liner.

The Ifni War

Frequently called the Forgotten War (and thus one of many in Atlantic history), this conflict arose over Moroccan pressure on Spanish North-west Africa in 1957–8. The Moroccan Army of Liberation, an anti-French militia, sought to gain Spanish territories in pursuit of Sultan Mohammed V's claims to them as historically and geographically part of Morocco. An insurrection in Ifni in 1957 led to Moroccan attacks on Spanish forces that were initially successful, but were subsequently held off, with the city of Ifni protected by trenches. The Moroccans then focused on the Spanish Sahara region, only in February 1958 for a joint Franco-Spanish force of 14,000 troops and 150 aircraft to drive them out. The Treaty of Angra de Cintra that April saw Morocco gain the region of Tarfaya (Cape Juby), but accept Spain's control of the rest of the Spanish Sahara and Ifni, which it only left in 1969 and 1976 respectively.

11

The Atlantic Today, 1991–

It was certainly crowded. Only 22 metres (72 feet) long, the Guyanese-built semi-submersible with its crew of three set off in autumn 2019 from Colombia to the Cape Verde Islands and then northwards, eventually along the Portuguese coast toward the *rias* (river valleys drowned when the sea level rose with the melting of the ice after the last Ice Age) of Spain's Galician coast. Hit by engine difficulties, bad weather and a shortage of fuel, the crew scuppered the submarine near Vigo; its cargo of as much as 3 tonnes of Colombia cargo was seized along with the first narco-submarine to have crossed the Atlantic and been caught in Europe.

Gander and Shannon

Once famous as a refuelling stop for transatlantic aircraft, airport construction began at Gander in Newfoundland in 1936. The site was chosen because it was close to the Great Circle air route between London and New York. Similarly, Shannon in Ireland became a stop on the transatlantic route in 1946. However, the greater range of aircraft affected transatlantic usage, so that a stop at Gander was no longer necessary for refuelling. The use of Shannon was also hit by the EU–US Open Skies Agreement coming into effect in 2008, putting an end to the requirement of a Shannon stopover. Gander played a major role in 2001 in housing a large

---

number of Americans and others whose flights were grounded in the aftermath of the terrorist attacks on New York and Washington. This hospitality is the basis of the musical *Come from Away*, which won the 2019 Olivier Award for Best New Musical.

Talk of 'the Pacific Century' can lead to a sense of the Atlantic as a secondary area of interest and concern. Indeed, the Atlantic can be seen as a leading news story of the last half-millennium that is being rendered redundant by the relative decline of the West, first of Europe and then of the United States, in the face of the rise of China and more generally of the Indo-Pacific region. That analysis has a measure of truth, but most notably so in relative terms and with reference to the greater economic and strategic significance of the Indo-Pacific. The Pentagon's 2020 annual report to Congress on China's military modernisation programme included on the Atlantic only Angola among the twelve states where China wanted bases to support potential offensive operations against the United States. In practice, China has also shown interest elsewhere, as in Equatorial Guinea and Mauritania, building the deep-water port that opened in the latter at Nouakchott in 1986 and American anxiety about a Chinese Atlantic naval base increased in 2021. Antigua and Barbuda, Dominica, Grenada, and Trinidad and Tobago signed up to China's Belt and Road infrastructure initiative in 2018, and Barbados and Jamaica in 2019.

Chinese low-interest development loans played a significant role, notably for ports in Antigua, the Bahamas, and Trinidad and Tobago. The Dominican Republic dropped its official recognition of Taiwan in 2018 after promises of Chinese investment. Guyana signed up to China's Belt and Road initiative in 2019, and China has agreed to loan money for a $46.7 million road improvement project that is designed to reach untapped markets in landlocked Brazil, and linking them to a rehabilitated port in Trinidad and Tobago.

The relative rise of the Pacific, however, does not mean that the history of the Atlantic is any less fascinating nor that developments there are without consequence. Indeed, the continued significance of Atlantic countries, politically, economically and culturally, was still very apparent in this period. It also remains an area of military confrontation, and notably so with the revival of Russian probing of NATO defences, as with the large Russian submarine drill in late 2019. In the Norwegian Sea extension of the Atlantic, Olavsvern, a major nuclear submarine base carved into the mountain near Tromsø, was reopened by Norway in 2020 in response to American requests. The base, which includes 3,000 square metres (32,000 square feet) of deep-water docks and is only 350 kilometres (220 miles) from the Russian border, had been closed since 2002.

An Atlantic Anomaly

Founded in 1884 as a small British colony, while the rest of modern Namibia became a German one, the administration of Walvis Bay was transferred in 1922 to South-west Africa which, as a result of German defeat in the First World War, had become a South African mandate. In 1977, South Africa transferred control of Walvis Bay back to Cape Province, a measure rejected by the United Nations. In 1990, when South-west Africa gained independence as Namibia, Walvis Bay remained under South African sovereignty, with South African troops present, and sovereignty was not transferred to Namibia until 1994.

There were, moreover, significant changes within the Atlantic world itself. In demographic terms, the relative decline of Europe was more than matched by the rise of Africa, a youthful continent with a lower share of people over sixty-five than any other. Nigeria in particular is due to have a major increase in population, and Lagos is the Atlantic city where development pressures are most acute. This rise in Atlantic Africa's population poses major issues for resource availability, public health provision and political stability. The large number of young men who have few employment opportunities can be linked to civil conflict since the 1990s, notably in Sierra Leone, Liberia, Ivory Coast and Nigeria. However, such conflict has a number of causes including regional separatism, as in Cameroon, while ethnic tensions are still a problem in states that avoid civil wars, such as Guyana, in that case between Afro-Guyanese and Indo-Guyanese, and Guinea in the case of the Malinké and Fulani, the latter contributing to violence at the time of a disputed election in 2020.

Coups, attempted coups and authoritarian government have all been a major part of the politics, even in states not noted for civil wars. Thus, in Mauritania, the president established a one-party state in 1964 only to be replaced by a military coup in 1978, which gave rise to others in 1979, 1984, 2005 and 2008, as well as to attempted coups, as in 2003. Coups occurred in Togo (1963, 1967), Congo/Zaire (1965), Ghana (1966, 1972, 1978, 1979), Sierra Leone (1967, 1997), Nigeria (1966, 1985, 1993), Equatorial Guinea (1979), Liberia (1980, 1990) and Ivory Coast (1999). In West Africa, only Senegal, independent from 1960, has not had a coup, but the election there in 2012 and referendum in 2016 were accompanied by violence, although democratic outcomes were obtained. In contrast, in Guinea-Bissau, coups in 1980 and 1998 were followed by five more in 2003–12. Elections there were repeatedly thwarted while the army profited greatly from its control of the drug trade. There have been no successful coups, however, in Morocco, Angola, Namibia and South Africa, although the coup attempt in Angola in 1977 led to large-scale slaughter by the Cuban-backed government forces of those considered suspect.

In the Atlantic New World, coups included those in Venezuela in 1948 and 1958, Argentina in 1955, 1962, 1966, 1970, 1976 and 1981, the Dominican Republic in 1963, Grenada in 1979 and 1983, and Haiti in 1991 and 2004. Some coups, such as that in Portugal in 1974, were followed by the establishment of democratic systems, but others were long-lasting, that in Brazil until 1985. Unsuccessful coups, in Argentina in 1956, Gabon in 1964, Angola in 1977, Spain in 1981, Gambia in 1981, Nigeria in 1990, Equatorial Guinea in 1997 and 2004, Guinea-Bissau in 2000 and Congo in 2004, were also an important part of Atlantic history, and helped to ensure that governments had to see coup avoidance as one of the most important tasks of their military policy. Moreover, demonstrations have been suppressed with violence, as in Haiti in 2019, Nigeria in 2020 and Venezuela, notably from 2014.

Coups and rebellions were made more serious by foreign intervention, as in Congo in 1997–2003, with Angola and Namibia among those who sent troops. In West Africa, in 2002–3, the Liberian government under Charles Taylor, whose seizure of power had originally owed much to backing from Ivory Coast, supported rebels in the three neighbouring states, Sierra Leone, Guinea and Ivory Coast, before being forced to step down in 2003. Guinea itself was linked to rebels against Taylor – Liberians United for Reconciliation and Democracy – a misnamed group of thugs, as was the army of Ivory Coast, where France had intervened in 2002 to support the government against rebels. Civil wars, which in Ivory Coast broke out in 2002 and 2010, benefited from the large-scale availability of small arms, and were financed primarily by criminal operations and extortion. The politics could be one in which individuals readily moved between being warlords, rebels, generals in government forces and presidents.

Despite its size, Mauritania is not an Atlantic state that attracts much international attention. Yet, it indicates the tension of large parts of Atlantic Africa, not least with the mistreatment of black Mauritanians, especially in 1990–1. At the same time, other parts of Atlantic Africa have seen dynamic growth without civil strife, and their cities, for example Accra and Dakar, cope with their population rise without breakdown. In 2011, as part of the 'Arab Spring', Muhammad VI of Morocco relinquished some of his powers in a successful attempt to lessen tension, followed by providing more food and fuel subsidies in 2012. However, democratisation led to rivalry between Islamists and secularists.

Environmental pressures in the Atlantic are in part linked to the massive rise in the coastal population, notably in cities. Waste dumping is a consequence. The population of Buenos Aires has risen from 2 million in 1930 to 15.2 million in 2020, and that of Rio from 1.5 million in 1930 to 13.5 million in 2020, the latter encouraging the development of slums (*favelas*), while the disruption of war in Angola in the 1980s encouraged a major growth in the population of Luanda. The rise in the population of Mauritania, from 0.7 million in 1950 to 4.3 million in 2018, has put particular pressure on the coastal capital, Nouakchott, as desertification from the early 1970s has led to a movement there from the interior, and slums have proliferated in this former fishing settlement. By 2012, Lagos was adding half a million people a year and was trying to reclaim land from the Lagoon, as well as to cope with terrible congestion, corruption, a poor power supply and the lawlessness also seen in other major Atlantic cities, including Miami, Rio and Cape Town. In Brazil, the drug gangs in the extensive *favelas*, notably in Rio, are a threat to the paramilitary police, which launched a 'pacification' policy in 2008, and there was repeated violence in the 2010s, although that also owed much to popular resistance to slum clearance.

Another product of population pressure is emigration. Opposition elsewhere in the world to large-scale immigration acts as a dampener and leads to illegal immigration. The most dramatic instance in the Atlantic is that of Africans in open boats from Morocco and places further south, especially Senegal, trying to make their way to claim refuge in the Canary Islands. Morocco, which ranks low in the United Nations' Human Development Index, has a high poverty rate and high youth unemployment, which leads to emigration, legal and illegal, to Spain.

Many have died in the process, as the boats are vulnerable to the Atlantic while the passengers face the problems of exposure, malnutrition and thirst. In the year from August 2005 to August 2006, 20,000 Africans arrived in the Canaries and up to 3,000 are thought to have died. The Red Cross estimated that one boat in four sank on a journey that might take up to ten days; from Senegal it is 1,530 kilometres (950 miles).

Thereafter, there was a decline in the route, with migrants instead going overland in the 2010s from sub-Saharan Africa to North Africa and Europe. Indeed, over 35,000 Gambians reached European countries by irregular means from 2014 to 2018. However, in 2019 there was a resurgence in the attempted emigration via the Canaries to Europe, notably from Senegal. In 2020, the existing crisis caused by conflict in the Sahel was greatly exacerbated due to the impact of the COVID-19 recession on African economies, while border restrictions hit overland travel. As a result, there was a sharp rise with over 7,500 people reaching the Canaries by October, two-thirds of them setting off from Western Sahara, a new departure point. Of those recorded, the largest categories were, in order, from Mali, Ivory Coast, Guinea and Senegal. Others died in boats that capsized, while some were detained by Mauritanian or Senegalese coastguards.

In Atlantic Europe, the pressures have been rather different, not least those of preserving social welfare systems and living standards in the face of competitive global pressures. Europe itself has focused economically on Germany, while the end of the Cold War and the inclusion of most of Eastern Europe in the European Union has helped move the latter's centre of gravity eastward. Thus, Slovakia is of greater interest for German investment than Portugal. The relative decline of the Atlantic can also be seen in the development of trade routes into Europe from the east, for example oil and gas pipelines as well as the Chinese Belt and Road infrastructure initiative launched in 2013. From this perspective, the Atlantic and its ports, such as Lisbon, can appear redundant or at least less relevant.

This does not mean that there is not economic activity of significance on Europe's Atlantic, for example with French ship-building at Saint-Nazaire. However, there is also a decline in traditional manufacturing, notably ship-related industries, along most of the Atlantic coastline. The emphasis, instead, is on tourism, as on Portugal's Algarve, which can compound the impression of a move away from an engagement with broader Atlantic currents. This impression is increased by the extent to which the EU's major Atlantic container port, Rotterdam, is not itself on the Atlantic.

Britain sees itself, not least as part of the Brexit narrative, as engaging with an outward-looking geography, and developments in Atlantic ports, notably at Liverpool, have been presented accordingly. It remains to be seen whether this account will be justified. Former imperial links have certainly been slackening, politically and economically, and, in 2021, Barbados is due to become a republic. Moreover, Britain's general presence has lessened. The decline of British diplomatic representation in Atlantic Africa was notable, with closures of embassies, including in Gabon, Liberia and Congo-Brazzaville in 1991, while the envoy in Cameroon also had to cover Gabon and Equatorial Guinea; also that decade, Togo was covered from Ghana, Benin from Nigeria, and Mauritania from Morocco. In contrast, Brazil increased its African represen-tation in the 2000s.

There was also an instructive shift in naval power. Commissioned in 1998, HMS *Ocean*, a landing-platform helicop-ter ship and, for a while, the British flagship, was sold to Brazil for £84.6 million in 2017 and became the *Atlântico*, the new Brazilian flagship. Brazil, which has the largest Latin American navy, had already bought in 2000 the French aircraft carrier *Foch*, which was renamed the *São Paulo*, becoming its flagship, only to be decommissioned in 2018 due to many problems with its serviceability. Prior to that, the Brazilians had purchased HMS *Vengeance* in 1956, using it as the *Minas Gerais* from 1960 to 2001 as a rival to the Argentinean *Independencia* (1959–70) and *Veinticinco de Mayo* (1969–97), both also formerly British carriers. Alongside the carrier *Illustrious*, *Ocean* had been used in 2000 in helping oppose rebel activity in Sierra Leone.

Colonial rule remained the case largely of islands, with Britain, France, Portugal and Spain retaining several each, albeit under very different governmental arrangements to the past. Denmark's role in Greenland and the Faroes ensures that it is the last of the old Atlantic empires still in evidence. In addition, on the mainland, Cayenne in South America remained under France and Ceuta in Africa under Spain. Founded in 1991, the Decolonisation and Social Emancipation Movement presses for independence for Cayenne, winning 17.3 per cent of the votes in the 2012 parliamentary elections. In 2017, there was a general strike, an occupation of the Guiana Space Station, and protests about a lack of investment from mainland France. Living standards are lower than in France. In 2020, the British government considered holding illegal immigrants on Ascension or Saint Helena, but decided not to do so, apparently largely for logistical reasons.

Ghana: From Chaos to Progress

Independent from 1957, Ghana, formerly a British colony called the Gold Coast, did not have a peaceful and democratic change of government until 2001. Initial hopes of progress were dashed by economic mismanagement, leading to a series of military governments. Alongside high

---

inflation and poor government there was discontent and coups, notably those in 1979 and 1981 that brought Jerry Rawlings, an air force officer, to power, leading to the execution in 1979 of three former heads of state. Instead of understanding that economic mismanagement was the problem, the focus was on corruption, and in 1979 Rawlings had the central black market in Accra blown up. After his second coup, Rawlings abolished the constitution and dissolved parliament, but in 1983 he changed policy (as did President Mitterrand in France), turning from left-wing economic (mis)management to free-market reforms. Coup attempts were suppressed in 1983, 1984, 1985, 1986 and 1987, but economic growth shot up, and with it stability. Rawlings returned to constitutional government and won elections in 1992 and 1996, and Ghana was cited in 1998 by President Clinton, alongside South Africa and Uganda, as evidence of an 'African Renaissance'.

Tourism

British tourists focus on the Mediterranean, but a large number make the flight to the Canaries, which are regarded in part as an extension of the Mediterranean. Thus, 858,118 visited Gran Canaria in 2017. Further afield, Florida and the West Indies attract many European tourists, not least as a result of the expansion of the cruise-ship industry. The number of all tourists in the West Indies rose from 1.3 million in 1959 to 25 million in 2013, although higher costs than in other beach destinations affected growth. Numbers increased to 2017 but were hit in 2018 and collapsed in the COVID-19 pandemic that began in 2020. The Dominican Republic, with 6.2 million stay-over tourists in 2017 (in other words, not cruise passengers), was the most popular.

Both Madeira and Cape Town have long been British destinations, while the Cape Verde Islands have become one, but, on the whole, the shores of the South Atlantic do not attract large numbers of European tourists, and there is no sign that this might change in a post-COVID tourist recovery. The islands of the South Atlantic such as Saint Helena are too remote and small to attract many tourists other than the most intrepid, although the Falklands became a destination when Antarctic cruises became popular in the 2010s. Meanwhile, COVID helped take the unemployment rate in Barbados in 2020 to near 40 per cent. In response, it, like Bermuda, sought to attract telecommuters.

The New World

North America has seen an increased move of power and wealth away from the Atlantic seaboard: alongside a revival of the American South has come the major growth of Texas and California, the last very much part of the Pacific economy. Nevertheless, America's Atlantic ports remain significant. New York, New Jersey, Norfolk, Baltimore and Miami expanded their facilities to take the larger container ships that, from 2016, were able to transit through the now larger Panama Canal, most of them bringing East Asian products to Atlantic markets. Moreover, there has been industrial growth in some east coast areas, as with the aircraft industry in Charleston.

Atlantic South America has not delivered on its potential. Each seriously afflicted by poor government and fiscal mismanagement, Argentina and Venezuela have declined, the latter becoming increasingly chaotic in recent years. Brazil was seen as one of the BRIC (Brazil, Russia, India, China) economies of major growth, a term coined in 2001. However, it has struggled to meet expectations and, as with South Africa which was invited to join in 2010, its divided politics is matched by a degree of dysfunctional government and economic underperformance.

Brazil under the anti-American Luiz Inácio Lula da Silva, president from 2003 to 2011, put considerable effort into developing closer links with Africa, and notably (but not only) with former Portuguese colonies, especially Angola. However, under the right-wing Jair Bolsonaro, who won the presidency in 2018, there has been a much closer alignment with the United States. This has been an aspect of a more assertive American attempt to lead Latin America, with, in particular, pressure under President Trump (2017–21) on the left-wing regimes in Cuba and Venezuela, and an attempt to lessen Chinese influence in the region.

Pressures

Poor government is particularly apparent in the Atlantic world in South America and Africa. It includes not only political instability and rampant corruption, as in Argentina and Brazil, but also serious fiscal mismanagement. Heavy debt-service payments due in 2021 included those from Angola, Ivory Coast, Congo, Cameroon and Senegal. Major falls in the price of oil have hit states, including Angola, Cameroon and Venezuela, heavily dependent on its export for their finances. Argentina, which has had frequent debt defaults, has faced persistent problems with poor government, corruption, economic performance and living beyond its means. In 2019, the official poverty and inflation rates rose to 35 per cent and 43 per cent respectively. In South Africa, poor fiscal management and excessive public spending, as well as corruption, led to a major increase in public debt in the 2010s and, in 2020, to borrowing from the International Monetary Fund, while recession was accompanied by rising unemployment. Unable to make its annual creditor payments, Puerto Rico was declared bankrupt in 2017.

Weak government is also a factor in the role of the Atlantic in organised crime, notably the movement of cocaine from South

America, particularly Rio, Colombia and Venezuela, to North America, Europe and Africa, and of cannabis from Morocco to Europe, especially Spain. Islands frequently serve as transit centres for drugs. For example, the Bissagos Islands off Guinea-Bissau, a state that, in addition to its significant production of cashew nuts, is regarded as an important centre for the drug trade.

There are serious environmental issues in Brazil, notably due to fires in Amazonia arising in large part from forest clearance, which became far more prominent from 2019, not least to clear land for soya cultivation and cattle. Environmental degradation is also very much seen in the Atlantic. The growing presence of plastic particles in the deep ocean is but one instance of the growing extent to which the mighty ocean is affected by human detritus, which has consequences for other animals living in and near the Atlantic. A 2020 study indicated that the Atlantic contained more than ten times as much plastic entering the ocean globally as the 8 million tonnes per annum estimated in a 2015 study; and with about 200 million tonnes of plastic in the Atlantic as a whole. Prolonged sub-lethal exposure to plastics hits ecosystems. The crisis is particularly present in the North Atlantic garbage patch that was first documented in 1972 and which is hundreds of miles across.

Other forms of pollution include oil leaks notably from offshore and coastal oilfields, particularly in Nigeria's Niger delta, but also from shipping, a tanker releasing 260,000 tonnes off Angola in 1991. Angola, Guyana, Mauritania (where production began in 2006) and Surinam all also have offshore oilfields. A chemical tanker ran aground off Galicia in 2019. Concern about pollution has led a Swedish company to design a transatlantic car transporter intended for production by 2024 that relies on the wind, with 100-metre (330-foot) high masts that swivel to optimise lift and smooth steel composite 'wings' or sails.

Cabinda, Offshore Oil Industry

North of the Congo estuary, four offshore oilfields are located in the Cabinda enclave of Angola. There are a number of oil companies involved, with the American company Chevron the most significant operator. The first offshore discovery was made in 1966, the first oil following in 1968; the first onshore well was drilled in 1958. In 1999, the first producing deep-water oilfield began operations and, in 2015, 5 billion barrels were produced from the offshore fields, while in 2018 Chevron's net daily production averaged 97,000 barrels and 324 million cubic feet of natural gas: liquefied natural gas was produced from 2013 from an onshore plant begun in 2000.

The Cabinda population argues with reason that it receives insufficient benefit from the oil, and there has been unsuccessful secessionist pressure, with low-level guerrilla violence.

The devastation of marine life takes a different form with over-fishing by giant factory ships that hunt shoals by radar and then hoover them up with suction devices or use massive nets. The impact, which attracted increased attention from the early 1990s with a major collapse in the north-west Atlantic cod fishery, is traumatic for fish stocks. The fall in the cod fishery has led to a turn to other fish, notably a massive expansion in the Atlantic squid catch from the 1980s, which, however, has affected seals and whales that otherwise feed on squid.

A Hazardous Ocean

The sinking of the *Andrea Gail* during the 'Perfect Storm' of 1991, the basis of the 2000 film of that name, indicates the continuing hazard of the ocean. The 92-tonne, 22-metre (72-foot)-long fishing boat, operating from Gloucester, Massachusetts, sank on 28 October 1991, its last reported position 290 kilometres (180 miles) north-east of Sable Island in the north-west Atlantic. The peak waves may have been over 18 metres (60 feet) if not higher. The crew of six were all lost. This is an indication of the danger facing earlier navigators.

Overfishing in the North Atlantic has been increasingly matched by factory fishing in the South Atlantic. This both hits the fish stocks there and affects the livelihood of coastal communities that rely on fishing and especially so in Atlantic Africa, for example in Namibia where Chinese and Japanese fishing vessels take advantage of the fish linked to the Benguela Current. Meanwhile, carbon dioxide absorbed by the Atlantic is making it more acidic, causing coral skeletons to corrode, which affects fish that spawn on deep-ocean coral. In addition, a 2020 study dramatically increased a 2015 assessment of the amount of plastic entering the Atlantic annually and estimated that there were about 200 million tonnes of plastic in the ocean. The strain on Atlantic ecosystems is unprecedented. It must encourage efforts to preserve them and, with that, opportunities for all. Separately, the La Niña weather pattern in the Pacific helped hurricanes by weakening the winds streaming high over the Caribbean and tropical Atlantic, which could otherwise kill off developing storms. Moreover, the vigour of the monsoon season in West Africa, as in 2020, set off strong easterly airflows that spawn Atlantic storms. The storms appeared early in 2020. Alpha in 2020 was the first recorded subtropical cyclone to hit mainland Portugal. At the same time, major North Atlantic currents have slowed dramatically as a result of climate change.

The Single-handed Transatlantic Race

Begun in 1960, and usually held every four years, this was the first single-handed ocean yacht race. Run from Plymouth to the United States, it is particularly difficult as the competitors sail into the face of the prevailing winds. There are different routing strategies, notably the Rhumb line, the Great Circle route, a northern route, an Azores route and a trade wind route; with trade-offs for each in terms of distance, the risk of encountering ice, and winds. Rowing the Atlantic has become more popular, with a now annual race from the Canary Islands to the West Indies launched in 1997.

Queen Mary II

Built at Saint-Nazaire, France, and launched in 2003, making her maiden voyage in 2004, the *Queen Mary II* became the Cunard flagship that year and has a tonnage of 149,215, a length of 345 metres (1,132 feet), 18 decks and, after its 2016 refit, a capacity of 2,695 passengers and 1,253 officers and crew. Powered essentially by four diesel engines, it was the largest and longest passenger ship built until the construction of the 19-deck, 3,634-passenger, Finnish-built Caribbean cruise ship *Freedom of the Seas* in 2006. However, the *QM2* continues to be largest ocean

---

liner ever built. When I crossed from New York to Southampton in November 2006, we hit a November storm or, rather, a storm hit us. With a cabin in the cheap bowels of the ship, I was interested to note that those in the most expensive cabins, faced by the greater rocking motion of the ocean (the higher up you are in a ship, the more you rock), took shelter for the night on the ballroom floor. The crossing provided an opportunity to read, write, go to a martini-making class, and spectate at an auction of the most unimpressive paintings I had ever seen. Among the reasons others gave for crossing were a break from work, a family-together holiday, an ability to take wheel-chair-bound relatives, a freedom to see your pets during the crossing, fear of flying, a need to smoke and unlimited luggage for emigration.

Postscript

....

Geography is not Destiny. Morocco is close to the shores of Western Europe like Japan is to East Asia. Neither have coal. Yet Morocco is no Japan. Indeed, the physical geography of the Atlantic, like that of other oceans, has been a setting for the very different development of societies, economies, states and cultures. There may appear to be a similarity when the same brands of hamburgers or makes of cars can be found in the cities of the Atlantic's four continents. Environmental pressures, whether climate change or overfishing, are problems that are widely shared.

A shrinking of the ocean is suggested, moreover, by its frequent overflying, and by communication satellites as well as aircraft. Individual ships now carry freight that a whole fleet would have transported half a millennium ago. Yachts cross the Atlantic for pleasure. Until the COVID-19 pandemic began in 2020, large numbers of passengers went to sea on cruise liners that represented a new iteration of the earlier passenger liners: the purpose now being solely to enjoy being on the ocean rather than to journey across it, the latter being done only by relatively few passengers, and notably on the *Queen Mary II* Southampton–New York run.

Yet, alongside these elements for convergence, as well as scholars' interest in 'transnational' links, past and present, there is the divergence arising from differing cultures, a divergence that was of more weight than generally allowed in the new field of Atlantic history that became more significant from the 1970s, with the key work being R. R. Palmer's *The Age of Democratic Revolution* (1959, 1964). This element of divergence will likely be accentuated by the varied impacts of climate warming, differential population movements and the decline of Western hegemony.

The Atlantic has been shadowed by the relative rise of the Pacific, but both links across the Atlantic and the divides it presents remain crucial aspects of the world.

Other Atlantics

The Cape Verde Islands

Portuguese from the fifteenth century, the Cape Verde Islands were a waystation on maritime routes to Africa, the Indian Ocean and South America. Visiting in 1702, Francis Rogers commented on Praia: 'a fine, fruitful, plentiful island, but hot, most of whose inhabitants are a sort of banditti (or banished, transported for crimes) or thieves, as an abundance of our countrymen can witness when they touched there for water or fresh provisions'. In 1669, Captain John Narbrough noted 'very good fresh water', but people 'much given to thievery'. Maize and bananas were grown. Now, very differently, tourism began in the 1970s on the island of Sal, and rose to over 716,000 tourists in 2017; 23 per cent were from Britain and 11.2 per cent from Germany. Portugal was the third largest source of tourists that year. Benefiting from a lack of rainfall, the tourists' focus is on the sandy beaches of the islands of Sal, Boa Vista and Maio.

St Pierre and Miquelon

With a population of just over 6,000 and an area of 240 square kilometres (93 square miles), this is the part of New France to remain under French rule. Long a fishing base, the islands benefited from smuggling during American Prohibition. The population have French citizenship and are represented in the National Assembly. The French maintain a patrol boat and have pursued a maritime boundary dispute with Canada.

Rockall

A granite islet, 30 metres wide and 20 metres high (100 feet by 70 feet high), this is a volcanic remnant in the north-east Atlantic, which was claimed by the United Kingdom in 1955, and made part of Scotland under the 1972 Island of Rockall Act. It is located 301 kilometres (187 miles) west of Soay, Scotland, and 423 kilometres (263 miles) north-west of Tory Island, Ireland, which rejects the British claim and, in 2019, there were Scottish complaints about Irish fishing in Rockall's waters. The island is uninhabitable, with large storm waves washing over it. Molluscs and whelks live there, while seabirds rest and have bred there. The annexation of Rockall in 1955 was the last territorial expansion of the British empire and was carried out to prevent use by foreign observers of British guided missile tests. This was another instance of a theme of this book, the importance of small islands. Aside from providing territorial claims to surrounding waters, they have also been bases for pirates, scenes of battles, tax havens, and a place of exile for Napoleon.

Selected Further Reading

The extensive and excellent literature on this subject grows annually and to suggest a small number of works is difficult. In line with the likely readership, the emphasis here is on English-language works and recent literature, as earlier studies can be followed up through those cited in this list.

Abulafia, David, *The Discovery of Mankind: Atlantic Encounters in the Age of Columbus* (New Haven, CT, 2009).

—, *The Boundless Sea: A Human History of the Oceans* (2019).

Armitage, D. and M. Braddick (eds), *The British Atlantic World, 1500–1800* (2002).

Bailey, C. C., *African Voices of the Atlantic Slave Trade: Beyond the Silence and the Shame* (2005).

Bailyn, B., *Atlantic History: Concepts and Contours* (2005).

Bailyn, B. and P. L. Denault (eds), *Soundings in Atlantic History* (2009).

Benjamin, T., *The Atlantic World: Europeans, Africans, Indians and Their Shared History, 1400–1900* (2009).

Blouet, Olwyn, *The Contemporary Caribbean* (London, 2007).

Brown, V., *Tacky's Revolt: The Story of an Atlantic Slave War* (2000).

Burnard, T., *The Atlantic in World History, 1490–1830* (2020).

—, *Planters, Merchants, and Slaves: Plantation Societies in British America, 1650–1820* (Chicago, Ill., 2015).

Butel, P., *The Atlantic* (1999).

Campbell, G., *Norse America: The Story of a Founding Myth* (2021).

Cañazares-Esguerra, Jorge (ed.), *Entangled Empires: The Anglo-Iberian Atlantic, 1500–1830* (Philadelphia, 2018).

Canny, N. and P. Morgan (eds), *The Oxford Handbook of the Atlantic World: 1450–1850* (2011).

Chet, G., *The Ocean is a Wilderness: Atlantic Piracy and the Limits of State Authority, 1688–1856* (2014).

Crosby, A., *Ecological Imperialism* (1986).

Cunliffe, B., *The Extraordinary Voyage of Pytheas the Greek: The Man Who Discovered Britain* (2001).

—, *Facing the Ocean: The Atlantic and Its Peoples, 8000 BC to AD 1500* (2001).

—, *On the Ocean: The Mediterranean and the Atlantic from prehistory to AD 1500* (2017).

Davids, K., *Global Ocean of Knowledge, 1660–1860: Globalization and Maritime Knowledge in the Atlantic World* (2020).

Davis, R., *The Rise of the Atlantic Economies* (1973).

DePalma, A., *The Cubans: Ordinary Lives in Extraordinary Times* (2020).

Diptee, A., *From Africa to Jamaica: The Making of an Atlantic Slave Society, 1775–1807* (2010).

Egerton, D. R. et al., *The Atlantic World: A History, 1400–1888* (2007).

Eichhorn, N., *Atlantic History in the Nineteenth Century: Migration, Trade, Conflict, and Ideas* (2019).

Elliott, J. H., *Empires of the Atlantic World: Britain and Spain in America, 1492–1830* (2006).

—, *The Old World and the New, 1492–1650* (1970).

Eltis, D., *The Rise of African Slavery in the Americas* (2000).

Fernández-Armesto, F., *Before Columbus* (1987).

—, *The Canary Islands after the Conquest* (1982).

—, *Columbus* (1991).

Garrow, D. and F. Sturt (eds), *Neolithic Stepping Stones* (2017).

Geggus, David, *The Impact of the Haitian Revolution in the Atlantic World* (Columbia, SC, 2001).

Gilroy, Paul, *The Black Atlantic: Modernity and Double Consciousness* (Cambridge, MA, 1993).

Goslinga, C. Corneliis, *The Dutch in the Caribbean and in the Guianas, 1680–1791* (Assen-Maastricht, 1985).

Green, T., *Brokers of Change: Atlantic Commerce and Cultures in Pre-colonial Western Africa* (2012).

—, *A Fistful of Shells: West Africa From the Rise of the Slave Trade to the Age of Revolution* (2019).

—, *Rise of the Trans-Atlantic Slave Trade* (2012).

Hanna, Mark, *Pirate Nests and the Rise of the British Empire, 1570–1740* (Chapel Hill, NC, 2015).

Horodowich, E., *The Venetian Discovery of America: Geographic Imagination and Print Culture in the Age of Encounters* (2018).

Klooster, W., *The Dutch Moment: War, Trade, and Settlement in the Seventeenth-Century Atlantic World* (2016).

Kupperman, K. O., *The Atlantic in World History* (2012).

Linebaugh, P. and M. Rediker, *The Many-Headed Hydra: Sailors, Slaves, Commoners and the Hidden History of the Revolutionary Atlantic* (2000).

Mancke, E. and C. Shammas (eds), *The Creation of the British Atlantic World* (2005).

Metzger, S., *The Chinese Atlantic: Seascapes and the Theatricality of Globalization* (2020).

Miller, J. C. (ed.), *The Princeton Companion to Atlantic History* (2014).

Morgan, P. D. and J. P. Greene (eds), *Atlantic History: A Critical Appraisal* (2008).

Newitt, M. (ed.), *The Portuguese in West Africa, 1415–1670: A Documentary History* (2010).

Nwokeji, G. U., *The Slave Trade and Culture in the Bight of Biafra: An African Society in the Atlantic World* (2010).

Osterhammel, J., *The Transformation of the World: A Global History of the Nineteenth Century* (2014).

Pagden, A., *Lords of All the World* (1995).

Paquette, G., *The European Seaborne Empires: From the Thirty Years' War to the Age of Revolutions* (2019).

Rediker, M., *Between the Devil and the Deep Blue Sea: Merchant Seamen, Pirates, and the Anglo-American Maritime World, 1700–1750* (1987).

Restall, Matthew and Amari Solari, *The Maya* (Oxford, 2000).

Saba, R., *American Mirror: The United States and Brazil in the Age of Emancipation* (2021).

Scammell, G., *The World Encompassed* (1981).

Schwartz, S., *Sea of Storms: A History of Hurricanes in the Greater Caribbean from Columbus to Katrina* (Princeton, NJ, 2015).

Seasholes, N. (ed.) *The Atlas of Boston History* (2019).

Smallwood, S. E., *Saltwater Slavery: A Middle Passage from Africa to American Diaspora* (2007).

Thornton, J., *Africa and Africans in the Making of the Atlantic World, 1400–1800* (1998).

—, *A Cultural History of the Atlantic World, 1250–1820* (2012).

Walvin, James, *Freedom: The Overthrow of the Slave Empires* (London, 2019).

Weaver, J., *The Red Atlantic: American Indigenes and the Making of the Modern World, 1000–1927* (2014).

Willis, S., *In the Hour of Victory: The Royal Navy in the Age of Nelson* (2014).

Index